Jane Miller was an English teacher in a London comprehensive school for several years before going to the University of London Institute of Education, where she is a Reader. She is the author of *Many Voices, Bilingualism, Culture and Education*; *Women writing about Men*; *Seductions: Studies in Reading and Culture* and *More has meant Women: The Feminisation of Schooling*. She has edited the Virago Education Series and *Eccentric Propositions: Essays on Literature and the Curriculum*, and she is currently editor of the journal, *Changing English*.

School for Women

JANE MILLER

A *Virago* Book

First published by Virago Press 1996

Reprinted 1996

Copyright © Jane Miller 1996

The moral right of the author has been asserted

A CIP catalogue record for this book
is available from the British Library.

ISBN 1 85381 713 9

Printed in England by Clays Ltd, St Ives plc

UK companies, institutions and other organisations wishing
to make bulk purchases of this or any other book
published by Little, Brown should contact their local
bookshop or the special sales department at the address below.
Tel 0171 911 8000. Fax 0171 911 8100.

Virago
A Division of
Little, Brown and Company (UK)
Brettenham House
Lancaster Place
London WC2E 7EN

For Anne Turvey and Sam Miller,
with love and thanks

Contents

Acknowledgements

This book has relied on other people and on their writing in unusual ways, so I shall begin from the oddest of my many debts. My great-aunt Clara Collet was a formidable figure in my life until I was fifteen, when she died. But my rediscovery of her work and her diary and letters six or seven years ago was fortuitous and a surprise to me. She was, it turned out, a formidable figure in other people's lives as well. I did not talk much with her in her lifetime, beyond a swiftly curtailed conversation about my future, when my admission that I wanted to be an Olympic diver drew from her only a dramatically despairing sigh. I have already written a brief biography of her in a book I wrote called *Seductions*. I never meant to write about her – holding no particular brief for genealogical studies or the like – yet she became an un-ignorable voice in all this. Here, I return to her as a teacher and a writer on education and on women's work, on which she became an expert. She has become a minor character in the book, and an exemplarily ambivalent and critical one, I hope.

I am constantly grateful for the support and knowledge and constructive criticism of my colleagues at the University of London Institute of Education. Not only have they given me the time to complete this book, they have also helped me with its argument. I especially want to thank Tony Burgess and Anne Turvey. I have had invaluable support as well from Josie Levine and Margaret Spencer and John Hardcastle and Ken Jones. Then Patricia Kelly, Sue Cranmer, Judith Benstead and Deanna Campbell have collectively taught me to use a computer, for which I thank them. My son Sam has helped me in innumerable ways: with the plundering and the interpretation of family archives and with reading drafts. I also want to thank Karl Miller, who always gives me good advice (though I don't always take it), as well as Georgia and Daniel Miller, Yvonne Andrews and Shireen and Ardu Vakil. I got more support than I deserved from them throughout the project. Then there are a number of writers and friends to whom I owe a great deal: Deanne Bogdan, Eric Korn, Harold Rosen, Suzanne Scafe, Carolyn Steedman, Mary Taubman and Emma Tennant, especially. René Weis helped even beyond allowing me to make use of his marvellous *Criminal Justice*, by lending me the records of Kensington Avenue School. Lennie Goodings has been an encouraging editor, and Marguerite Nesling a meticulous one. I needed them both.

I have always learned enormously from my students. Teaching teachers must be one of the best kinds of teaching, for my students are already experts at what they do. Here I particularly want to thank those of them who have let me use their work in a variety of ways in this book. They are Anita Barley, Sabrina Broadbent, Beverley Bryan, Celia Burgess Macey, Jo Cross, Jenny Daniels, Michael Hamerston, June Levison, Moya O'Donnell, Gill Plummer, Kate Pugh, Chris Raeside, Sue Smedley and Elena Zervou.

Introduction

There is wide-spread dismay about schools these days, as there has often been, which makes it all the more striking that so little is made of the most impressive educational achievement of the last 150 years. Educating girls has changed the world, and many would say that the change has been for the good. Yet it has often been greeted with a wringing of hands and a reminder that what girls have gained, boys have lost.

Sixty per cent of all teachers in this country are women: 74 per cent of primary-school teachers and 45 per cent of secondary-school teachers.[1] That presence, and its distribution in terms of schools and age range, is barely acknowledged in public discussion of education. Those figures have a history, which is also usually ignored, and three immensely significant questions have their source in that history. There is first the effect on children's lives of being brought up by women and then taught by women. There is the effect on women's lives of having access to this developing form of employment, and third, there are the consequences for all forms of higher education and training of the demand for women teachers. Those themes run through this book, linking past and present and suggesting how important to contemporary debate the history of women's involvement in schools has been.

Classroom teachers have a contradictory public image,

especially at the moment. They are often presented, for instance, as the best possible models of knowledge and practice for teachers beginning their careers, and a huge improvement on teacher trainers, who are, of course, ex-teachers, but instantly tainted by thought and ideology on their translation from school to higher education. Teachers are at the same time regarded as responsible for all that is wrong with schools and education. The knowledge they are thought to possess naturally – and this is in the benign view – is inarticulate, untheorised and experiential: mercifully uncontaminated by ideas, reading, ideology and contest. These non-intellectual, non-political, apparently safe teachers – and they are usually imagined as women or as conservative men – are at the same time the unspecified but constant target of almost all official and unofficial public criticism of what are characterised as low, and sinking, educational standards. Why does teaching and why do teachers get such a bad press? And has the fact that a majority of teachers are women got anything to do with that bad press? Those too are questions I shall try to answer.

Women teachers are figures of such impossible familiarity that it can seem inappropriate to train any sort of searchlight on them. They have not, as workers, been inclined to court celebrity or seek public vindication. Most of them have become used to regular doses of obloquy and unthinking condescension from many quarters. Yet it is necessary to try to understand their history. It is necessary for the women themselves and for their thousands and thousands of pre-decessors, and it is essential for education, for schools and for the children going through the school system, some of whom may well become teachers themselves. We may learn a good deal in the process about the values of a society which is prepared to hand over the education of most people's children to a group of adults whose powers of mind and character and whose qualifications for the job are so consistently distrusted and traduced.

There are one or two useful recent histories of women's education and an accumulating store of studies by historians and sociologists on aspects of women's work as teachers here and – more often, in fact – in North America. I have made use of that work, but I am not in the business of either reproducing it or wishing to outdo it. If not quite unexplored territory, women teachers are a curiously neglected subject. Serious research is still published on almost every aspect of state education, which makes no mention of women's presence within it, whether as students or teachers. It is rarer still for anyone to pay attention to the actual women who have chosen to teach and to how they thought of that choice, how they prepared for it, and the lives they have led as teachers. There are, it is true, the somewhat despairing accounts of schoolteaching and governessing included in the novels of, for instance, Charlotte and Anne Brontë, and governesses are certainly to be found in the novels of Maria Edgeworth and Jane Austen and other writers. Many women grew up on a diet of boarding-school stories, where teachers, occasionally romantic figures, more often despicable or even monstrous ones, lurked as shadowy warning to the more vivid adolescents in their care. But how those women had come to be there and what their lives consisted of was usually outside the story's frame of concern, unless, significantly, it was set in America or Canada, where the prospect of girls becoming teachers, if only temporarily, was firmly registered by writers like the authors of *Anne of Green Gables*, for instance, of *The Little House on the Prairie*, and, of course, of *Little Women*.

You need to look further for recognition that by the middle of the nineteenth century there was a whole new group of women teachers, drawn by and large from better-off working-class or lower middle-class families, who were being recruited into the schools which, from the 1870s onwards, became part of educational provision for all children in this country. Teaching was (relative to other occupations for women) well-paid work, and women were relied on to staff first elementary schools for all children and then, after 1902, the beginnings of a system of secondary schooling. The importance of this cannot be exaggerated. Not only were schools increasingly staffed by women, who were more and more likely to teach boys as well as girls, but in addition, a whole edifice of further and higher education developed in response to this new demand for educated women. The teacher-training colleges, the first of which had opened in the 1840s, became part of a general expansion of higher education: undergraduate courses in universities, the setting up of university departments of education, a proliferating collection of ways for mature students to top up on their schooling before embarking on degree courses. These developed – with mostly grudging local and central government support – in response to the recruitment of women into teaching. And supply has characteristically created further demand. This country still languishes behind most European countries in the amount of higher education it offers and the general level of education and training provided for young people. It resembles those other countries in that it was the need for teachers which spurred development and growth in the first place.

It is characteristic of much history about women that it should be difficult to assemble as a coherent, linear narrative. Not only are the sources of information sparse, erratic and inconsistent, there are variations which are hard to interpret and incorporate into a history already dredged out of absences and denial. Nor can a story like the story of women teaching be told as one which affected women uniformly. The difference between teaching middle-class girls in girls' secondary schools, whether independent or state-funded, and teaching in elementary schools, was as vast as the difference between the kinds of education received by girls from the middle and the working classes. Where there are histories of elementary schooling, for instance, girls and women simply disappear into the figures and the arguments. Official school records survive – I include a little of one of them here – and they do give some sense of how teaching was organised in schools and how this changed over time. But I wanted as well to get a sense of how, in the past and now, women teachers have thought and think about their work. Not all women teachers, of course, but some. In wishing to challenge what have often been damaging representations of teachers, I have tried to focus on the specific experiences of certain women now and in the past. So there are noticeable gaps: the increasing number of women, for instance, who are now heads of co-educational secondary schools, and teachers in subject areas other than English. Such teachers may not find themselves spoken for here, though my hope is that they will recognise aspects of their own lives in parts of the book.

I have made use of all kinds of testimony. Above all, I have wanted to hear the voices of teachers themselves, and this book has grown out of my work with teachers and out of my reading of fiction and memoirs and history written by teachers. For many years I taught English in a London secondary school. For the last twenty years I have taught in the University of London Institute of Education, where my work has involved training English teachers for secondary and further education and also teaching experienced teachers on masters courses or supervising their research. I have been very lucky. I have found myself working with experienced and talented students in an area which has engaged their intelligence and interest and commitment. From that position it has been strange to read the diatribes of journalists week after week and in all sections of the press against precisely such teachers: teachers of English, for instance; or primary teachers engaged in teaching children to read and write; or teachers who are expert at supporting bilingual pupils, or other pupils who have difficulties with reading and writing; or teachers of literature working with older teenagers or adults in further and higher education. My sense of these teachers (and the majority of them are women) is of flexible, knowledgeable people, who are different from some other intellectual workers only in being practical and pragmatic, as they are required to be in response to the needs and the problems of the young people they teach. It is true that some of them lack confidence in themselves as thinkers and writers, which is not surprising, given how little they are encouraged to see themselves as either. And that needs remedying, not simply for their peace of mind, but for the light they are thereby enabled to throw on teaching as work and on schooling as a more or less efficacious process. The voices and the writing of women teachers are at the heart of this book. My purpose has been to do more than quote from these teachers. I have wanted to incorporate their evidence and their arguments into mine, as demonstration and embodiment of some of the lives and knowledge and thought that have been left out of most educational discussion. Also woven through the chapters are episodes from my own life. So that narrative, autobiography, memory[2] take their place – as I am certain they should – alongside argument and analysis.

More than twenty years ago I wrote an article about my life as a teacher in a large London secondary school. It was the first opportunity I had ever had to do so. Few teachers ever get such a chance. The article, which I called 'Tell him, Miss'[3], recalls the debates of the early seventies. It was written in angry response to *The Black Papers* and to what I read as a patronising attack by Professor John Carey on schools like mine and, as I saw it, on teachers like me.[4] *Plus ça change*. I am surprised to find that many current preoccupations were already in place in even this short characterisation of one lesson.

Winston was back. Small, spherical, black, he shimmies round the classroom, singing quite loudly about imagined sexual encounters between the two smallest boys and the two largest girls. He had already been ejected from one school when he came here. A month ago he was suspended, and efforts were made to find a place for him in a special school, which he is thought to need. The efforts failed, as such efforts usually do, and he is back again. He has no mother, and his father has already caused permanent damage to his other son's left eye. Winston's style of perpetual motion, a version of what Muhammed Ali goes in for, but closer to the ground, makes a good deal of sense, since he often has to parry blows. The emission of continuous sound serves a similar purpose; he has no reason to suppose that an interval of silence might be filled with words he'd like to hear. Today I have given him a tape recorder to talk into, and he patted me, tenderly, though fairly hard, on the head. For twenty minutes this reduced his noise level to what is called in teaching 'an acceptable hum', and concentrated it into one corner of the room. Then, tired of having no audience for his boasting tales of triumph, intellectual and physical – he is neither strong nor brave – he wandered across to a girl with neat handwriting and rested his bum winningly on her folder.

'Tell him, Miss', she said wearily. I told him, and led him back in a sort of foxtrot to the tape recorder. He recorded a story about a 'wicked' West Indian lady setting about him with a rolling-pin at the door of a youth club he was trying to get into. He is banned from most such clubs. He does a good imitation of a Jamaican accent. His own is clear and London. At the end of the lesson I asked him to play me the best thing on his tape. He turned up the sound, and we all listened to his blow-by-blow account of beating his brother to the point of gibbering surrender. 'He is a weed', the story ended.[5]

I tried to interpret that scene and others like it in my article in terms of the pressures on education in the early seventies and in relation to contemporary arguments about 'sheep and goats' and selection versus 'mixed ability'. The pressures on teachers and on their students are far, far greater now, and arguments about school organisation and the curriculum have become narrower and more circumscribed. Yet many of the same dilemmas persist. Indeed, I planned at one point to recycle that article's title as a title for this book, as mournful acknowledgement of some grim continuities, and as apt injunction from a girl pupil to her woman teacher to stop a troublesome boy doing whatever he was doing and tell the world what it was like to be a girl in that classroom. However, what was bizarrely imperceptible to me in the early seventies was the character of my own presence as a woman in that classroom, and the meaning of that for educational debate, for accounts of classrooms and for the children going through them. Winston and Jackie (who wrote so neatly) could easily have children of their own by now, children old enough to have reached the same stage of their schooling as Winston and Jackie had reached then. It would be good to feel that they were getting more and doing better than their parents were twenty years ago. Good, but unrealistic. Schools have not become better places for most children since then. I offer this book in the hope, nonetheless, that future generations of girls and boys will one day get something better.

I

Culture and Paradox

Whereas most societies have held back from educating girls, they have relied on women in a variety of ways to educate their children, and that in its turn has unsettled the notion of what a teacher is, making it simultaneously honoured and despised as a social role. Women have always been the first teachers of children, and this may explain their invisibility. They are there and not there. For, disconcertingly, the story of women as teachers has always shifted between home and school, between mothers and not mothers, between the private and the public, between the unpaid and the paid. Charting these activities as a history marks out the work itself and those who have performed it as inaccessible, unreliable and apt to vanish beneath layers and indeed generations of disparagement and suspicion. Whatever it is that women do when they teach children could be better done by men, the story seems to go, if only people were prepared to pay men the going rate to do it.

This, then, is a slippery tale but an important one. Teaching children plays a decisive part in the cultural life of all societies, because it embodies a society's methods of inducting new generations into shared practices and values. It also measures out women's scope for participating in the culture and the ways in which the character of that partici-pation may be checked on and supervised. So much cultural activity originates in the procedures a community devises to regulate women's sexual energies and productivity. Think of the significance of rituals celebrating the coming of age of boys and girls, the lengths to which societies will go to preserve young women's virginity and to guard against female adultery. Think of weddings and their attendant paraphernalia of dowries and symbols of innocence. Yet it is also characteristic of the ways in which all that cultural activity has developed historically that it should exclude women: whether as priests or artists or scholars or judges.

That ambivalence generates others. In trying to tell a small part of this story, it is to that primary tangle I return again and again; to the meanings of the discrepancy between a reliance on women as teachers of children, on the one hand, and the doubts surrounding the value of teaching girls, or even the benefits of regarding women as equal actors in cultural life, on the other. I shall concentrate on England, and most of my examples, though not all, will come from the nineteenth and twentieth centuries. So that there will be, inevitably, a somewhat local and particular cast to my argument and my illustrations. However, a comparison with the way state schooling developed in North America will suggest both the general character of much of my argument as well as the quite different and illuminating directions events have taken elsewhere.

Teaching is probably the best example of the ambiguities inherent in all paid work performed by women. Their qualifications for doing such work at all have usually rested on what they were thought to know and be able to do 'naturally'. This often meant no more than an extension of what they were in the habit of doing anyway: bearing children and looking after them up to a certain age, providing and preparing food, making and maintaining clothing and keeping things clean. In many societies women have also farmed, built houses and produced everyday necessities like pots and fabrics. However, the kinds of work which are nowadays thought of as 'women's work' are usually extensions of those traditional activities. Gradually, it is true, jobs like nursing and social or secretarial work developed beyond domestically acquired skills and the similarly acquired capacity to support men in their working lives. There were new technologies, and these were not considered part of women's 'natural' armoury. The important point is that work regarded as traditionally women's terrain has not, for the most part, been thought to need much formal training. Though in those professions which are popular with men as well as women – medicine, psychoanalysis,[1] law and so on – the long training has served to deter a good many women, almost as if without such a deterrent women might imagine themselves better suited to the work (by virtue of their experience or because of popular stereotype) than men.

Views on the education of girls have often been polarised between the need for something minimal and instrumental at one end of the spectrum, and for a kind of luxuriant 'finishing' at the other. The struggle has been to achieve an educational offer which was at least as varied and flexible for girls as for boys and which envisaged the same kinds of work and leisure possibilities for them in adult life. The principal problem with that aspiration, of course, is that most boys are themselves in receipt of a great deal less than that. So that my discussion of women teaching and girls' education will be conducted – of necessity – within an often unedifying account of how little of anything this country has been ready to invest in the education of all its children.

I have been a teacher for more than a quarter of a century and a woman for many more years than that. Women teachers have a long history, and a choppy one, as I have suggested, but women and teaching have not always been a bad fit, by any means, either for the women themselves or for those they have taught. Yet the confusions at the centre of that pair – woman teacher – are apt to erupt periodically, and to reveal in the process some difficult cultural and educational dilemmas. In attempting to address those dilemmas and to set them within the historical and contemporary contexts which they are able, in their turn, to illuminate, I want also to characterise those contexts and hear the voices of some of the women who have spent years of their lives as teachers, tussling with the contradictions inherent in doing so.

For most of the time the fact that a majority of school teachers are women and have been for more than a century is something people know but barely reflect on. From time to time, however, a spate of stories will appear in the press expressing what may be widely held anxieties about women's predominance in the nation's classrooms. In the last two years – a period of great turmoil in education generally – there has been a number of such scare stories. First, there was the sudden and pressing need to recruit more men into teaching and the apparent difficulty of doing so. The man responsible for the entry of potential teachers into training institutions in this country was reported to be

> worried that the knock-on effect of a predominantly female teaching force will be to stereotype the profession further, and deprive children of male role models. A number of recruitment strategies have been tried, for example sending male teachers to talk to would-be recruits, with seemingly little success.[2]

He was joined by an even more vociferous professor of education to become 'only two of many' – a typical sleight of hand – 'who fear that the shortage of men may also impair the education offered to children'. This was feared as a possibility for a number of reasons. The absence of a male role model (sometimes thought important for all children, but more often simply for boys) was one. A bias away from science and technology was another. A suspicion 'that

women teachers may have been gradually, and unknowingly'
– another nice touch – 'moulding education and assessment
to suit their gender' was another.[3]

Other themes have received a good deal of attention
recently. There is a concern that unemployment is becoming
more of a male problem than a female one. There is also,
as the *Independent* put it at the end of 1993, 'ample further
evidence confirming the trend towards employing women'.[4]
This does not simply mean that women now support their
families by working when their husbands are unemployed,
though it can mean that. It is more likely to mean that families
have either two earners or none. This has to do with the
decline in manufacturing industry, the growth in the services
sector and women's greater flexibility and willingness to
work part-time and outside conventional career structures.
The effects of this are far-reaching, but the concentrating
fear is, as it has usually been, of 'an ever-growing pool of
virtually unemployable young men'. That fear is exacerbated,
explained and glossed by another current concern: that girls
are now performing better in public examinations, represent
at least half of those competing for places in higher education,
and that schools are therefore becoming increasingly in-
hospitable to boys. A series of articles about women teachers
seducing their male pupils and even marrying them is icing on
the cake, perhaps, but well aimed to terrify parents who
might otherwise have supposed their children's teachers to
be on their side. Such stories also carry a more serious allusion
to the supposed dangers of leaving boys to the predatory
attentions of young women teachers; and I shall return to
other manifestations of this fear.

When I began teaching English in the late sixties it was in
a large, mixed comprehensive school in London. I had gone
to a co-educational and so-called 'progressive' boarding
school myself, and was taken aback by assumptions that I
might find it difficult to teach boys. There were even people
who expressed fear for my safety amongst all those large and

violent boys they expected me to find in my classes. I was once introduced to Arthur Koestler, and I remember that when I told him I was a teacher he seemed genuinely surprised and dismayed to hear that I taught boys as well as girls between the ages of eleven and eighteen. He objected to my calling myself a teacher, preferring 'schoolmistress', which I think of as having had something of a gartered and saucy ring to his ears; and he did not at all fear for my safety, but for the safety of the boys I taught. How could more or less fully grown and possibly even intelligent young men expect to learn from a youngish woman they could only relate to sexually and who could not conceivably be equipped intellectually to prepare them for university, let alone for adult life? Koestler's patrician candour is likely to have originated in Hungary rather than Britain, but his view has a long history and is one I believe to be shared (if not openly) by a good many men in this country. Moreover, it has powerfully influenced government policy during the eighties and early nineties.

Of course, I did find some boys difficult to teach, and some girls too. There were, for instance, the 'fourth-year leavers' in those days, with their cropped hair, cropped jeans, large boots and braces. 'Bovver boys' is how they were described by the press and how they cheerfully referred to themselves at times. Many of them looked forward eagerly to their fifteenth birthday and the end of school. Some of them anticipated this happy day by months, if not years, and were more likely to be found working in the market than in school. In those days we did not expect boys to be unemployed when they left school, and when they did come to our lessons they were given to marvelling at our willingness to work so hard for so little, when they could have fixed us all up with something far more lucrative in Shepherd's Bush market.

Most of the teachers in that school were women, as were one of the two deputy-heads and two of the eight heads of houses. Apart from that, the school was run by men, and the only department headed by a woman until many years later was the Maths Department. Even then, though, the women teachers felt there was some strength in numbers; and it was women who campaigned to end corporal punishment (which had only been administered by men, anyway) and to change from an organisation of twelve streams in each year to twelve 'mixed-ability' classes. When the school-leaving age was raised to 16 in 1972, it was principally the women in my school who developed Mode 3 CSE[5] examinations, in the belief that their emphasis on coursework assessment would be more attractive to our new fifth-year pupils, and more productive of good teaching and learning.

Such reforms have been thought of as 'cranky' or 'ideological'. However, it would not be true to say that in the late sixties and early seventies we were consciously fighting on a feminist ticket, either on our own behalf or on behalf of our girl students. Nor did the moves I am describing always meet with the approval of other teachers on the left. Indeed, the consequences of those campaigns were later anathematised as amongst those tactics of containment (especially the containment of boys) which masqueraded as progressive and humanising, when they were in fact patronising and out of sympathy with the real-life needs of working-class boys heading for unskilled work in manufacturing industries or for the army or the police. Many women of my generation would have to confess – as I confess – that we were moved above all by a desire to establish bearable relations with the boys in our classes rather than by any thought of doing better by the girls. But the girls were, in fact, doing better, as they have continued to do better whenever they are offered more: better, that is to say, than they had hitherto. Raising the school-leaving age, unstreaming, coursework assessment: these have improved the performance of girls noticeably and unequivocally, as they have the performance of boys, though less dramatically. Even the government was prepared to concede in 1991 that the plan to reduce the coursework element of examinations at GCSE (in the interests of a necessary 'stiffening' and 'rigour') was likely to reduce girls' scores by at least half a grade. The hope that this would redress the balance in favour of boys has not so far been realised.

In the early seventies, research and public discussion of education focused on violence and truancy and discipline, and therefore on boys. The left was just as likely as the right to question teachers' enthusiasm for collaborative rather than competitive kinds of teaching and for more open-ended forms of assessment, which were supportive of the curriculum rather than independent of it. Women teachers were often characterised as indulgent towards boys, motherly when they should have been realistic, kind when they should have stood firm. I remember that not long after I began teaching I was visited by an especially lumbering Head of House, who assured me that if any of the 'lads' in my classes gave me either lip or steel boot, he'd thrash them to within an inch of their lives. The control of working-class boys was understood to be the principal problem for schools like mine, and, of course, a particular problem for their women teachers. And we did worry about boys: about the numbers of them who failed to learn to read and write fluently, about their truancy and their disruptive behaviour in class. When the English Department decided to take over and teach the 'remedial reading' required by a good number of children in the school, it was boys who appeared in our classes; hardly ever girls.

Yet we never congratulated ourselves on the girls, and I wonder whether we even congratulated them. There they were, rarely causing trouble, finding school perfectly acceptable for the most part, even gathering qualifications for more education or for work, and we did little more than breathe sighs of relief. Sometimes they even brought younger brothers or sisters to school with them, because their parents expected them to give that sort of a hand.

State education in Britain is provided by women to an extent which is rarely acknowledged. Indeed, virtually all schooling for young children, whether public or private, is provided by women. So that parents who pay for their sons' education may be paying for an absence of women, amongst other things; and that may be just one of the more visible signs of the unease produced by women's presence in schools: an unease that has been widely felt and expressed for as long as there has been a state system of schooling. The periodic spasms of alarm and criticism levelled at state education in this country are hard to understand without a sense of how gender has always – covertly as well as openly – articulated with views of culture and of the upbringing and education of children. Women are made responsible for the transmission and mediation of the central themes and values of the culture: for what is regarded as necessary knowledge, for morality, for language and accepted forms of social behaviour and for beliefs about family, religion, nation. Yet the fact that this process is submitted to constant surveillance and continuous legislation – and with minimal consultation with classroom teachers – is an indication of how little women are trusted to take responsibility for the system within which they work.

It is not far-fetched to see the frenzies of legislation and revision undertaken during the late 1980s and the early 1990s in Britain, in the name of 'standards' and the market, as a response to what can seem like the feminisation of education, and, by usually unspoken extension, its infantilisation as well. The hostilities are deep-rooted, and contemporary versions of them may actually be disguised by the evasions entailed in paying lip-service to Equal Opportunities. A strange nostalgia persists for schooldays when boys were boys and teachers were men; though that is not, in fact, a time that many people can actually remember if they were not educated privately. Nor, of course, have all men who taught escaped the patronage and contempt meted out to their female colleagues.

When politicians fulminate these days about 'woolly' educationalists and poorly trained teachers, they are, in fact, attacking a predominantly female workforce and even traditions of research and practice which have in some cases been initiated and implemented by women, though usually under the management and guidance of men. But politicians do not say much about that; any more than they say who they mean by parents. Teachers and parents are apparently ungendered and beneficent categories of people, until, that is, they evince opinions of a professional kind as teachers or lack male partners as parents. Yet the blameless parents who are invoked as emblematic of the new accountability of schools (and as stand-in for tax-payers), active consumers and participants in their children's schooling, most likely to support schools as governors or fundraisers or even as classroom aides, are much more likely to be women than men. Just as teachers are. And how easily that parent is transformed into the unmarried teenage mother, callously milking the system, while the idealised teacher, mercifully uncontaminated by ideas or reading or ideology – and consequently the perfect model for the next generation of teachers – loses her innocence as soon as she claims knowledge, ideas, an intellectual life of her own. Can parents really want their children to be taught by teachers who are 'passive, unintelligent and accommodating'?[6]

It is the contrast between the passionate thinking and feeling that she remembers in herself as an intelligent and creative young woman, who was reluctant in many ways to become a teacher, and the silence enjoined on her as a teacher, which informs this moving passage from Carolyn Steedman's 'Prisonhouses'.[7]

> I don't care any more about sounding pretentious, so now I tell people who ask at parties why I did it for such a very long time, that it did seem a way of being a socialist in everyday life. I believed immensely in their [the children's] intelligence, thought I could give them

peace and quiet, a space of rest from the impossible lives that many of them had to lead. I read everything there was to read, later was to make myself a minor expert on children's writing. No one cared – indeed, no one knew – what social and political theories informed my classroom practice: I only looked like a good teacher, doing what all the textbooks said I should. I think with great fondness now of my little socialist republic, that intensity of use of time and space, the pleasures of its working, my clear-sighted refusal of all the liberal notions of false democracy that the official pedagogy of child-centredness provided me with. What mattered was that they could do it: learn, learn to read, defy the world's definition of them as deprived, pitiful, social priority children. And I kept the door shut, and the children quiet.

We are returned to the overlap between those twin spheres of women's influence on children – families and education – as crucial to the contradictions of women's paid work in schools. The world nods approvingly at a good teacher. The world does not want to know what she thinks she is doing. Then there is the manipulating of notions like 'nature' and 'culture' to become coterminous with the maternal and the paternal. Such abstractions have recoiled on the ambiguous teacher/mother figure: a figure at once known by each of us – impossibly familiar – and yet bizarrely suppressed within so many public accounts of what culture is, and what education and schools are for.

Fear of women's influence as teachers and of girls' academic successes at school (and some sense of a possibly sinister link between the two) is by no means a new fear. Its contemporary manifestations are unprecedented only in so far as they are disguised by the apparent even-handedness of current ways of discussing the subject. In the past, access was denied to many girls on the grounds of their 'natures' and presumed future needs as wives and mothers. Nowadays, the arbitrary insertion (or omission) of an occasional 'she', like so much Equal Opportunities rhetoric, can work to deny specific and telling gender differences in the disposition of power in schools, in teaching, learning, curriculum, management and academic outcomes, and, most significantly, in the debates and documents accounting for them.

Women have in the past been blamed for the poor health and low spirits of the young men the nation needed for the army and the empire.[8] Now they are blamed as parents and as teachers for the weak wits and inadequate technical achievements of yet another generation of (mainly) boys; for girls are doing demonstrably better and, of course, offering serious competition to their male contemporaries. The blame is continuous and opportunistic. Only the pretexts for that blame change. Though, perhaps fortuitously, the two periods most marked by this sort of paranoid distrust of women were the 1880s and 1890s and the 1980s; very different periods, of course, though each was presided over by a woman: by Queen Victoria and by Margaret Thatcher.[9] It may even be this which helped to produce such paroxysms of defensive suspicion of women.

It is hard to explain the contempt directed at women teachers, hard to explain and hard to characterise. It is useful to do so, because it is irrational and ill-informed and linked irrevocably to the low esteem in which teaching is held generally. Public contempt is also experienced, painfully and often angrily, as part of all the other tensions inherent in their role, by women who become teachers. The contempt has been capacious, inescapable, but always contradictory. For instance, teachers have been thought sexually repressed and sexually repressive at precisely those moments when they were also being prevented from marrying by the exercise of the 'marriage bar'. They have been found perilously pretty and culpably ugly. Fault has been found as easily with those thought winsomely permissive as with those thought grimly disciplinarian. They may be imagined as meek and biddable, or as battleaxes. There has also, of course, been a consistent tradition of thinking teachers stupid and anti-intellectual, mouthpieces of prevailing dogma or, on the contrary, hopelessly outdated in their ill-considered adherences. Yet a parallel but alternative fear persists that they may, in fact, be far too opinionated and political and in a position, therefore, to be of considerable danger to the young. Their commitment to their work may be read as evidence of a narrow, unworldly and ignorant enthusiasm, but their inability to do any other kind of work leads also to their being cynical and lazy. And so on.

Accompanying these fairly widely held views are slightly more nuanced ones. The teachers of the youngest children are always the stupidest. They teach children rather than subjects, in the current lingo. This accords neatly with the more likely presence of women in classes for the youngest children. The intelligence of teachers is thought to increase with their pupils' ages and in relation to the amount of money parents pay for their children's schooling: you will get a better class of teacher, according to this view, in an independent school (where, incidentally, teachers may teach without a qualification to do so). And that progression is also gendered. The teacher of young children has often been thought motherly but/and brainless, and many are the university tutors' references I have received recommending a student for teaching, but suggesting that her shyness, her apparent interest in 'other people' and her anticipated lower second indicate that she would do better as a primary teacher. Men are usually recommended for secondary teaching, whatever their degree.

Teachers are not only targets for the right, of course. They are frequently envisaged as conspiring with their political masters. For Louis Althusser, all but a very few 'heroic' teachers (and those I think were not pictured as women) were implicated in the repressive intentions and procedures of schooling. I remember several (always male) student teachers in the late seventies drinking in, with almost sado-masochistic fervour, the message of his famous aside on the subject.

> I ask the pardon of those teachers who, in dreadful conditions, attempt to turn the few weapons they can find in the history and learning they 'teach' against the ideology, the system and the practices in which they are trapped. They are a kind of hero. But they are rare and how many (the majority) do not even begin to suspect the 'work' the system (which is bigger than they are and crushes them) forces them to do, or worse, put all their heart and ingenuity into performing it with the most advanced awareness (the famous new methods!). So little do they suspect it that their own devotion contributes to the maintenance and nourishment of this ideological representation of the School, which makes the School today as 'natural', indispensable-useful and even beneficial for our contemporaries as the Church was 'natural', indispensable and generous for our ancestors a few centuries ago.[10]

I suppose Simone de Beauvoir's account of her time as a teacher in a girls' *lycée* could be said to belong within such a 'heroic' tradition, though I wonder exactly what was learned by her pupils apart from strategies of resistance.

> On such subjects as labour, capital, justice, and colonialism I said what I thought, and said it passionately. Most of my listeners rose in rebellion at this. Both in class and when writing their essays they belaboured me with their fathers' carefully polished arguments, which I then proceeded to demolish. One of the most intelligent girls left her seat in the front row and went to the very back, where she sat, arms crossed, refusing to take notes and glaring at me with stony hatred.[11]

Such hubris in anyone else, and especially in Miss Jean Brodie, would run the risk of being ridiculed.[12] Women teachers are more likely to be taxed with ignorance. Even for Valerie Walkerdine, whose imaginative classroom research has meant a great deal to many of them, teachers are deluded and collusive and usually, as it happens, women: middle-class, by virtue of their work, the enemies of working-class mothers and their daughters, and gullibly cornucopian in their patience and generosity towards boys.[13] For the American feminist, Madeleine Grumet, who is on her side,

> it is the female elementary schoolteacher who is charged
> with the responsibility to lead the great escape. At the
> sound of the bell, she brings the child from the concrete
> to the abstract, from the fluid time of the domestic
> day to the segmented schedule of the school day, from
> the physical work, comfort and sensuality of home to
> the mentalistic, passive, sedentary, pretended asexuality
> of the school – in short, from the woman's world to the
> man's. She is a traitor, and the low status of the teaching
> profession may be derived from the contempt her betrayal
> draws from both sexes. Mothers relinquish their children
> to her, and she hands them over to men who respect the
> gift but not the giver.[14]

The dislike and suspicion of women teachers have been translated into varieties of self-disparagement. Nell Sampson remembered the frame of mind in which she began her teacher training in the first year of the First World War. Her tone of self-denigration has a generic rather than an individual ring to it.

> My father died when I was seventeen and still at school,
> money was scarce and it was imperative that I should
> earn as soon as possible. Those in authority pointed out
> that I would be useless in an office as I was hopeless at
> figures and couldn't spell; that owing to my propensity

to day-dream I should probably kill anyone I attempted to nurse; but that as I had passed exams, I could at least teach. So in September 1914, full of doubt and fore-boding, I entered St. Matthias College.[15]

Brains, looks and clothes become interchangeable terms in the covert regulation of women teachers and their potentially wayward sexuality. Some of us asked in the early seventies if we might wear trousers to work. To do so was regarded as brazen, unprofessional and political. So several already 'naturally' trousered persons gave much judicious thought to the issue. The decision eventually went our way, but was relayed to us with a list of caveats evincing a positively unseemly interest in anatomy and current fashion. Trousers could only be worn as part of what was known then as a 'trouser suit'. Bums must not be seen. And there was also a list of the kinds of trousers we might absolutely not wear: ones made of denim or jersey, for instance, and ones which were either tight or flared. It was not, of course, that any of the women who availed themselves of these new liberties bothered much with the detail. But we yielded to the convention which lets men wear what they like, so long as it includes trousers, while exercising what is allowed as control over female dress in the interests of professionalism.

This may seem unimportant. It stands in, however, for some central ambiguities. The possible sexual provocations of a young woman teacher may be used to cancel her professional competence and judgement. Just as the absence of sexual provocations in an older woman teacher may exile her from the human altogether. Both are assessed not as workers but as more or less desirable women and as more or less well adjusted to a small number of fundamentally sexual roles. And since a woman's actual sexual relations (like a male teacher's) are not ones she is likely to trail into school with her, she is often found sexually unsatisfactory.

Many women have wanted to think of intelligence as

ungendered, to believe, with Mary Wollstonecraft, that 'mind has no sex'. That would only be plausible within a view of intelligence as wholly innate and impervious to development, education, culture and all the uses our lives allow us to make of our minds. Teachers are occupationally inclined to regard intelligence as capable of growth and change, and as always embodied. And minds develop within bodies, which are gendered, and therefore profoundly influenced by whatever that may mean in a particular society. Certainly, the invoking of something called a 'female mind' has not as a rule been benign. It has usually been treated as a troubling entity: at once liable to fevers of hysteria and debility if overtaxed in any way, and when apparently able to withstand life's hazards likely to be thought 'unfeminine' and even freakish or monstrous. The uses of the female mind, some might claim, are clear and negative; for if it did not exist it would have to be invented, as the norm against which rationality and common sense have come to be defined. And even 'common sense' itself, that stony and immutable quality we know so well, slips tellingly within contemporary debate between absolutely opposite meanings. There is, first, the *natural* rapport with children, the intuition of the woman primary teacher: properties, indeed, which justify her overwhelming presence in classrooms filled with young children. Yet within regulatory government policies, another kind of 'common sense' is able to transform those 'natural' teacherly talents into 'new-fangled', 'progressive' and insufficiently rigorous or consistent practices, requiring the attention of outsiders (men, for the most part), who become, for this purpose, the repositories of common sense, intuition and a natural and traditional concern for the nation's children.

One training college, which was determined to increase the recruitment of teachers for country schools, published its plans for doing so in 1865. The following paragraph gives some idea of the state of popular prejudice at the time and a characteristically lack-lustre attempt at combating it in the interests of encouraging entry into teaching.

> Unfortunately the idea is still too prevalent, that a young woman who is broken down in health, or too delicate for household service – a cripple, perhaps, or deficient in one or more of her organs, who can get no other employment, may, as a last resource, become a schoolmistress. Others imagine that, although a girl has no special inclination for teaching, yet, if she is a good girl, she ought to be a teacher. Undoubtedly goodness and piety are prime qualifications for a schoolmistress, but they are not the only ones. A schoolmistress must be strong in health, pleasant in her manners, fond of children, sufficiently well-informed, and apt to convey her information in simple and attractive language. It should also be borne in mind that, as country children are generally more dull of comprehension than those that dwell in towns, it needs clearness of head, with patience and tact, to teach them.[16]

Thousands and thousands of girls and young women went into teaching from the second half of the nineteenth century with such views ringing in their ears. What I have wanted to know, and have tried to find out, was how that decision to become a teacher looked to them; what alternatives there were for most of these women; what kind of life they anticipated as teachers. And what the satisfactions and the disappointments turned out to be. In the pages that follow, the voices of teachers themselves will take over the narrative at times, with their own accounts of how they have confronted the tensions inherent in the work they do. Teaching has usually been better paid than other work for which women were thought eligible, and it often allowed them to gather more education and to gain some independence and flexibility in their lives. Many women – and I include myself amongst them – have enjoyed teaching and felt pleased to be doing well what seemed to them valuable work. Women who were bringing up their own children have, since the Second World War, found that teaching chimed with the demands and rhythms of that period of their lives. This in itself has been held against them. But teaching also cast them, whether as unmarried working women in the past or now, or as married women with children since the 1940s,[17] into a social limbo, defined by the contradictions and the disparagements women, and women doing this particular kind of paid work, tend to attract to themselves.

Though some middle-class girls have been going into elementary and then primary teaching since the 1930s, most teachers of young children and of older working-class children have come from working-class or lower middle-class backgrounds themselves, so that teaching was seen to offer them advantages and freedoms of a particular kind. Yet what teaching also entailed was becoming the embodiment for most children and their parents of middle-class men's views of child-rearing. These views were usually quite outside the teacher's own experience, and they were to be implemented within what were seen as potentially coercive relations with the working-class children she taught. More than that, it meant the upholding of a view of culture and of education which was in principle at loggerheads, not only with the culture of the children, but often with her own cultural experience as well.

That tension has been at the heart of teaching, I believe, and it has acquired a special importance for women teachers. The best things that go on in classrooms are always in some sense an articulation and working through of that tension. There have, of course, been teachers and writers on education who have felt able to side-step that dilemma: clear in their own minds that schools were there to provide versions of knowledge and skill which can be agreed beforehand and independently of who the children in the classroom may actually be. Different accounts of that view of schooling – from Mr Gradgrind's to those of a long line of recent secretaries of state for education – promulgate for their time, it might be said, a view of schooling which ignores how children learn and ignores the culture of their families and communities, which may well be in unproductive conflict with the culture schools promote.

When, on the contrary, teachers have faced the implications of cultural and class conflict in the classroom and engaged with that conflict as necessary and potentially productive, they have been able to feel surer of their ground. When, in addition, they have set their own experience as women – and as women with particular class and race allegiances – within an analysis which acknowledges the strangely entangled histories of state education and the educating and professionalising of women, then we begin to have some understanding both of the obstacles to creating the best possible system of schooling, and some ways forward.

Perhaps the closest parallel to the contradictions embedded in the teacher's role has been the position of the policeman. Carolyn Steedman has written of the formation of provincial police forces in this country between 1856 and 1880,[18] and has characterised the working-class policeman as 'the good and docile and comprehensible servant', with his carefully circumscribed powers and duties, and his right, for instance, to whip juvenile offenders: a combination which made him, though always anomalously, a figure of authority, able to inspire fear and dislike. Policemen too 'were placed in a position of deep conflict', as Steedman writes, employed in part because of what they were seen to have in common with the criminal classes, but there too to uphold the values of the property owners with whom they had little in common themselves. And *their* account of things has not been much heard. Less even than teachers have policemen written about their work and their lives. It is a parallel which takes us only so far, however, since gender inevitably unsettles it. Yet questions of authority, class, race, gender are played out to this day in classrooms, in ways which can never be simply resolved or refereed.

Take Anita Barley, for instance, who teaches English in an East London girls' school, where almost all the pupils are Asian or Afro-Caribbean. She recently completed a study of her own teaching of literature in that school, and she began it with moments remembered from her own childhood and schooldays.

St. Joseph's Convent, St. Lucia. 1976. A young black teacher stands before a class of twenty-five second-form students reading from an anthology of traditional English poetry, entitled *A Choice of Poets*. Today's reading is 'The Darkling Thrush' by Thomas Hardy . . .

During the last week or so, we have been studying some nature poems, 'English' nature, and I am even more excited about Hardy's poem as its focus is winter. I try to snuggle comfortably into my hard, wooden seat, and pray that the oppressive heat, both in and outside, may subside by the time the bell rings for home time. I use the word 'snuggle' because my mind, momentarily, would like to enter the English rural countryside of say, Dorset, where Hardy was born and presumably the setting of his poem. 'Snuggle', because dreaming of ice and frost, I too, for a change, like Hardy and the men he writes about feeling cold, wish to seek the 'household fires' which he speaks of in his account of winter drear.

My attempts at entering Hardy's world are futile since it is impossible to escape the penetrating rays of the afternoon sun which have chosen to filter through the open doors and window. The sweltering heat descends mercilessly upon the white-walled building, engulfing us all, drowning us all in a sea of sweat, where all I can do is crouch helplessly behind a loose-leafed exercise book which serves as both fan and Hardy-note-taking paper. I can no longer imagine frost being 'spectre gray', the 'tangled bine-stems' which scored the sky, nor the 'bleak twigs' among which the old, frail thrush rests and sings 'Of joy illimited'. Instead, my thoughts have wandered over to Ma Roy's grocery store, where, instructed by my father, I will buy 'salt-fish' to make *accra*, a local fish cake, for tomorrow's religious observance of Good Friday – a day when Catholics (the majority of St. Lucians are Roman Catholic) abstain from eating flesh of any kind, except of course fish, as a mark of respect for the suffering of Christ crucified and nailed to the cross.

As my English teacher moves to a discussion of the poem, I am suddenly drawn back to Hardy's winter forest and I again have a desire, an uncontrollable one, to feel cold and to experience snow. You see, though I was born in England, I spent most of my early life in the Caribbean after having emigrated with my West Indian parents to the tiny island of St. Lucia, my father's home-land (my mother was Guyanese). This happened when I was seven. I am now at this convent school receiving a rigid and formal education, very English in its ethos, as St. Lucia has not yet broken ties with England.[19]

This, remember, is a young black woman teacher recalling her own formation in a school where she was taught in English by black Catholic women on an island where French Creole was the language spoken at home by most families, in addition to the English learned in school. Anita Barley's experience seems a good place to start, for it carries the peculiar treacheries of an English education on its travels from the mainland to the colonies or ex-colonies, and back again. It also allows us to see the tensions embodied in that woman teacher, as she offers up the riches of Hardy's poetry and of the English language and landscape to girls growing up on this tiny and beautiful Caribbean island. For Anita

Barley's own family, as for the school, these discrepancies were unspoken, as were the egregious differences between the world of English literature that she is excitedly encountering and the physical world she inhabits. The differences are not made accessible to discussion in the classroom, are not there as part of the curriculum, whether under the rubric of history, geography, English, religious education. And the effect is to rule out even as useful benchmark the imaginative energy of her experience of, amongst other things, her own language and landscape. Yet Barley's study also takes pride in the pleasure her parents felt that she should be reading English literature, and respects the similar and often passionately expressed wishes of her pupils' parents in this country that their children will read Shakespeare, for instance, at school.

What is learned later, but painfully and often angrily – and too late for many children – is the history that has submerged one kind of experience and culture beneath another, and has then invoked transcendant values as justification for that history. Barley's study and her assembling of isolated memories from her own childhood gather new meanings within an accumulating sense of her life as a detail and a paradigm of imperialism. Her memories catch a central trans-action within the history of British imperialism: the faith in English literature as bond and emollient, and a readiness to leave that process in the capable hands of women. Her memories continue,

> the lesson on Hardy's poem continues long after the school bell has rung. Yes, as I lick the spiced-accra juices dripping down my fingers and hear the delicious melodies of 'patwa' spoken by men and women who have gathered under a nearby lamppost to discuss the deteriorating political scene in St. Lucia, I am sitting in the coolest part of our balcony, aware of other pleasant sounds – the swish and sway of banana leaves in our yard and the night cries of frogs and crickets both near

and far. It is in this location, against this type of distinct cultural setting, that I choose to write my own nature poem, a homework assignment set by my English teacher, which would later complete and complement the literature essay on style. I write about winter and snow. Although I have no copy of the poem I wrote, I can remember vividly writing of snow-covered fields and dales ('dales' is not a St. Lucian word, 'valley' is), bare branches, grey and white, and apple trees in orchards, clearly a marked contrast to my own cultural surrounding and experiences. I had grasped something of English culture and my writing of things 'English' confirmed a desire to be not only successful at English, but also to be a better person.[20]

What becomes possible for Anita Barley and for other women teachers as they put the complex memories of their own schooling and its cultural anomalies into the analysis they need as teachers, is reflection as well as new texts. Barley's study goes on to describe the introduction of West Indian, Indian, African and Afro-American texts and writers to young people, not in the spirit of 'the threatened replacement of *Beowulf* by *The Color Purple*', as Peter Conrad once reductively put it,[21] but deliberately adding to the literature syllabus, in the interests of developing the scope and the repertoire of the girls she teaches. In their various ways her students may (or may not) 'take to' these books, as coming out of, or reflecting, lives which may be closer to their own than those assumed by or evident in texts which are more conventionally taught in school. But that cannot be straight-forwardly anticipated. And much more important, in any case, is their gathering sense (illustrated through transcripts of classroom discussion and through examples of writing) of the history that has divided the cultures they are coming to know, as well as united them. What Barley's study demon-strates above all is that she has as a teacher a personal and intellectual interest in expanding on what these girls are offered, in developing their own critical powers and their knowledge and their sense of the constraints and the possibilities of their own lives.

At the end of her study, Anita Barley draws on Edward Said's analysis in the final chapter of his *Culture and Imperialism*, where he argues for a broader, more capacious and dynamic and, indeed, transformational, sense of culture, as necessarily hybrid, and always 'encumbered, or entangled and overlapping', within which literatures and their readers and writers are always connected and interdependent.

> But reading and writing texts are never neutral activities: there are interests, powers, passions, pleasures entailed no matter how aesthetic or entertaining the work. Media, political economy, mass institutions – in fine, the tracings of secular power and the influence of the state – are part of what we call literature. And just as it is true that we cannot read literature by men without also reading literature by women – so transfigured has been the shape of literature – it is also true that we cannot deal with the literature of the peripheries without also attending to the literature of the metropolitan centres.[22]

We need to extend that sort of analysis of literature to education, to an understanding of how discussion in both areas has so often started from assumptions about the inferior cultural capacities of readers (or learners) and the need to submit the minds of such inferior beings to versions of what is then asserted as unarguably the best in the world. Literature and culture within such a dispensation can be expected to deliver an instant and magic improvement, it seems, in these same inferior minds: a careless and perfunctory kind of optimism, which is uncharacteristic of teachers, I would have thought.

Gauri Viswanathan has also made use of Said's analysis in

her study of the moves made by successive British governments to introduce literature into Indian schooling during the
middle decades of the nineteenth century. She writes in *The
Masks of Conquest*,

> A vital if subtle connection exists between a discourse in
> which those who are to be educated are represented
> as morally and intellectually deficient and the attribution
> of moral and intellectual values to the literary works they
> are assigned to read.[23]

As a teacher of literature in a secondary school, in this country
or in St Lucia, Anita Barley is supported and enlightened
by such rebuttals. They give history and perspective to her
own childhood and to the complexity of what she is now
aiming for in an East London girls' school. But in different
ways both Said and Viswanathan leave her out, leave teachers
out. As principal targets of both curriculum policy-making
and imperial take-over, teachers disappear into their own
educational histories, into the material and the texts they
teach, into their own pedagogic designs on those they teach
and into the political plans and purposes of the masters and
architects of a society's schooling. Yet teachers, whether they
are the Indian teachers of English literature in India or the St
Lucian women who taught the poems of Thomas Hardy to
Anita Barley and the other girls in her class, are themselves
snagged on the ambivalences of their own education and
professional training and on their own oblique and uneasy
relation to the powers and the virtues that all education
promises its pupils.

2

The Feminisation of Schooling in Two Countries

The invisibility of women teachers in most available accounts of nineteenth-century life is partly due to the social limbo they were likely to inhabit. Their isolation from families and even within the communities they served put them outside any recognisable class identity. This has made it difficult to discover very much, either generally or in detail, about the lives of the increasing numbers of young women who trained as teachers and worked in schools, sometimes throughout their lives. If they were occasionally somewhat glancingly remembered by their pupils, it was often as figures either of caricature, or of some entirely natural, and also entirely unfamilial, provenance, rather than as individuals who had chosen – it is true, from a somewhat limited set of possibilities – to teach in elementary schools. Such work offered itself, if only temporarily, as an alternative to marriage and looking after families, as often other people's as their own. Yet the choice of teaching was a revealing one, involving often pressing and contradictory motives in the woman herself, which are able to tell us a good deal about women's experiencing of class and poverty and family and sex.

Jessie Chambers, the friend and lover of D.H. Lawrence's youth, who wrote *D.H. Lawrence: A Personal Record* in answer to the disparaging version of their friendship that has been read into Paul Morel's friendship and brief love affair with Miriam in Lawrence's *Sons and Lovers*, gives us a startlingly vivid sense of the link for a girl like her between becoming a teacher and getting an education for herself in the early years of this century.

> At that period I was in a state of furious discontent and rebellion. I was the family drudge and hated it. My lack of education was a constant humiliation. The desire for knowledge and a longing for beauty tortured me. I came to the conclusion that unless I could achieve some degree of education I had better never have been born. I quarrelled continually with my brothers, who tried to order me about. I felt an Ishmael, with my hand against everybody, and everybody's hand against me. I did not know that Lawrence was aware of my state of mind, but one day he suddenly took an end of chalk from his pocket and wrote on the stable door:
> *Nil desperandum.*
> 'What does it mean?' I asked, although I knew.
> 'Never despair,' he replied, with an enigmatic smile, and ran away.
> Eventually I succeeded in making myself so disagreeable that mother in desperation sent me back to school and I became a pupil-teacher. Then began an arduous life of studying, teaching, and helping with the housework, which still somehow left time for the most exciting games.[1]

Jessie, the third of the seven children of a tenant farmer, whose wife was a friend of Lawrence's mother, was barely fifteen when she won this concession from her mother. She remembers getting her first wages – five gold sovereigns, which was, incidentally, double the going rate of the 1880s – fifteen months later, and she was seventeen when she was first sent by the local education authority to the Ilkeston Pupil-teacher Centre, to which Lawrence was also sent as a pupil-teacher; though his three years at Nottingham High

School meant that, unlike Jessie, he was able to prepare at once for the King's Scholarship[2] and matriculation. Both of them knew that the education and training they were being offered was wretched in many ways, always qualified by the disdain and the niggardliness of those concerned with the delivery of education to working-class children. Yet these were also wonderful times, as Jessie wrote.

> I knew quite well that the manner of our education was a beggarly makeshift, but for me it was wealth beyond price. We went for only two and a half out of the five school days, having to teach in school on the other days. But to sit down in a class and be taught, no matter how crudely, instead of struggling all day trying to teach children, or sitting alone at a table in the middle of a noisy schoolroom 'studying'; to mix with a number of girls of my own age and occupation; the long early morning walk to the railway station, and the novelty of the short journey by train, these things filled out the days with wonder and delight. And when the mellow chimes of the church clock drifted across the market square to us in our classroom, I could not escape the feeling that in spite of the meanness of our situation, we were the heirs, and in a sense the fellows of the scholars of all time.[3]

The Chambers family were always poor, certainly poorer than the Lawrences. By 1907, when Jessie was twenty, two of her brothers were working as coal-miners, another was a farm worker, and she and her oldest sister were school-teachers. Lawrence's sister Ada also became a teacher, as Lawrence did himself. In fact, most of the young women who were his friends were teachers at one time or another, several training as pupil-teachers with Lawrence and Jessie Chambers. Indeed, it is possible to see that centre in Ilkeston, and others like it, as pivotal to a period of significant change in working-class life. Such centres stood simultaneously for

the effects of this new need for elementary teachers and the
new demands made on the education system by children
who had done well in their elementary schools, and were
demanding more. Thereafter, children like these had either –
in what were still rare cases – gone on to some form of
secondary education, or, by staying on in elementary schools
as pupil-teachers, earned the right to some further training
in the new centres or training colleges, or (as happened to
Lawrence) in the newly created education departments of the
developing university colleges, like the one in Nottingham.
It is difficult to exaggerate the effect of these openings and
possibilities, not just on women, but on families, on relations
between men and women and, inevitably, on the character of
education and of work.

There is no question that, just as Lawrence makes Ursula
in *The Rainbow* think of her own education as a way into
the professional classes, so he and the women teachers he met
in college and the schools where they taught, saw teaching as
a way into a new class and a new way of life.[4] Yet Lawrence
also experienced this, as many teachers have, as a paradox.
For if teaching was a way of moving into another class, this
was a process often dramatised by its involvement with and
proximity to communities and families living in extreme
poverty. Elementary teachers often came from the industrial
or rural working class themselves, though most commonly
from the better-off families within that class. Yet their
education, training and work in schools usually involved
them in mediating a world which was reluctant to accept
teachers as bona fide members of the middle class, while
requiring them to transmit middle-class culture to children
from the poorest families. And even their own access to
reading and to other aspects of middle-class culture was
constrained by the meagre character of what was offered by
most forms of teacher training. The sense of cultural and
class incongruity, and their own uneasy relation to that, was
often felt by teachers to be a serious problem, one which

was to be met by some through socialist politics and union participation, and by others through the kind of individualism that Lawrence confers on Ursula.

Nottingham University College, which was formally opened in 1881, was in some ways characteristic of the technical and philanthropically supported colleges being opened in many Midlands and northern cities during the 1870s and 1880s.[5] Most of these new colleges began from attempts to meet the particular technical needs of each city's local industries. The Nottingham college could be said to have grown out of the impressive traditions of the Mechanics' Institute, which had for years encouraged missionary young scholars, from Cambridge particularly, to give public lectures for working men in Nottingham. But the inspiration behind the setting-up of these institutions had more sources and explanations than that. There was, for instance, a general and growing anxiety that England was lagging seriously behind most European countries, particularly Germany, in the education and technical training it offered the industrial workforce. There was as well a new civic pride in Nottingham's cultural institutions, which now included an art school, a handsome museum and a library. There must also have been a new breed of manufacturers (Sir Jesse Boot was Nottingham's original benefactor), who wished to commemorate themselves through donations to a local college or even a university.

Gladstone had attended the original stone-laying for Nottingham College in 1877, and had on that occasion uttered the words, 'What we, and those who promoted that movement wished for, was that every human being should get all the cultivation of which he was capable.' There were to be no religious tests for entry to the college and no distinctions between men and women students. In its earliest days, the college catered largely for students who had not had a secondary education, so that the level of study was often deplored as scarcely superior to what might be found in a grammar school. And as, predictably, women formed the majority of the students in many areas of its work, particularly amongst the 'day students', their greater numbers were linked to what was regarded as the college's poor academic reputation. One history of the college puts it like this, 'There was a considerable pool of leisured, and no doubt often bored, young females who must have welcomed the opportunities the College offered, if only to get a respite from domestic chores and the vacuity of the contemporary drawing-room.'[6] How painfully often that kind of disparagement served to homogenise and divert attention from the numbers of young women who sought an education.

The development of a department which would train teachers was an essential part of the evolution of the Nottingham college towards university status, and the history of that development illuminates one strand of the preparation of teachers in the last decades of the nineteenth century.

> More important than any of these was the inauguration of classes to train elementary teachers – a development which led eventually to the establishment of an education department. This began in a small way in 1885 with a few evening classes on the science of teaching and school management. Two years later Professor Symes approached the Board of Education to use the College officially for the training of teachers. A royal commission on elementary education, which reported in 1888, favoured the idea of sending a limited number of students who were intending to become teachers to be trained at university institutions where they might acquire a better and a broader culture than that given in the restricted and specialized atmosphere of the average training college. In 1890, when day training colleges were established at the universities, Nottingham was among the first five to be accepted.[7]

D.H. Lawrence spent two years at Nottingham University College, years which were, after his time at Ilkeston Centre, a horrid disappointment, despite the fact that they were years of astonishing intellectual growth for him in other ways. His memory of the college remained sour, however, caught at the end of *The Rainbow* in Ursula's thoughts about her time as a student,

> This was no religious retreat, no seclusion of pure learning. It was a little apprentice-shop where one was further equipped for making money. The college itself was a little, slovenly laboratory for the factory.[8]

That sense of disappointment reverberates through many teachers' accounts of their own education and training. Their dreams of learning and knowledge – gathered, no doubt, from the romance of dreaming spires in cities expressly fortified to keep women out – are swiftly dashed by the adulterated fragments of high culture they were given, by the brisk and practical demands of a training course, and by the disparagement of their own capacities and interests, which students soon learn to read into that bias. Nonetheless, Jessie Chambers, in a moment's admission of despair in 1909, at her relationship with Lawrence and at the tedium of her life, asked to be sent to teach in a school in Nottingham, so that she might attend evening courses at the college.[9]

Any consideration of the relation between what would now be thought of as the 'clients' or 'customers' of this University College and the intentions of those who were working to transform this institution into a full-blown university, able to hold its own with others all over Europe, reveals predictable tensions. Nottingham University, like all the other city universities founded in the late nineteenth century, began from and depended upon developments in, first, elementary education and then secondary education. The new colleges were also intended as places where specialist training could be offered in the industrial sciences and technologies relevant to the local industries – lace-making, in the case of Nottingham. Also, and quite differently from Oxford and Cambridge, women were envisaged as potential students from the beginning. Yet the centrality of teaching training and of women to these early foundations seems also to have been seen as a problem, as committing them instantly to the second-rate. The slaking of Jessie Chambers's passionate thirst for knowledge sits oddly with the fact that in 1907, for instance, two members of the College Council resigned in protest when the students organised a lecture by Christabel Pankhurst, with the rigid rules of dress for women, and even with the remark made in 1915 that 'the girl who is seen talking in hall or corridor with a man is not regarded favourably by those in authority'. These new institutions could not have flourished without their female students; but their presence was grudgingly tolerated, it seems, and they were never treated as the equals of the male students. During the Second World War the proportion of women students to men increased enormously on all courses, not only amongst those in education, so that in 1944 the ratio was something like 184 women to 43 men. One historian's comment is worth savouring, I think.

> The crabbed might mumble that they were being cloyed with over-sweetness, and rueful jests were made about this new manifestation of Gresham's Law, whereby the bad currency was driving out the good. But that was mere common room babble. The arts departments owed a great deal to these girls who filled the depleted lecture rooms, and brightened a sombre passage of time with their zeal and charm.[10]

The condescension is lacquer-hard and impenetrable. Even women's pleasure at being in a university and being able to study and read is made to seem shallow in its naive optimism. More than that – and there are prefigurings here of much contemporary debate – women serve as fig-leaf to the uneasiness of any temple to learning which must compete and sell itself in order to get enough students to break even.

Neither zeal nor charm is adequate to suggest the vitality and appetite for study of women like Jessie Chambers or the other young women Lawrence trained with and later taught with. Nor were any of these women the repressed and sexually inexperienced spinsters of hope and legend, but in many cases sexually active women, with strong intellectual interests and an impressive history of reading. Lawrence knew from his own experience that many women hated what Ursula calls 'the bondage of teaching' at times, but that marriage too and even love could spell bondage as well. Their own childhoods told them that.

America developed a system of public education earlier and more quickly than England. It was, nonetheless, the expansion of public education in both countries during the nineteenth century that – by vastly increasing the need for teachers, particularly teachers for younger children – was also responsible (at first, perhaps, as an unpredicted by-product) for increasing demand for and provision of all levels and forms of education for women. Not only were these developments linked; they powered, as twin engines, the growth in educational provision generally from that time. Things did not proceed in the same way in the two countries, however, and though my focus here is on women teachers in England, it is useful to set that history alongside a history which has so much in common with ours, while also differing in significant ways. It should also be said that wherever elementary education for all has been proposed and implemented, this has entailed the massive recruitment of women as teachers, a move that has invariably been fraught with contradiction and subjected to an odd assortment of rationales.

In England – a highly stratified and already industrialised society – public education, in the sense of a national system, could be said to start from the 1870 Education Act, when local school boards were first enabled to open elementary schools and fund them through a specially raised school rate.

This did not bring about an instant transformation, but certainly by the end of the century there was at least an adequate number of school places, even if they were not all in the right places or actually filled. From that moment something resembling a system of universal and enforceable compulsory elementary education was created out of a disparate and uneven pattern of schools already in existence, most of them fee-paying, however small the fee.

It is important to get some sense of the scale and variety of educational provision before 1870, however, since this accounts for the heterogeneous traces of that provision as they have survived into the twentieth century and, indeed, into contemporary schooling. Most popular education in the nineteenth century was provided by the voluntary societies. Schools were owned and run either by the National Society or by the British and Foreign School Society, which represented, respectively, the Anglican Church and the Nonconformist churches. From 1833 successive governments did contribute small sums of money to these societies, though it has been pointed out that

> by 1861 total government spending on education was only £250,000 compared with the £600,000 which was spent by the smaller Prussian state thirty years previously, and by 1869 still two-thirds of school expenditure came from voluntary sources.[11]

An important point is that these 'voluntary' schools, far from withering, actually grew within the semi-public and hybrid system which resulted from the 1870 Elementary School Act, and that by 1881 there were 14,370 voluntary schools to the 3,692 public board schools created since 1870, and attendance at voluntary schools was double that for the board schools. Secondary schools continued to be exclusively private until the 1902 Act, after which the first public grammar schools were formed, 'exactly one hundred years after Napoleon created the state *lycée*'.[12]

And within that broad picture, a working-class girl might have attended one of a number of schools: a dame school, which was usually run by one woman in her own home, a Sunday school, a charity school, a factory school, a ragged school provided by a philanthropist for children 'too poor and dirty' to be accepted elsewhere, or, of course, one of the day schools run by one or other of the voluntary societies.[13]

This history of heterogeneity has affected state education to this day, leaving us with the remnants of a patched-up operation and its haphazard accretions, in the form of largely unbridged differences and inequalities of provision across the country, a thriving sectarian tradition, a large and currently government-underpinned private sector, and a legacy of cynically differentiated establishments for the education of working-class children. And that is before we have begun to consider the development of state provision of secondary schooling after 1902, its absorption of the old grammar schools, and governments' pretty consistent determination to avoid instituting compulsory secondary education for all children until after the Second World War.

We have in the process become accustomed to the endless tinkering required by a system which was never conceived as a whole, but assembled in this piecemeal and minimalist way. Issues of curriculum and pedagogy and funding have been debated and reported on, and there has been a whole series of properly critical commissions and investigations: but the provision of education for working-class children has been thought of instrumentally, for the most part, as social engineering, rather than as likely to contribute to the life possibilities of the children themselves. And if provision for working-class boys at least made some of its purposes visible – towards specialised and local work possibilities, for example – provision for girls was constructed out of what it was not to be or to contain. The curriculum for girls was to be neither academic nor vocational. Such 'training' as girls might receive should be general and domestic. No future way of life was envisaged for girls which would not benefit directly from a course made up principally of good manners, good hygiene and a daily diet of needlework.[14]

It is important to start from the haphazard character of this process of accretion and assimilation, because it illustrates and accounts for the extraordinarily perfunctory way in which women were prepared for and recruited into teaching from the middle of the nineteenth century and thereafter. Even by 1870 and the Forster Education Act, there were about equal numbers of women and men teaching in elementary schools, and by 1913 three-quarters of the 163,000 elementary teachers were women.[15] Yet the training provision for all teachers, and particularly for women, was wholly inadequate. In 1900 over half of all certificated women teachers had not been to college, and even in 1913 one third of women elementary teachers were still uncertificated.[16]

In America, a new country in the process of vast territorial expansion and resettlement during the first half of the nineteenth century, the establishment of schools for all children – 'common schools' – was a vital step in the creation of new communities. From the 1830s onwards the recruitment of an increasingly female teaching force was allied to the need to develop first high schools and then 'normal' classes within them (intended especially for those expecting to teach), which could prepare pupils, mainly girls, to be teachers.[17] That, in its turn, led to the setting up of separate institutions of higher education and training. If teaching also 'suffered' in America from being women's work for the most part – poorly paid, that is, disparaged and so poorly supported – it was recognised from the beginning as a distinct career for a woman, if only for the few years before she married. To teach in a publicly funded school was to teach most of the community's children, not, as in this country, what were in effect the children of the poor. Yet having insisted on such a contrast it is also necessary to remember the injustices inherent in the poverty of the schooling available to black and Native American children. Indeed, the 'common' school was originally a way of asserting the shared character of white culture and white values. It is also worth reminding ourselves that much internal criticism of the American school system is inspired by what is seen precisely as its failure to cater for an elite, indeed by the very democracy that has been so markedly absent from the system in this country.

Quite apart from those young women who entered teaching as a lifetime's career, there were those who became teachers as preparation for occupations other than running families. A woman teacher could expect to acquire invaluable skills and experience in the classroom: organisational and public-speaking skills, for instance, and experience of managing people and budgets. Though a majority of women who left teaching did so in order to marry and have children, some also moved into politics and local-education administration.[18] This seems to have been rarer amongst women teachers in this country, where their unmarried state was likely to be held against them in the world outside school.

North American children's books are full of girls whose early playing at school anticipates their careers as teachers. Jo March of *Little Women* marries and creates with her husband a school for poor and orphaned boys, her *Little Men*; and her school comes to symbolise the possibilities of combining the domestic and the maternal roles with service to the community. Jo's responsibility for the boys' moral welfare and her husband's responsibility for their academic work also prefigure a recognisable division of labour in schools to this day. The Canadian Anne of Green Gables eventually becomes the Principal of a high school on Prince Edward Island,[19] after taking her degree and before leaving teaching to marry. And Laura Ingalls Wilder, the author of that long series of stories about her own childhood in a family which moved circuitously through northern and midwestern America during the 1870s and 1880s, starts school herself with the three books her mother has kept from her own years as a teacher, 'One was a speller, and one was a reader, and one was a 'rithmetic'. The teacher in her first school, in Minnesota,

> was a beautiful young lady. Her brown hair was frizzed in bangs over her brown eyes, and done in thick braids behind. Buttons sparkled all down the front of her bodice, and her skirts were drawn back tightly and fell down behind in big puffs and loops. Her face was sweet and her smile was lovely.

And the schoolhouse was

> a room made of new boards. Its ceiling was the underneath of shingles, like the attic ceiling. Long benches stood one behind another down the middle of the room. They were made of planed boards. Each bench had a back, and two shelves stuck out from the back, over the bench behind. Only the front bench did not have any shelves in front of it, and the last bench did not have any back.
>
> There were two glass windows in each side of the schoolhouse. They were open, and so was the door. The wind came in, and the sound of waving grasses, and the smell and the sight of the endless prairie and the great light of the sky.[20]

When Laura is fifteen, her father takes her by sleigh across the twelve freezing snow-packed miles separating their home from a tiny settlement and schoolhouse, where she is to teach five girls and boys, between the ages of nine and seventeen, three of them older than she is.[21] Living now in another part of the prairies, Laura is still a schoolgirl herself, though she is also the possessor of a provisional certificate allowing her to teach her 'first school' for eight weeks or so of the winter. She lodges unhappily with the school's builder and principal parent benefactor and huddles round the stove of the school-room with her pupils, learning 'to manage' the maverick boy amongst them and 'hearing' them recite their lessons. For her first eight weeks as a teacher she earns $40. Later, she is paid $25 a month, which is somewhat less than she believes she could earn by other means. Laura does two more short stints as a teacher, separated by a return to her own school and successfully passing two teachers' examinations. She has never really enjoyed teaching, and is pleased when she is able to earn money by needlework and by living-in as a companion to a woman and her children. And not long after she gets married she gives up work, just as her mother had. Teaching makes a kind of break or bridge between childhood and marriage. She grows up, gains confidence and refuses to promise 'to obey' her husband, though she is certain that she doesn't want the vote.

On the day when Laura and her friend come to school wearing engagement rings, there is a conversation amongst their friends, which gives some sense of how a group of seventeen-year-old girls thought about teaching as work in rural America in the 1880s.

Mary Power and Florence and Minnie could hardly wait until recess to pounce upon them and admire their rings. 'But I'm sorry you have them,' Mary Power said, 'for I suppose both of you will be quitting school now.'

'Not me,' Ida denied. 'I am going to school this winter, anyway.'

'So am I,' said Laura. 'I want to get a certificate again in the spring.'

'Will you teach school next summer?' Florence asked.

'If I can get a school,' Laura replied.

'I can get the school in our district if I can get a certificate,' Florence told them, 'but I'm afraid of teachers' examinations.'

'Oh, you will pass,' Laura encouraged her. 'There's

nothing much to it, if only you don't get confused and forget what you know.'

'Well, I'm not engaged, nor do I want to teach,' said Mary Power. 'How about you, Ida? Are you going to teach for a while?'

Ida laughed, 'No, indeed! I never did want to teach. I'd rather keep house. Why do you suppose I got this ring?'

They all laughed with her, and Minnie asked, 'Well, why did you get yours, Laura? Don't you want to keep house?'

'Oh, yes,' Laura answered. 'But Almanzo has to build it first.'[22]

In Britain, the need to recruit girls as pupil-teachers was officially acknowledged, if grudgingly, by the mid-1840s. The training of girls, working-class and lower middle-class girls, as pupil-teachers, was initially for elementary schools. In the first half of the nineteenth century the training of teachers consisted mainly of what might be picked up on the job within schools which were still in many cases operating the monitorial system of teaching, with its admirably cheap 'cascade' model of training.[23] But in the wake of the creation in the 1830s of a government education inspectorate, a system of apprenticeship or pupil-teacher arrangement was introduced, so that by the 1840s it was possible to move from working as a pupil-teacher in school to normal schools or training colleges on a Queen's Scholarship; even though, as I have pointed out, there were never anything like enough teacher-training places for the numbers actually qualifying and, indeed, going into the classroom.[24]

The first teacher-training colleges to which women were admitted were opened in the 1840s and were usually intent in the early days on offering a narrowly based vocational training rather than an education from which a girl might

herself benefit. Frances Widdowson refers in her study of
early women's training colleges, for instance, to one young
woman 'being hauled in front of the Principal at Salisbury
College as late as 1885 for reading a novel by Dickens'.[25]
One play or one poem was thought quite enough for the final
year of study. Another memory from the earliest days of
Homerton College in Cambridge is of more enlightened
teaching and reading, but also of the mindlessness of the
textbooks they were required to read.

> One of our founts of wisdom was a book by Fitch,
> which seemed to cover every possible want, but much
> of it seemed silly to us even then, and we were in
> the spirit to get as much fun as possible. A book on
> 'Class Management' (which was apparently a special
> branch of educational science) gave a great many hints,
> one of which made me dubious about the rest: 'Avoid
> unconscious humour.'[26]

A constant complaint from those who taught in these
colleges was that the girls came from backgrounds which
were not middle class, so that training entailed, above all, the
instilling of ladylike ways. Widdowson goes into some detail
about the efforts that were made to encourage middle-class
women to go into elementary teaching. The salary for a
certificated teacher in the 1840s and 1850s was about
£30 to £40, often in addition to free accommodation, while
a governess was unlikely to earn more than £35 a year. Yet
it was virtually unheard of for a middle-class woman to
consider elementary teaching. By the end of the century, and
partly as a consequence of the campaigns organised by first
Angela Burdett-Coutts and then Louisa Hubbard, there had
been a slight change in the class background of some of the
young women going into elementary teaching, though the fact
that middle-class women had not been pupil-teachers and
were therefore worse prepared for the Queen's Scholarship,
worked as an additional deterrent. And there was always

some sense that this was not work for young ladies. However, as Frances Widdowson puts it, by the end of the century,

> a new kind of elementary schoolmistress had emerged. As recruits increasingly came from a higher social class it was no longer necessary for them to be indoctrinated with bourgeois morality and manners as part of their course at training college – many were already middle-class by birth, albeit of the lower strata.[27]

What had also changed by the end of the nineteenth century was the possibility of some post-elementary schooling for girls. This often took the form of middle schools, which were private (though, as we shall see, there were also free schools set up at the beginning of the twentieth century, which catered for girls from eleven to fifteen or so) but which offered some scholarships to the children of poor, if not the very poorest, families. And it is clear that where such schools were in operation, elementary teaching was the most likely occupation for such girls after leaving school.[28]

Despite large regional variations in America, more than two thirds of all the school teachers in the country were women by 1900 (in Massachusetts the percentage was 90.5), in a system which catered in principle for 90 per cent of all school students. Historians of American education are inclined to be critical of much that went on in the common school, and certainly the use of women teachers was advocated openly as a way of saving money, as it was in this country.[29] However, there was some sense in America of constructing a system that might be both coherent and democratic, rather than the cheapest possible method of supplying basic literacy and numeracy skills to working-class children. Partly because of the presence of girls and the need to recruit and train a good many of them as teachers, the development of elementary and secondary schools for all children soon led in America to the creation of colleges and universities. The presence of girls within secondary, as well as elementary schools, that is, was inseparable from America's earlier commitment to secondary education for all and from co-education. *Faute de mieux*, perhaps, for co-education was for the most part a necessity in a country where the population was still too low in most places to allow for the 'luxury' of single-sex schools outside the major cities. It seems clear that co-educational arrangements in America released the curriculum – and particular teachers' experience of it – from the undermining separation of boys and girls in this country, where a girls' curriculum prevented most of them from getting much academic study at all and, therefore, from the possibility of entering institutions of higher education or training. It is worth recalling that in the final novel of the four she wrote about the March family from 1868 onwards, *Jo's Boys*, Louisa M. Alcott wrote about a boys' school which had recently become first a co-educational school and then a co-educational college. Jo March, the heroine most admired by generations of English and American girls,[30] is the moving spirit behind this, and it is her old admirer, Laurie, now her millionaire brother-in-law, who becomes, through her inspiration, the college's private benefactor.

The dependence of the American system on women teachers was acknowledged from the beginning, and not always positively, of course. The 'schoolmarm' was an ambivalent figure in the community, as we know, though far less anomalous and socially isolated than her counterpart in this country. The marriage bar was not used officially, for instance, and the effect of the woman teacher's presence on the structure and the delivery of the curriculum and on expectations that girls would do well at school and might become teachers themselves, was included in that ambivalence. Also, the existence of co-educational secondary schools led to the early establishment of co-educational colleges and universities: a development which was also in sharp contrast with much of what happened here.

Yet, as in this country, public discussion about the different kinds of education which were appropriate for boys and girls

could proceed, strangely unimpeded by the fact that more
and more of that education was in fact in the hands of
women teachers. There was always the fear, expressed by
women as well as men, that 'femininity' might be impaired
by too rigorous an education. In America, the Salem School
Committee report of 1840, which argued for the adoption
of sewing classes, could comfortably assert that:

> it is a matter of complaint in our city, and seemingly
> just, that girls have too much intellectual and too little
> home education ... Boys need, strictly speaking, a
> more intellectual education than girls, since the latter
> are destined to the duties of the home, while the main
> province of the former, as men, is ever abroad, in the
> complications of business, requiring the rigid analysis
> and calculation happily spared to the wife and
> mother.[31]

Or, as Clara Collet put it – rather more succinctly, though no
less devastatingly – in the chapter she wrote on the secondary
education of girls in Charles Booth's *Labour and Life of the
People*, 'a boy's education is civic, a girl's domestic'.[32]

Another important difference between the two countries
lay in perceptions of how these newly independent women
would influence the consumption as well as the delivery of
education. Because of the class origin of the new female
teaching force in Britain, there remained a gap, in duration
as well as social distance, between the training of teachers
and the first moves towards women's entry into higher
education. And though it became possible from the 1870s
for some women – those who had had a good deal of
secondary schooling themselves – to take external BA degrees
while they were teaching (mostly through London University
and its proliferation of affiliated colleges across the country)
this was a minority of women, who were, for the most part,
teaching secondary-age girls in what were still private schools.
The high failure rate in the early part of this century amongst

student teachers trying for a degree in only two years in addition to working for a teaching certificate, became a weapon in what was in effect the relegation of teachers to 'professional' as opposed to 'academic' courses.[33] (Incidentally, 70 per cent of the men failed this compared with 50 per cent of the women.) So it would be some time before most women teachers in the state sector would be seen as potential consumers of higher-level education for themselves; just as it was often thought unnecessary for graduates to be prepared in any way as teachers. Yet it is worth noting that in contrast to secondary-school headmasters, the leading headmistresses all supported professional training for secondary teachers. Indeed, Miss Buss, the founder and first head of the North London Collegiate School and the founder of the Camden School for girls, famously asked in 1891 whether there was anything to be done 'to avert this growing danger that the teaching profession should fall into the two classes of those who were highly educated and not trained and of those who were trained but not highly educated?'[34]

Many young women who went into teaching in America, however, expected to continue their studies, and a whole range of relatively flexible forms of provision, in colleges and universities, eventually enabled them to do so while they were working. The effect of this was to produce a larger number of educated women than men, so that, as one American historian has put it,

> The unheralded result has been that some American women have always had to marry men with less formal schooling than themselves. This education gap set up hostility on both sides, and it may be the reason why American women seem bossier and more demanding of their men than women in countries where men are generally better schooled than their wives.[35]

Whether or not that is fair to American women, there remained, of course, gross inequalities of pay and prospects between women and men, and, as in this country, the availability of teaching for women depressed its status as a career and a profession, with women largely in the classroom and men running schools and school boards. Yet, a majority of boys in America must have grown up knowing from their own experience that girls were as likely to do well at school as they were, and expecting to be taught by a woman during most of their schooling. Arguments used to justify different or reduced educational provision, on the grounds of the different needs and inferior capacities of women, had at least to be more deviously promulgated. It may be that this explains the somewhat different paths taken by feminist educators in the two countries during the second half of the twentieth century; paths which might be characterised as more confident and essentialist in America, more conciliatory but also at times more politically radical in this country.

It was not, of course, that women's role as educators of boys – particularly of large boys – was accepted as unproblematic in America. Indeed, much public anxiety about the standards of education on offer was expressed in relation to this issue, and women's influence in the classroom was deliberately circumscribed by the establishment of an almost entirely male administrative structure. One New Jersey superintendent's objection to the 'feminisation' of teaching must have been fairly typical:

> I am strongly in the opinion that the presence of women as teachers of boys in the upper grammar grades, and even in the first and second year of the high school, causes thousands of boys to become disgusted with and to leave the schools. Of my own knowledge, many young men have been driven from school because of their intense dislike to being (using their own words) 'bossed by women.'[36]

Alison Prentice and Marjorie Theobald include Canada in their account of the ways in which the idea of the woman teacher was politically manipulated in North America, to fill the gap between rhetoric and reality. As they expressed it,

> much of the rhetoric surrounding women's own education in the nineteenth century was directed to the preparation of women to play a highly idealized and romanticized role as teachers of their own and, more often, other people's children. Historians soon discovered difficulties with an undue focus on ideology, however. As the Canadian case demonstrated, leading promoters of school reform accepted the doctrines idealizing the schoolmistress very reluctantly, and only when the numerical dominance of women teachers in the state elementary schools was already a reality.[37]

Public education in America may be seen, then, to have accompanied a territorial and demographic expansion: a shift from a predominantly agricultural economy to an industrialised one, and as one amongst several key agencies in the forging of a nation out of diversity and dispersal. In contrast, the development of public education in this country during the same period is better understood as a series of halting attempts to contain urban anarchy and – but only incidentally – to inculcate those skills thought useful to the labour force in a period of massive – though perhaps by then already incipiently flagging – industrialisation. The training of teachers – and particularly of women teachers from the working class or lower middle class – was designed to maintain order rather than to expand minds. And the use of the 'marriage bar' to regulate the numbers and the cost of women teachers illustrates how little teacher training was intended to prepare young women for independent and fruitful lives.[38]

The narrow aims of much teacher training and the low expectations of what teachers might know and think, did not, of course, prevent large numbers of women from making impressive use of the training and the work they embarked on. In addition, it should be remembered that the vast expansion of the teaching force had the effect of opening up an avenue of social mobility for many clever working-class children. Gillian Sutherland, a historian of education, suggests how important that was as an aspect of the moves made to professionalise elementary teachers in the 1840s,

> The effect of all this was to endow elementary school teaching with a status, financial attraction and security which it had hitherto entirely lacked. This greatly improved both the numbers and the quality of the recruits; and the apprenticeship arrangement ensured that the improvement would immediately have an effect at school level. . . . The pupil-teacher system also formed probably the most important single contribution towards the development of elementary education as a mode of social control – although it is not clear to what extent contemporaries realized this. The system formed a limited little career ladder for working-class children to move to lower-middle-class white-collar respectability.

I shall return to the theme of teaching as a profession in another chapter. However, in drawing our attention to these new possibilities Sutherland makes the essential connection between changes taking place in schools and the wider social and educational effects of those changes.

> Giving the teacher a place in the social structure was at least as important in controlling the effect the school had on children as any external regulations about teaching methods or curriculum content.[39]

Despite official purposes and the exiguous character of much of their training, many of these young women experienced their entry into teaching as an escape from the drudgeries of family life and a welcome postponement, or even refusal, of marriage, into work that offered them interest, a sense of usefulness, some genuine independence and an introduction to a public and political world. They came to stand as models for the possibility of escape and independence for thousands and thousands of girls, models at once baleful and encouraging. Most of these teachers came from backgrounds offering women little opportunity for independence or intellectual growth. It is not surprising, therefore, that many of them were to engage in political and cultural activities inside and outside the school, and to make themselves responsible for the liberalising of pedagogy and a broadening of the curriculum. Women teachers have often thought of themselves, and been thought of, as less authoritarian, less orthodox, less hierarchical than men: more interested in new ideas and methods, and readier to collaborate with others. They have also stood for compromise and realism.

A history of the last 120 years reveals a recurring pattern of utopian ambitions amongst women teachers for their working-class pupils, alternating with periods like the one we are currently enduring, when a barrage of criticism is levelled at what are seen as the 'soft' centres of education. 'Basics' and a 'stiffening' of standards are opposed to a presumed laxness. Frugality replaces prodigality. The curriculum is reduced, classroom practice standardised, assessment forms and procedures multiplied. 'Pleasure' becomes a dirty word, and all that is 'hard', 'difficult', 'demanding', will be set against the 'informal', the 'progressive' and the 'popular'.

In considering the parallel yet very different nineteenth-century histories of state education in America and in England, as these have determined the ways in which teaching as a profession for women has developed, and in focusing for a moment on one or two young women who became teachers,

I have drawn attention to some crucial issues. First, I have wanted to reverse the possible expectation that to talk about women teachers in the nineteenth century is to talk only about those women who, as governesses or schoolmistresses, taught the daughters of the middle and upper classes. Then, I have stressed the importance of teaching as work for women; as the site on which a women's politics has been conducted; and as an area accessible to their cultural intervention. Women's presence as teacher has above all been a shared experience for almost everybody, altering class and gender relations irrevocably. I have also suggested what kinds of connection exist between women's increasingly dominant presence as teachers in schools and developments in other sectors of education: in further, adult, higher and alternative forms of education. Finally – and most historians of education have agreed about this – increased provision has always preceded, indeed produced, increased demand, despite a constant and residual reluctance on the part of many parents in the past to send their children (and particularly their daughters) to school. *More* has meant *more*, not *worse*. Indeed, more may very well be said to have meant women.[40]

The expansion of public education during the nineteenth and twentieth centuries here and in America is a phenomenon which cannot possibly be considered – though it often has been – without taking women's participation in it into account. Even the figure of the heroic autodidact has been stereotypically a male one, though, as Ursula Howard has shown in her study of literacy, and particularly of writing, in the lives of nineteenth-century women, 'the nature of their lives made women, ironically, more likely to be isolated learners than men'.[41] June Purvis, in her history of working-class women's lives and education in the nineteenth century points to a significant take-up of any access offered women by the Mechanics' Institutes and the Working Men's Colleges.[42] Margaret Bryant, another historian, describes how quickly women responded to the equal access offered them by the

London Polytechnics at the end of the nineteenth century and by the civic and the new universities in the early years of this century.[43] The creation of the 'new universities' in the 1960s, the huge success of the Open University, the continuing interest in extra-mural, adult education and other alternative forms of education have depended to a great extent on women's appetite for more and more education.

Women's massive take-up of all these forms of adult education during the second half of the twentieth century has occasioned chagrin amongst some of their male tutors. Women have often returned to education in order to acquire further qualifications or to resume an education cut short by family expectations, by poverty or marriage or childbirth. Often, however, it has also been for the pleasure of learning and studying, of enhancing leisure as well as earning power, of deepening knowledge for its own sake. Sometimes, of course, this kind of study is undertaken because women have reason to lack confidence in their ability to compete in the world and to expose themselves to the competitive expectations of students and teachers in more traditional kinds of educational enterprise. Typically, moreover, it is in these kinds of teaching that women then find themselves too. Most of the innovative pedagogic experiments of recent years have been conducted by feminist teachers in marginalised or alternative areas of further and higher education. Women's relegation to the peripheral sectors of education is certainly both undesirable and undesired. Yet these kinds of education also suit the less competitive motives which many women value in themselves and in others and which are undoubtedly the object of suspicion from policy-makers and educational hierarchs.[44]

Women's desire for education has been pursued in a context of largely unchallenged dogma about their weaker minds and bodies and the moral and intellectual inadequacies (even as breeders and carers of their own children) of working-class women. Educated women who have argued for the benefits of educating girls have usually echoed aspects of those beliefs. Mary Wollstonecraft begins her proposal for the education of women with an acknowledgement of their damaging inadequacies, and even Clara Collet at the end of the nineteenth century could make her case in the light of her certainty that 'the rather-above-the-average woman is quite on a level with the average man'.[45] Such confident assertions of female inferiority, and the longevity of such assertions, are what are often forgotten in the current terror that girls are now doing better than boys. The recruitment and training of young women from poor (if not the very poorest) families was consistently regarded as regrettable but necessary, as women increasingly took over from men as the teachers of the very young and as teachers responsible for small village and parochial schools. And though the colleges hoped always to attract girls from middle-class families, and scarcely managed to do so until the beginning of this century, they continued in most cases to limit their responsibilities to the transmission of the basic curriculum material any young teacher would herself be expected to impart. This was accompanied by a regime, usually regarded as of far greater value, which was designed to instil habits of cleanliness, godliness and frugality in these student teachers. The pay was poor, often less than half what a man doing the same work would earn, though as the fifth most common recorded occupation for women of twenty or over in 1841, it was probably the best paid.[46] The other commonest occupations were, first, domestic service, then dressmaking, working in the cotton mills and laundry work.

Absent from my account is the setting-up in this country, from 1850 onwards, of secondary schools for girls from middle-class backgrounds, schools like North London Collegiate School and South Hampstead High School. That is not a development I want to ignore, not least because the success of those schools powerfully influenced the 1895 Bryce Commission into secondary education, so that secondary provision for girls had, as a result, to be considered alongside secondary provision for boys.[47] This also encouraged the creation of some co-educational secondary schools, and many of the existing girls' schools were eventually incorporated into the state system through grants. Yet the optimism and the expansion signalled by these changes to the schooling of a minority, and a minority made up almost entirely of middle-class girls, must emphatically be seen in the context of a system of public provision always intended as a limited project, which would take the majority of children to the age of eleven or twelve, but no further. And if the prospect of teaching was not always welcomed by those girls who were headed for posts in the private and secondary sector, there remained a gulf between those who were known as 'assistant schoolmistresses' (secondary-school teachers, who were more and more likely to be graduates) and the young women who were to become elementary teachers.

For, as Clara Collet pointed out – and she had taught for seven years in a secondary school before she finally acknowledged that teaching was not for her – 'the mass of parents do not wish their daughters to be teachers', even though 'teaching may be regarded as a life work well worth the doing for its own sake'. In her *Educated Working Women*, written during the 1880s and published in 1902, she usefully focuses on these contradictions and on the growing gap between the minority of teachers in schools offering a secondary education to girls and the vast majority of women teachers, who were to work in the elementary sector.

> In these schools, of which a considerable number are under the management of the Girls' Public Day Schools Company and the Church Schools Company, while others are endowed schools or local proprietary schools, some University certificate of intellectual attainment is

almost invariably demanded, and a University degree is more frequently required than in private schools or from private governesses. These assistant mistresses have nearly all clearly recognised, even when mere school-girls, that they must eventually earn their own living if they do not wish to spend their youth in maintaining a shabby appearance of gentility. They regard marriage as a possible, but not very probable, termination of their working career; but for all practical purposes relegate the thought to the unfrequented corners of their minds, along with apprehensions of sickness or old age and expectations of a legacy . . . In the majority of cases they are devoted to their profession, for the first few years at least; and they only weary of it when they feel that they are beginning to lose some of their youthful vitality, and have no means of refreshing mind and body by social intercourse and invigorating travel, while at the same time the fear of sickness and poverty is beginning to press on them. There are not 1,500 of them in all England, and their position is better than that of any considerable section of the 120,000 women teachers entered in the Census of 1881.[48]

In America as in Britain, public education has always existed alongside an elaborate range of private schooling at all levels and in different relations to religious institutions. And if, for women teachers, the connections between the private and the public education sectors have necessarily taken a different form, that does not mean that women's education has been any less decisively determined by class and economics than men's has. Indeed, the policies and the ideologies surrounding the employment of women as teachers take us into central questions about the living of gender and class; and this will be a theme of future chapters.

One consequence of this separation on class lines and its relation to age level and public and private provision was that while women teachers in America might expect to teach boys as well as girls throughout their schooldays, women in this country taught only young children or those girls who went on to secondary schools. A system designed to educate children according to their social class was also split along gender lines, so that though women were entering the profession in great numbers – by 1875, 54.3 per cent of elementary teachers were women – they entered those parts of the system with the lowest status and the lowest pay. This has left a significant legacy, which has affected more than women's careers as teachers and girls' achievements at school. It has reinforced a polarisation within education (between primary and secondary, for instance, between the 'academic' and the 'vocational', or between the 'academic' and the 'pastoral', and between what have been thought of as female and male subjects) and within public discussion of education. That legacy has been harmful.

As I write of these things I experience a curious doubleness. How obvious women's presence in education is for all of us. Yet how suppressed and ignored and manipulated and finally ambiguous that presence is. I think of the letter written to the press in 1991 by one of the 'Three Wise Men' commissioned by the government to look into the problems of primary education, and his insistence that research into the subject is likely to discover that 'the causes of the problems we identify lie partly in the professional culture of primary education.'[49] A professional culture which is, of course, a women's culture, though he doesn't say so.

As a teacher in higher education now, whose students are almost all women, I am daily reminded of such anomalies, for myself and for my students, who are teachers. Most women teachers have been afflicted by such doubleness, by the simultaneous belief in something called teaching, as an ungendered and therefore primarily male calling, and in the

possibility that what they might offer as women was importantly different and yet all too likely to be disparaged for being
so. There has been a dividedness too in women teachers' sense
of what education and schools could be and, especially, of the
importance of educating girls. They could simultaneously
want to offer girls the same academic opportunities as boys,
for instance, and fear the consequences of educating girls out
of their anticipated roles as wives and mothers.

And yet many of the most important battles round girls'
education and the conditions of work for women teachers can
well seem to have been won. Access to higher education is now
in principle the same for women as for men, and despite some
striking discrepancies between the actual careers in teaching
pursued by men and women, and the sectors and levels where
women are more likely to be found, Equal Opportunities
policies have done something to redress the balance in terms
of promotion possibilities for women. After years of using
the marriage bar whenever it was useful to regulate possible
unemployment amongst male or single female teachers, the
last of the local authorities finally abandoned their erratic
reliance on it in the late 1930s. Then more than half of this
century was spent in a struggle between teaching unions and
government to introduce equal pay for women teachers, a
battle which was finally won in 1955, though the process
of bringing women's salaries into line with men's was not
completed until 1961.[50]

These were hugely significant reforms. Yet there are ways in
which they served to disguise continuities almost as effectively
as they actually transformed education. For schools and
schooling have turned out to be extraordinarily impervious to
fundamental change, or perhaps they are simply ineradicably
marked by the ways in which gender is organised in the wider
society. All women who perform paid work are subjected to
unhelpful views on the assumed duality of their position. More
than that, though, women frequently experience themselves
as 'at fault', hybrid, unnatural, for this doubleness. It is a rare

woman who thinks of herself, and is thought of, solely as a working person, independently of her sexual relationships and the roles these may be thought to entail. Yet it is likely that it was in the hope of being thought of *simply* as good teachers that many women went into schools in the first place. Most women in teaching have wanted equality with men rather than supremacy.

It is not surprising, therefore, that whereas in their battle over equal pay the anti-feminist NAS union continually stressed the danger for boys of being taught by women, insisting that 'If boys were to be trained to become men they must have manly instincts implanted in them, and these could not be produced by women teachers', their principal opponents, the NUWT, always argued for *minimising* the difference between the sexes and the curricula for boys and girls.[51] It is interesting to compare the inflammatory language used by the NAS to oppose women teachers' aspirations to equality, and their warnings against juvenile delinquency and instant national decrepitude, with the measured tones of the NUWT president at the union's annual conference in 1930.

> We ask that in all schemes of reorganisation our predominantly male reorganisers shall remember they are catering for girls as well as for boys, and that the interests of neither must be subordinated to those of the other. The existence of the mixed school in which these conditions do not obtain is at best an unsatisfactory compromise, and in cases where women are excluded from the headships constitutes an abiding injustice to successive generations of girls trained in an atmosphere where one sex perpetually dominates – and that not their own.[52]

Indeed, it could be said that it has always been a central tenet of feminist teaching that sexual stereotypes of any kind should be resisted at all costs: that too much was made of the absolute differences between girls and boys and the polarising images of how girls and boys were likely to spend their adult lives. Yet it has also to be conceded that it has not only been male teachers who have warned of the damage women teachers might inflict, nor have boys been the only ones thought to have been vulnerable to the undermining effects of being taught by women. Women teachers have been taken to task by some of their girl pupils for inept or zealous transmission of the more irrational and oppressive ideologies of femininity, and there is an interesting literature on this subject by women who were educated in convents, for instance, which I shall consider in the next chapter. Indeed, many accounts by women of their growing up make the woman teacher a central and emblematic figure in their memories of division and ambivalence. Muriel Spark's Miss Jean Brodie and the wicked and delicious Mlle Julie in *Olivia* by Olivia, are examples. And whether such figures were adored or hated, they were always enigmatic figures, possessors of unknown and perhaps unknowable sexual secrets, at once a danger to girls and a source of otherwise inaccessible wisdom and knowledge. They were also, of course, alternative mothers and possible versions of our future selves, and therein lay both their excitement and their capacity to inspire fear. Mary Evans, in her memories of her 1950s grammar-school days, writes of the girls' 'great respect' for the young, married women on the staff' and remembers how the girls 'entertained a romantic fascination for the teacher whose fiancé had been killed in the Second World War'. Yet she expresses a ferocious contempt for other teachers.

> So when we looked at our teachers what we saw was a model of adult existence that was both frightening and unattractive. We said of our teachers that they 'only had their jobs' and we turned to the ideas of home and family as areas of richness and fulfilment. Being adult, married women seemed extremely attractive when set

against the lives of the unmarried teachers that we knew. These women seemed to be concerned about little except endlessly demanding of us the orderly presentation of tasks. The quasi-rational world that they appeared to defend and represent was deficient, to us, in human interest, in vitality and in enjoyment.[54]

Doris Lessing, too, in the first volume of her autobiography, a fiercely truthful account of her growing up on a farm in southern Rhodesia in the late twenties and early thirties, can concentrate astonishing venom into her portrait of a remembered teacher.

Sometimes they failed to get a husband. There was one, not young, perhaps forty or fifty, a grey cold lean woman who always wore flat walking shoes and thick stockings. She taught history. When we heard her steps outside the classroom we all froze, including the girls who had such a bad tone. Why? She never hit us, or even threatened to. It was her personality, contemptuous, sarcastic, angry. She would stand, ruler in her hand, and direct her gaze at the bad-tone girls, first on one, then another, saying calmly they were riff-raff, they were rubbish, they thought they were clever but that was only because they did not see how silly they looked to someone with education. The cold eyes would then travel slowly, all the time in the world, from one face to another through the classroom.[55]

Not only has this woman 'failed to get a husband' – a bizarre charge to hear from Lessing – she is a dull, bad teacher into the bargain, and Lessing makes it clear that she distrusts teachers. In remembering bullies at her own school, for instance, she reminds herself that bullying is now infinitely worse than it was, and 'that teachers seem unable to stop it. Perhaps they are not unable, but even like the idea'.[56] I think of all those teachers who have read Doris Lessing's work seriously and with pleasure – for teachers must represent an impressive proportion of her readers, I imagine – and who have introduced thousands of delighted children to her stories and her novels. I remember a lesson in a Hackney boys' school, where a wonderfully gifted woman teacher was reading one of Lessing's *African Stories* with a class of mostly Jamaican twelve-year-olds. Most writers would be proud that their work was read with that kind of intelligence by anyone anywhere. I am shocked and angry at the casual inhumanity of Lessing's suggestion and at the chasm between that and my own sense of how teachers struggle daily to stop bullying. Yet the venom is not really casual at all. Lessing's mother, she tells us, 'never ever lost an opportunity for instruction',[57] and was for her daughter one of the 'two clever women whose lives did not permit them to use their talents',[58] so that the writer grew up resisting with all her strength what she saw as 'all the pathetic identifications of a woman whose gratification is only in her children'.[59] The mother's identification with her daughter becomes a terror of invasion and possessiveness and rivalry, and the daughter must leave. Her flight from the mother is flight from the pedagogically inclined woman and even from herself as a writer, who is both didactic and wary of didacticism, particularly in a woman, and who resembled both her mother and her teacher in so many ways.

The terror and the ambivalence start in our own child-hoods, as uncertainty about our futures, about what and who we may manage to be. For girls know from an early age that the economic and sexual aspects of women's lives are alarmingly entwined and all too susceptible to disintegration and loss of control. Teachers have inspired love and admiration in their girl pupils and they have certainly offered models for emulation. Yet what may seem like power and independence have rightly struck some of their pupils as won at too great a cost. The relation of women teachers (even those who are married and have children) to the women children know outside school, is surely seen by children to be unequal and ambiguous. For women who do paid work are required to split themselves, for fear that mothering be tainted by contamination from any potential monetary value that may be put on it. So that if girls learn from teachers that they too might be teachers, the lesson they learn is not unequivocal.

3

Children's Teachers

There was Miss Cocker, for instance, with her strong calves, rolls of grey hair and narrow face. She could tell at a glance that I wasn't a serious scholar or anything like as good at swimming as my namesake, Jane Chapman. Miss Cocker taught the top juniors, and was acquainted, therefore, with genuine maturity and sophistication, of the kind possessed by those much older children I avoided in the playground, for fear they would find me out. Mr Toes, as we called him, who looked after the bee hives, and Mr Messingham,[1] who ran the workshop and was thought to wash out the mouths of swearers with carbolic soap, were, in my eyes, practical people, who knew about nature study and lathes, but were hardly intellectuals and certainly not eagle-eyed seers into children's souls. Miss Clarke was the headmistress and a gentle presence in her elegant knitted suits, silvery and belted, matching her naturally curly hair and flattering her small waist and large bosom. 'Matching' and 'flattering' were very much the fashion imperatives of my youth. She lived in a splendid wing of the school, with sofas and whatnots and a glass case of treasures, from which I once stole two Chinese dolls: to be apprehended (and forgiven) before I had even got them home for lunch. Her soft voice was never required to compete with ours, for her appearance at the door of the classroom was enough to produce an instant and absolute hush.

The memories we have of our first teachers – and they are likely to be of women – must surely be important ones. They will be overlaid by now, confused, distorted, reduced by time and age and the learning of many kinds of disdain for unmarried women who have worked all their lives with children and were probably quite poorly qualified. Yet that sort of knowledge cannot quite make its peace with the memories I still return to. I have, for instance, the clearest possible memories of those women's legs, of their strong calves and neat ankles and second-best shoes with small heels. Though Cor, who ran 'the barn', where we wove our mothers' kettle-holders, wore Clarks sandals and ankle socks and had slightly fallen arches and an absence of calves, and Alison, who taught us eurythmics, wore ballet slippers, with elastic across the instep. I could go on. There were the subtlest distinctions for us between those teachers we called by their first names or even by nicknames and those we believed to possess no such names at all. No doubt I spent many hours cross-legged on wooden floors gazing at adult women's legs, though never, so far as I remember, wandering in imagination or otherwise beyond the hems of their dirndls or their gor-ray skirts, though it is true that knickers were much on our minds. Those women were large and impressive, admirable and enviable and all-knowing. They were women who seemed to me to have choices and to have chosen, amongst other things, not to have husbands and not to have children of their own. In this and in other respects I thought them superior to my parents, who were to have three children, yet could not – by any stretch of the imagination – be thought to possess an exceptional talent for bringing them up. Also, I believed that what ordinary adults knew and did was fine for them, but uninteresting for us. What teachers knew was likely – for what was school for, if not? – to be right and a good deal more worth listening to.

So there was nothing either serious or modest about my wanting to be a teacher as a small girl, nor much thought for the children I might teach, or what I might teach them. It was the status and the limelight I was after. In fact, I didn't want to teach so much as to run (and perhaps even own) a school. A favourite book was *Ameliaranne Keeps School*, in which a very young girl gets the chance to practise 'minding children', which is useful as she's going to 'keep a school' when she grows up. It was this moment that caught my own ambitions exactly,

> Ameliaranne was rather clever at painting, and she walked about among her pupils, flourishing a paint-brush, and mixing a colour here or putting in a line there. When she found Bobby Binns and Wee William painting each other's faces to look like Red Indians, she marched them to the wash-basin and washed them with a *very* firm hand.[2]

'Keeping school' was definitely what I was after: the opportunity to explain what was what to children younger than myself, to adjudicate sagely and to ordain how time should be spent and space occupied. It was clear to me from a pretty early age that 'keeping school' had everything: power, glamour, rooms and rooms which belonged to you, the right to speak at all times and to demand a hushed silence as you did so, a fleet of children to run your errands, presents brought from home, and unstinting admiration. You were also in a position to bestow or withhold favour as you saw fit. Teachers had a lot more going for them than parents. They knew, for a start, how to handle children, and since that included children much older than I was, like the ones in Miss Cocker's top class, that meant that you had earned the respect of the gods themselves. Parents – in my experience, at least – were often at their wits' end. Indeed, I realised that teachers could put your parents right about all sorts of things, and parents might very well not answer back when they did. Mrs Ormorod, for instance, who wore her hair in plaited 'ear-phones' and gave some of us remedial classes for our flat feet – I write as a person who is uniquely practised at picking up fir-cones with her toes – could, according to my mother, be deaf to all she wished not to hear: a condition I associated with unusual will power and the peculiarities of her coiffure.

I worked out quite soon too that there was a lot more to teaching than to learning. It was much easier, for a start, and you got paid for doing it. You didn't see teachers sitting down and doing tests all the time, as we did. We often did tests: not just IQ tests, but what were called for some reason 'industrial tests', which told you what you would be fit for in adult life. I assumed that teachers were beyond all that, and must know all they needed to know by now.

I began my school life, somewhat untypically I now think, by finding it wonderful; perhaps because I started rather late, between six and seven. Before that and for nearly a year, between the ages of five and six, and from a moment early in 1938 when my father was fearful of sending me to Switzerland because of the possibility of war, I stayed in a semi-detached villa in Broadstairs. Here, two pious sisters cared for about eight young people who were convalescing from TB. I think that I was the youngest, and I thought of the oldest as being at least twenty. Age meant a great deal to me, and my own has usually been something to be ashamed of: always too young or too old.

One room of the house was a schoolroom, with a large oblong oak table and two glass-fronted cupboards of the same stingily varnished wood. These contained rather little: a globe, some exercise books with magenta marbled covers and alternating pairs of narrow and broad lines ruled in pink inside, some pencils and a small pile of tattered blue hymn books. Here some of us worked during the mornings, more or less on our own, as I remember it. I learned to read and write during that year, though I remember the writing better than the reading. I practised in an old diary and in one of the exercise books, biting my lip until the blood came as I struggled to fit the round bits of letters between the narrowly ruled lines, leaving the tails and loops free to shoot above and below them. When writing was 'free choice' I simply wrote 'history' and 'geography' over and over again in my diary. Indeed, I was never to get the hang of what was meant by creative or imaginative writing, then or later.

At the end of the year, trailing whiffs of godliness which were to be peremptorily expunged, I returned to my family, who had moved while I was away, from London to a small Hampshire town. There I found a younger sister I had forgotten I had, preferring to imagine my parents bereft and comfortless. She had had whooping cough, so that for another week or two I glared stonily at this small interloper at the far end of the upstairs landing. But now that I was no longer the youngest in the family, my teacherly purposes could at last be realised. For a few happy months she became my bewildered pupil as I taught her all I knew and a good deal that I quickly invented in order to keep her there: principally a language I made up, and taught her to read and write in, but also how to run a shop, how to avoid going to bed, where to hide her savings so that I could borrow from them but no one else could, how to do a whole string of cartwheels with your skirt tucked in your knickers and how to dance like a fairy to a record of Miss Gibbs's Lancers.

My sister was an excellent student: too good, in fact, for she quickly outstripped me in virtually every area of my own curriculum, as students do. When we started proper school in the Autumn, together, despite the three years difference in our ages, I was a seasoned teacher in my own eyes, but an anxious student.

I remember my surprise at finding that Simone de Beauvoir's memories of teaching her younger sister were so like mine and yet so unadulterated by the embarrassment that colours mine,

> Teaching my sister to read, write, and count gave me, from the age of six onwards, a sense of pride in my own efficiency. I liked scrawling phrases or pictures over

sheets of paper: but in doing so I was only creating imitation objects. When I started to change ignorance into knowledge, when I started to impress truths upon a virgin mind, I felt I was at last creating something real. I was not just imitating grown-ups: I was on their level, and my success had nothing to do with their good pleasure. It satisfied in me an aspiration that was more than mere vanity.[3]

The school that I went to with my sister was the junior part of Bedales, the oldest of the so-called 'progressive' co-educational boarding schools in England, where my parents had met and where my father now taught music. Because of that we had free places as day girls in a school with high fees and a somewhat unusual and rarefied atmosphere, characterised more than anything else, probably, by a belief in cold baths, fresh air and the virtues of woodcutting, and by a suspicion of sex, city life and competitive examinations (as opposed to diagnostic tests). I was least convinced by this last part of it, since all it really entailed was taking our 'effort' marks more seriously than our marks for achievement: a difficult injunction, if, like me, you were given D1 for the violin, and the 1 was the top mark for effort, while the D stood for where it had got you. I think it likely that none of the teachers in the junior school where I began had a degree, and that though there were some teachers who had been trained in the Montessori methods (I can feel those extravagantly san-serif capital letters made of sandpaper and the frames strung with buttons and buckles and bows for us to learn to manipulate) most of the teachers had drifted into teaching out of an interest in crafts or child art and probably some sort of psychology or even psychoanalysis. The curriculum would be thought unusual nowadays, and methods were eclectic. We learned a good deal about bees and their ways – as a blueprint for a human heaven, I assumed – about the history and geography of Hampshire and about the properties of lead, which we melted and poured into wooden moulds we'd made with Mr Messingham. We made more than kettleholders in the barn. We made egg cosies, trayclothes, shoe bags and, later, lengths of abrasive, mud-coloured tweed: sometimes spinning the thread and always weaving the cloth. We hung from our climbing frames and tore about the fields beneath the doodlebugs making their erratic way to London. And in the early autumn we lifted potatoes. We wrote stories about witches and dragons and illustrated them, and we did sums and worried at 'problems' as other children did. As it happens I knew 'other' children, for we lived in the largest house in a working-class part of the town, and our friends were our neighbours. I knew as well that they thought little of the school we went to and only a little more of the one they went to themselves, which most of them left for good when they were twelve.

My school was both odd and conventional. We wore uniform, though some girls wore boys' uniforms, and we had assembly every day, though God was never mentioned, as a civility to non-believers, for which I've always been grateful. These occasions could nonetheless be marked by a Nonconformist fervour of a quite unspecific kind, so that children might rise to their feet and tell us whatever they chose: that they had eaten chicken and carrots for lunch when taken out by their parents on Sunday, and had later produced a stool of a quite satisfactory consistency; or the history and all the successes ever enjoyed by Arsenal Football Club, accompanied by a résumé of their last match (delivered in impressive commentator style) and brief biographies of the players.

Between those earliest schooldays, when school itself – its buildings and inmates and rules and order – so delighted me, and the time, not so many years later, when I had learned to relegate teachers along with almost all other adults to a limbo of dull irrelevance (a position I had to unlearn eventually, if only to save my bacon), I read all the school story-books

I could find: those written for boys even more avidly than those written for girls. I have memories of lying on the floor with my girl cousins, our feet roasted to chilblains by an ancient art deco electric fire I still possess, as we read *Teddy Lester's Schooldays* and *The Fifth Form of St. Dominic's*. And during all that time I laid plans to convert every large house I saw into the perfect school. For to create the perfect school was to possess and exert maximum power and creativity. An ideal school stood for me as the model for a kind of utopia: the kind, I think incidentally, where women might run the show and teach their hearts out.

In 1938, the year before I started school, Ruth Adam's second novel, *I'm Not Complaining* was published.[4] It is the story of a young woman of thirty, Madge Brigson, who teaches in an elementary school in the poorest district of a Midlands town. Ruth Adam herself taught in a Nottinghamshire mining village for some years after attending a boarding school for the daughters of clergymen and then undergoing a typically brief college training. The novel's narrator ends her tale with her rejection of a proposal of marriage and the prospect of a lifetime working as a teacher: not such an unusual ending to a woman's novel, as it happens, and one which recalls the moment when Charlotte Brontë has Paul Emanuel die at sea as Lucy Snowe settles into her sanctuary with the encouraging words, 'my school flourishes, my house is ready'. Madge explains her decision not to marry as at least partly due to her ambition to become a headmistress and also to her sense that by now she is too used to her independence, too 'fixed in my ways, trained from my childhood in the school house for this one job',[5] as she puts it. The last paragraph of the novel manages, in its melancholy way, to suggest the charms, the achievements, the securities of the job, while also conveying the sad strandedness of all women whose professional work is the care of children who will grow up and leave. The classroom is a refuge and protection against the ferocities of the outside world. Yet there is also a clear recognition of how entirely that outside world impinges on and penetrates the classroom, in a manner she welcomes as much as she regrets.

> September. There are new faces in my class, new faces in the staff-room, new babies in the infant-class. The whistle blows, they march in orderly rows and line up for prayers. Registers are marked in identical red strokes, with black noughts added half an hour later – neither more nor less. Books are given out, taken up, we march into the yard for drill, have singing in the hall and tea in the staff-room at break. And beyond our little island of order and quietness, where the three hundred voices hum with the steady monotony of bees in a hive, is the maze of mean streets and dark yards swarming up to the green-painted fence like the jungle round an outpost of civilisation. Day by day we take them one more tentative step on the difficult and dangerous path to maturity. There may be an Adolf Hitler or a Joseph Stalin staring at me from those orderly rows. There may be a poet who will never be forgotten while men still use human speech. There may be a scientist who will draw stars from their courses and make a suburbia of the mysterious universe. But long before then I shall have forgotten their faces, lost the sense of their personalities, and even their names in the register will have vanished as though they had been written in sand.[6]

When the novel opens it is the early thirties. Madge has already taught for 10 years in this school with nearly 300 children between 5 and 10, and 5 teachers, all of them women: so classes of more than 50 children. Her closest friend is Jenny, a pretty, clever girl from a working-class family, who is fiercely aware of all she has avoided by going to college and becoming a teacher:

I went to a council school and lived in a slum. I only got to college because I was top girl in the class and got a scholarship to the secondary school, and a Government loan to train as a teacher. If I hadn't – I should have been what my sister is now. You've never seen her, and you're not likely to, because I keep my family circle separate – but she works in a factory, six days a week, folding cardboard boxes into the same shape, and she drops her 'h's' and reads *Peg's Paper* and picks up boys in the street.[7]

Jenny herself has picked up her college lecturer, who is married and by whom she is now pregnant. She is prepared to go to any lengths to have an abortion, which was still illegal at the time. The novel revolves round the different class expectations and morality of the two young women. Madge, as the somewhat sceptical and agnostic daughter of a schoolmaster, is clear that as teachers neither of them 'rank as employing classes',[8] yet as a second-generation professional she believes that her friend's desperate plans should be resisted, as illegal and dangerous. She also keeps her distance from the middle-class world, and particularly from that world which is characterised in the novel as influenced by reading Nottingham's own D.H. Lawrence and consequently devoted to the causes of 'free love' and progressive education. A conversation with the tense but compliant wife of the adulterous lecturer catches Madge's ironic amusement at the concerns and remoteness from reality of those parents who might well have sent their children – as mine did – to Bedales.

I asked where their child was, and she said he was at school. It was a very enlightened co-educational boarding-school, she hastened to add, where there was no nonsense about segregating the sexes and thus putting impure thoughts into the children's minds. I said that we didn't have any nonsense about segregating the sexes at our school either, but that, so far as we could judge, the impure thoughts were in their minds all ready-made. She started to explain to me, in a long harangue, how, in a state of society where children were not repressed at all ante-natally onwards, the thing would work all right.[9]

It is interesting in retrospect to reflect on the chasm that existed between these two views of education, and on the fact that many of the 'cranky' ideas first put into practice by 'progressive' schools have, nonetheless, been taken up since the thirties, in modified form, by schools in the public sector.

Ruth Adam's novel is peopled by those who still span, or hover between, classes, and whose work might be said to police the boundaries between the ruling classes and the working class: teachers, minor civil servants, minor clergy, the police force itself. The lives and work of such people are seen to entail particular kinds of compromise and ambivalence. Madge finds herself upholding values which seem to her to be quite inappropriate at times for the children she teaches. Yet she is also uneasy with many of the working-class parents, aware of how potentially unpopular teachers can be with them. She is uneasier still, however, with the Lawrentian middle classes and their insensitive freedoms. She is often admiring of her colleagues' professionalism, their pride in their work, their exasperation at the inadequacies of their own training and the impossible task they are set. Yet she is also self-consciously aware that the professional concerns of women teachers in their staffroom are not generally thought exciting.

I know that conversation about teaching is supposed to bore outsiders, but I never can see why it should be so much more a matter of reproach to discuss it than for actors and actresses, for instance, to talk shop, which is supposed to be rather Bohemian and intriguing of them. Anyway, Miss Jones and I got very friendly over the progress of the Top Infants.[10]

Jenny marries and will leave teaching and not be happy. Madge will teach and live alone and miss out on marriage and motherhood, but with a strong sense that that is not all loss. The novel does not idealise teachers. In suggesting the satisfactions of the job, the tensions and constraints are made clear too. Nor is Madge some sort of self-sacrificing or 'natural' teacher, suffering little children, but very much someone who has learned to do the job well through thought and experience, if not training.

The living of class ambivalence by women teachers, the independence, derived precisely from an escape from the narrowness of many middle-class women's lives and the poverty of working-class life, has been painfully won and painfully sustained. The hostility of many working-class parents to their children's teachers is part of that. So too is the sense of teachers having started on an education for themselves, of becoming students and readers and then having little or no opportunity to pursue their new interests. There is the question always (as there still is) of what kind of work this really is: mental, intellectual work, skilled, requiring training and a sense of belonging to something like a profession, or an activity which relies on 'natural' female characteristics and talents and the possession of what may generally be thought an appropriate personality. Sue Smedley, who was once a primary teacher and is now a teacher trainer, read through the references written for the young women who were applying for a degree course in primary teaching. She summarises them like this:

Applicants lacking in analytical powers, intelligence or the ability to argue their case, made up for it by being able to 'brighten your day'. 'Enthusiasm, energy, good humour' all appeared as desirable, even necessary and should be coupled with 'pleasant personality, cheerful disposition, strong character'. But, surely, I didn't expect to read about the ill-tempered, sour and lethargic.

Suitability for teaching was indicated by describing the student as 'organised, calm, personable, patient, even-tempered'. All very commendable traits. She was also frequently 'charming, polite, co-operative, sincere and well-balanced'. And a 'neat and tidy appearance' completed the outward manifestation of inner teacher-liness.[11]

There is never the hope or the expectation that young women going into teaching might be, and need to be, intelligent, intellectually alert and critical or, indeed, interested in anything in particular, except, in some wholly unspecifiable way, children. Critics of primary teachers in particular are capable of simultaneously deploring their low levels of literacy and announcing that teachers whose job it is to introduce the young to literacy do not anyway require – let alone possess – very high levels of literacy themselves. Representations of teachers on television or in films are almost invariably of bad-tempered and irrationally unpleasant women, who have no sense of humour and a built-in distrust of children. The wearing of spectacles and hair drawn fiercely back from the face are meant to suggest a grim serious-mindedness rather than a lively intellect.

Yet despite this continuing history of disparagement there has been from the beginning a sense of women participating for the first time in a form of public life, in debate, even in local and national politics. The Depression and its politics are never simply background information in Ruth Adam's novel, but intimately part of Madge's life and work, not least through their effect on the children she teaches.

Flora Thompson, who wrote the extraordinary autobio-graphical trilogy, *Lark Rise to Candleford*, also wrote a novel, *Still Glides the Stream*, which returns to the Oxfordshire village of her childhood in the 1880s, but sees it this time through the eyes of Charity Finch, who, in the

1940s, just after the Second World War, remembers her childhood as it contributed to her becoming a teacher and spending fifty years of her life in a school.

> Long years which had turned the little Charity, or Cherry, as she had then more often been called, into the elderly Miss Finch. Years of hard work and many disappointments, a typical schoolmarm's life. But there had been compensations. One here and there of her pupils had shown the sudden gleam of comprehension, the mental and spiritual response to her teaching which sometimes in her lighter moments she had referred to when talking to her colleagues as 'plugging in', or 'taking the bait', but which in her secret thoughts she had treasured as her most precious experience. That, and the privilege of fostering such promise, had been the chief joy of her life; but there had also been material advantages, personal independence, a home of her own, books, friends and holiday travel. She had planned for herself a trip round the world the year she retired, but by that time the world was at war, and travelling impossible.[12]

Flora Thompson did not in fact become a teacher, but – like her Laura in *Lark Rise* – an assistant postmistress (a new area of possible employment for literate girls in the 1880s, which the trilogy describes very well), who married the postmaster. So the novel stands in relation to the auto-biography as a kind of exploratory fantasy, about teaching and about not marrying. Like Ruth Adam's heroine, Charity rejects marriage, to her mother's grief and chagrin; for a rejected husband is a wasted husband, and she has always abhorred waste.

In both books, though, the novel and the autobiography, Thompson writes with sympathy and interest of a village teacher and her life in the last fifteen years of the nineteenth century. Charity, in the novel, comes to love Miss Fowkes –

who is plain and given to buying hats and other garments that do not become her – and to wish for a life like hers. A life, for instance, in which it might be possible to close the school for a day after a gruelling inspection and stay in bed with a pot of tea and a Jane Austen novel. When Charity is thirteen, Miss Fowkes pays her £2 10s. a year to be her monitress, and then her pupil-teacher, before she goes off to teacher-training college on a scholarship.

Girls like Charity and Laura grow up in a village where 'there was no girl over twelve or thirteen living permanently at home'.[13]

> After the girls left school at ten or eleven, they were usually kept at home for a year to help with the younger children, then places were found for them locally in the households of tradesmen, schoolmasters, stud grooms, or farm bailiffs. Employment in a public house was looked upon with horror by the hamlet mothers, and farm-house servants were a class apart. 'Once a farm-house servant, always a farm-house servant' they used to say, and they were more ambitious for their daughters.[14]

Eventually, these girls might marry, perhaps even come home to do so, but they might also move to positions in large houses further from home, and perhaps eventually even become 'upper servants'.

> The boys pulled forelocks and the girls dropped curtseys to the upper servants, for they came next in importance to 'the gentry'. Some of them really belonged to a class which would not be found in service today; for at that time there was little hospital nursing, teaching, typing, or shop work to engage the daughters of small farmers, small shopkeepers, innkeepers and farm bailiffs. Most of them had either to go out to service or remain at home.[15]

Charity's family belong to a somewhat poorer class than that, to what Thompson writes of as 'the comfortable poor'. Yet she is never in any doubt that the life of a teacher is more attractive than the prospect of being a wife or a servant, even an 'upper servant'.

Once again we see the anomalous position of the woman teacher, this time in a village setting. In *Lark Rise*, one of Laura's teachers, Miss Shepherd, votes Tory and lives in a two-roomed cottage, meanly furnished by the school managers 'in the manner they thought suitable for one of her degree'. She is 'artistic', however, as well as a Tory, and she adorns her rooms and lives her life in such a way that it is clear to Laura (as it was to me) that a teacher may at least enjoy freedoms that are denied her pupils:

> The mistress was at liberty, too, to look out of the window, which they were not, and she made the most of this advantage, tiptoeing to open or shut it or arrange the blind whenever voices were heard. On one of these occasions she looked round at her scholars and said: 'Here, now, are two respectable men going quietly to vote, and as you may guess they are voting for law and order.'[16]

Yet Laura also registers that her teacher was not asked to tea at the Rectory on election day 'as she had hoped', and both books record the small slights these women endured at the hands of their pupils' parents, though also from the representatives of the Church, the squirearchy and the Inspectorate.

Miss Holmes, Laura's first teacher, is an ambiguous figure as we first see her: 40 years old, small and plain and neatly dressed, playing the harmonium at morning prayers, then teaching all the classes simultaneously a diet of reading, writing, arithmetic, scripture and needlework, while each day the Rector would arrive to teach scripture to the older children. Miss Holmes could be seen as a figure of authority, feared and rebelled against and distrusted, yet she is also seen as on the children's side. And despite her austere and alarming countenance, engaged for years, it turns out, to the squire's head gardener, whom she finally leaves teaching to marry.

> As Miss Holmes went from class to class, she carried the cane and laid it upon the desk before her; not necessarily for use, but as a reminder, for some of the bigger boys were very unruly. She punished by a smart stroke on each hand. 'Put out your hand,' she would say, and some boys would openly spit on each hand before proffering it. Others murmured and muttered before and after a caning and threatened to 'tell me feyther'; but she remained calm and cool, and after the punishment had been inflicted there was a marked improvement – for a time.[17]

Yet even as she holds her own with the boys and their parents and manages, with her small team of 'monitors', to get most of her pupils to read, if not to want to read, we see her always as an object of regulation. There is the squire's lady, who visits the school once a year to inspect the needle-work and provide the meagre and only treats the children get at school. There is the Rector, with his superior gifts and knowledge. There is Her Majesty's Inspector,

> an elderly clergyman, a little man with an immense paunch and tiny grey eyes like gimlets. He had the reputation of being 'strict', but that was a mild way of describing his autocratic demeanour and scathing judgement. His voice was an exasperated roar and his criticism was a blend of outraged learning and sarcasm. Fortunately, nine out of ten of his examinees were proof against the latter. He looked at the rows of children as if he hated them and at the mistress as if he despised her . . . The mistress did not have to teach a class in front of the great man, as later; her part was to put out the books required and to see that the pupils

had the pens and paper they needed. Most of the time she hovered about the Inspector, replying in low tones to his scathing remarks, or, with twitching lips, smiling encouragement at any child who happened to catch her eye.[18]

It is possible to see the education provided in the 1930s for the children of the poor in a fairly large Midlands city and for the rural poor of Oxfordshire in the 1880s as linked above all by its class character. In both schools, boys and girls up to the age of eleven are submitted to a regime that has been designed to deliver the most basic of literacy and numeracy skills – and a little perfunctory Christianity – and which is controlled and regulated by established institutions: government, the Church, the squirearchy, the Inspectorate, in the interests of limiting the offer, keeping down costs, narrowing the curriculum and maintaining discipline. And, of course, the employment of young women (even, in the case of the Lark Rise school, girls of thirteen at a shilling a week) becomes part of this. It is hard not to see the limited training on offer as part of the same desire to patrol the edges, the borders of this class experience, to ensure that none of these children would take from their education anything that might encourage them to widen their horizons or look beyond the possibilities of life and work outside their own class. The irony was, however, that the young women who were pivotal to this process were themselves at risk of having their horizons widened and of wanting and asking for more. And central to the satisfactions of the job was the possibility of finding amongst their pupils those who were interested in reading and study and might go further with their schooling.

Michael Apple, who has written about the connection between the employment of women as teachers and what he has called the 'proletarianization' of teaching in this country and in America, goes so far as to describe women as 'the first industrial proletariat in the United States', the group most easily exploited by the fact that they are usually 'both paid and unpaid workers'.[19] In charting the way in which women gradually came to form the majority of teachers in both countries, he situates his story within a changing economy as well as a changing educational system, so that as men might leave teaching for more lucrative work, in the last quarter of the nineteenth century, and compulsory schooling landed local education authorities with growing costs, the employment of women became a way both of controlling costs *and* of keeping control of the system itself, which threatened at times to implode. Women were cheaper teachers (between 1855 and 1935, they never earned more than two-thirds of men's salaries) and, as Apple puts it, 'once a set of positions becomes "women's work," it is subject to greater pressure for rationalization'.[20] Men, as he points out, did not all leave education. Rather, they moved into newly created levels of management and supervision, while women filled the classrooms.

This seems to me an essential insight. It has been all too easy to picture women's arrival in teaching and their numerical dominance since about 1870 (though this has been more or less confined until recently, of course, to the worst paid and least prestigious positions in teaching) as random, a matter of individual need or choice. In fact, the orchestration of these developments and the anomalies attendant on women's presence in classrooms in this country have been central features of the kind of state system of education successive governments have been prepared to provide.

It may at first seem paradoxical that the employment of governesses in middle and upper-class families should illustrate a similar point. Yet there is no question that the employment of middle-class women as governesses was also an exercise determined above all by a need to maintain class boundaries. Not only was elementary-school teaching virtually out of bounds for middle-class women until the end of the nineteenth century – so that governessing was defined, amongst other things, as *not* elementary-school teaching – but the only serious qualification required by a governess was that she should herself come from a middle-class family. As Kathryn Hughes puts it in her study, *The Victorian Governess*, many governesses had 'nothing to offer, but their ladyhood and their desperation'.[21] And within the quite different world of the wealthy and the servanted, governesses found themselves at least as dislocated in relation to family and servants and class and economic need as young working-class women could find themselves in their village schools. Significantly, as Hughes points out, the employers of governesses were as suspicious of training as employers of teachers in the state system have usually been. It seems to have been understood by both kinds of employer that women were better teachers in their 'natural' state than in a trained or 'professional' one. Besides, the girls who went into governessing could not have afforded the fees at teacher-training colleges and were unlikely to win scholarships, since they had not as a rule been to school themselves.

In some ways the lives of elementary-school teachers and the lives of governesses may be thought of as inhabiting utterly different and separate worlds. Yet, as Hughes makes clear, the 'plight' of the pensionless and retired governess was alarming for its reminder and prefiguring of other plights.

The governess' situation provoked a reaction in her contemporaries which cannot be accounted for by the material facts of her existence. What was shocking was not the conditions of her life *per se* but the contrast that these presented with the normal expectations of a woman of her class. Her presence in the household acted as a reminder that no woman, even the thoroughly genteel, could automatically assume the life for which she had been educated. The young woman who today received instruction from her governess might tomorrow be providing that same tuition in someone else's school-room. The governess gave the lie to the construction of the home as a place beyond and above the market place and suggested that it too might be touched, if not overwhelmed, by the social and material hungers so graphically expressed in the waves of industrial unrest which marked the first part of Victoria's reign.[22]

As we saw in the last chapter, there were powerful reasons for encouraging middle-class girls to consider elementary teaching for their own sakes, and it is worth referring to the arguments for their doing so put forward by Louisa Hubbard in 1872 in her proselytising publication, *Work for Ladies*.

Why should a lady be less esteemed as a village school-mistress than as a governess in a private family? We trust that we may be able to show . . . that there is not only no reason why she should not live as suitably to her tastes and condition under her own simple roof in the village school as in the schoolroom of the parson or squire, but there are some respects in which her position there may even be preferable . . . after 4.30 p.m. at the latest, the mistress is free for recreation and a few pleasant visits to the parents of her scholars, or to her richer neighbours in the cool summer afternoons, or to such repose and self-improvement in the way of books or music as the wintry evenings may bring.[23]

The remarkable achievement of Flora Thompson's *Lark Rise* is to have charted change in her account of a village and its life which have been conventionally read as 'timeless'. After Miss Holmes gets married, Miss Higgs arrives, 'fresh from her training college, with all the latest educational ideas'.[24] These include wanting to 'be friends' with the children. The chaos that follows her arrival is discovered by the Rector, who puts an immediate stop to it.

> Then, after a heated discourse in which he reminded the children of their lowly position in life and the twin duties of gratitude to and respect towards their superiors, school was dismissed.[25]

Miss Higgs is dismissed too, and Miss Holmes, now Mrs Tenby, is brought back until a new teacher is found. The gentle Miss Shepherd is less of a disciplinarian and something of an idealist (a Tory idealist), who encourages the children to believe that they might rise by their own efforts.

> She would read them the lives of some of these so-called self-made men (there were no women, Laura noticed!) and though their circumstances were too far removed from those of her hearers for them to inspire the ambition she hoped to awaken, they must have done something to widen their outlook on life.[26]

If not a Tory herself, certainly a traditionalist, Flora Thompson represents these changes as undermining of the class certainties which had made the curriculum so easy to enforce.

> Meanwhile the ordinary lessons went on. Reading, writing, arithmetic, all a little less rather than more well taught and mastered than formerly. In needlework there was a definite falling off.[27]

School is seen by the pupils' parents and by most of the children as largely irrelevant to their lives. 'Boys who had been morose or rebellious during their later schooldays were often transformed when they got upon a horse's back or were promoted to driving a dung-cart afield.'[28] What Thompson in her autobiography and Charity, the heroine of her novel, offer us is the sense that while school is experienced as a clumsy and irrelevant intrusion in the lives of these boys, which may humiliate them and so bring out an ugly rebelliousness, its meanings may be different for girls. The image of the teacher may even be attractive to some of them, though it will also be shot through with questions about their own future sexual and social status. However, there is less ambiguity about the curriculum. Needlework was regarded by many of the girls as tedious but useful, and Thompson herself gives us an unusual insight into the ways in which the girls of her generation, and their mothers, made use of the literacy they had acquired at school. I shall return to this in Chapter 6.

There remains, though, the question of how the job of teaching was perceived, and what its prospects for girls were thought to be in the 1880s. Flora Thompson was in no doubt about the anomalous social position of the village school-mistress.

At that time the position of a village schoolmistress was a trying one socially. Perhaps it is still trying in some places, for it is not many years ago that the President of a Women's Institute wrote: 'We are very democratic here. Our Committee consists of three ladies, three women, and the village schoolmistress.' That mistress, though neither lady nor woman, was still placed. In the 'eighties the schoolmistress was so nearly a new institution that a vicar's wife, in a real dilemma said: 'I should like to ask Miss So-and-So to tea; but do I ask her to kitchen or dining-room tea?'

Miss Holmes had settled that question herself when she became engaged to the squire's gardener. Miss Shepherd was more ambitious socially. Indeed, democratic as she was in theory, the dear soul was in practice a little snobbish. She courted the notice of the betters, though, she was wont to declare, they were only betters when they were better men and women. An invitation to tea at the Rectory was, to her, something to be fished for before and talked about afterwards, and when the daughter of a poor, but aristocratic local family set up as a music teacher, Miss Shepherd at once decided to learn the violin.[29]

Thompson's tone of affectionate ridicule can sometimes obscure her own view of these things: yet the novel in which she imagined teaching as a lifetime's occupation was written after the trilogy and its portraits of the women in her childhood who inspired such contrary and disconcerting reactions in their pupils and in the community they served. Besides, Thompson's ambivalence is to be found in a thousand other memories of schools and teachers, for it reflects the bewilderment of girls and young women confronted by women teachers, who can seem to be at once the embodiment of authority and its absolute denial. The woman teacher is simultaneously the object of admiration and suspicion, of emulation and dread.[30] She has asserted herself, evaded the constrictions of class and family, and she has exiled herself from the world which might validate her as a woman in the process. She represents the scope of learning and knowledge, its potential excitements and satisfactions for girls and young women, as well as the waterings and winnowings exercised in the interests of controlling what these new women teachers might minimally offer the children of the poor. She is also perceived by her pupils as having attracted to herself, knowingly or not, the opprobrium of men and their fear or disgust of learned, accomplished women, who can seem not to need men. That opprobrium is likely to be sharper still in relation to women who may be thought to possess only pretensions to learning and accomplishment, and who are, in addition, anything but middle class or economically secure. Learning, study, doing well at school may be reduced by this to no more than the tainted baggage of spinsterhood, gentility and solitude: a suspect collection of constraints and embargoes.

Women who have been educated by nuns in convent schools provide us with vivid accounts of that doubleness, and its relation to those outside worlds which undertake to validate nuns and their work, while also submitting both to the most exigent forms of regulation. Nuns could be said to be multiply caught by these confusions about women and work. The 'families' or communities they set up and maintain borrow titles and relationships from the families they have chosen to leave. And their presumed 'vocation' as religious women and as teachers marks them off from the professional teacher, while also offering an idealised image of the teacher/mother, who works for love rather than money.

Women have chosen to enter religious communities since the fourth century, and probably earlier, and though by the middle of the sixteenth century there had been a shift from those orders where women might have lived alongside men in 'monasteries', and where, for instance, women might have taught boys as well as girls, the tradition of teaching orders and of convent schools has had something like a continuous history to the present day. Since the changes introduced in the late 1950s and early 1960s as a result of 'Vatican II',[31] some of the more extreme traditions of convent schooling have been relaxed. Possibly as a consequence of that, fewer nuns go into teaching, and the figure of something like 1,000 teaching nuns (out of a total of 12,000 Roman Catholic and 950 Anglican nuns in England and Wales[32]) in the early 1990s represents a drop of 80 per cent since 1964. What has been continuous, however, has been a serious commitment to the education of Catholic girls, which has been uneven in its offer, often vitiated by social snobbery and certainly open to criticism for some of its assumptions about what educating girls could be expected to achieve. But a commitment, nonetheless, unequalled within the mainstream Protestant tradition and probably exceeding at times even the provision made for girls within Nonconformist families and communities.

The forms of convent education have varied. Long before the Middle Ages, convents were already offering a refuge for rich young women and widows, who chose the religious life and who made use of the often exceptional facilities to study and write and teach or work in other ways. Many convent schools were set up in the first instance to educate the daughters of wealthy Catholics, and there have been those of their ex-students who saw the purpose of such schools as being principally to prepare girls for a materially good marriage or, in rare cases, to encourage those with a vocation to join the community itself, perhaps even as teachers. One nun in her forties has written recently of her own debt to the nuns who taught her:

> they were *amazingly* attractive. They were fun, they laughed a lot, they liked each other. They were intelligent, they were gifted, they were happy, they were devout. There are many natural causes for any religious vocation, and I'm sure one of the natural causes for me was the sense that I would like to be like these women.[33]

It is clear from this testimony and from others by women who have chosen to pursue a religious life, whether as a teacher or not, that space and time in which to think, and the sense of living a significant and worthwhile life won a fairly easy victory for these women over the attractions of marriage and motherhood. But what emerges from the passionate accounts, favourable as well as critical, that women have given of their schooldays in convents, is the excruciating tension they are encouraged to experience in their efforts to meet both the exalted educational and spiritual ambitions of some of these schools and the crushing regime of humility which formed a central part of those ambitions.

Antonia White's novel, *Frost in May*, reverberates with that tension. The mother superior can claim, for instance, that 'We work to-day to turn out, not accomplished young women, nor agreeable wives, but soldiers of Christ, accustomed to hardship and ridicule and ingratitude.'[34] She can also insist on the need to break the spirit of the girls in the process. The novel's heroine, Nanda, is a convert, who is finally expelled from the convent for writing a novel of her own, but not before she has tried most desperately to make up for her unfortunate beginnings, and filled her head, and pages and pages, with meditations like these:

> Rich and poor, however, a divine dispensation. Must not try to alter natural order of things. Abominations of socialism, freemasonry, etc. Trying to do God's work for Him. Women's votes unnecessary. Let her use her great influence in her own sphere. Modesty more effective than desire to shine. Our Lady had no vote and did not want one.[35]

A recent anthology of memories of their convent schooling by a number of well-known women, called *There's Something About a Convent Girl*, contains an astonishing variety of strong feeling on the subject, from bizarre complacency to bitter rage. There is a general sense of gratitude for the time and care the nuns put into their teaching, the sense that this was a total way of life for them, not a nine-to-five job, as it would be for 'ordinary' teachers in what many of the women grew up to think of witheringly as 'high schools'. There is the sense that this is what teachers ought to be: mothers, full time, unpaid, living on the premises, utterly absorbed by the life of the community. Yet 'the huge bonneted figure of a nun' sometimes troubled their sleep and their hopes. Germaine Greer realises now that she 'had a terrific education', though with characteristic perversity she attributes her current position as 'an atheist Catholic' to the nuns being 'dreadfully incompetent at teaching Catholic philosophy . . . The Jesuits on the other hand are very good at it, and if I'd been taught by Jesuits I'd probably still be a Catholic.'[36]

For Polly Devlin, the nuns who taught her were bent above all on undermining heterosexual womanhood, though she is also able to suggest that the passion with which they did so may be responsible for her own somewhat overheated and even Lawrentian commitment to sex and sensuality.

There was something so sexless about that face. People talk about the serenity and the purity and the feeling of peace that came out of it. I never did find that serenity. I just found those hooded black things like vultures, about to pounce on me. The swish of their huge wide-bodied skirts as they came round the corner still gives me a chill when I think of it. They had a scapula that fell from this white, chaste thing that covered bosom and breast, so that what you saw was a black bird-like figure, completely sexless, coming at you – and these were our mentors. Girls who were budding into adolescence and into womanhood were being taught by these extraordinarily mediaeval figures, jumped out of some extraordinary Gothic painting, telling them how to live. These were women who had eschewed all spirit, all sensuality, turned their backs on earthly delights, had taken a vow of chastity and who, in every possible predication you can think of, were held up to us as being better than our own mothers, as having made the greater choice, the Marys, rather than the Marthas.[37]

Such differences of view are not exclusive to women who were taught by nuns, though it is possible that the rest of us were spared (or perhaps missed out on) such extremes of moral and intellectual struggle and such contradictory metaphors for powerful and adult womanhood. Certainly, though, women teachers do present us with complex images of authority and subservience; of independence and weakness; of intellectual adventurousness and timidity; and even of sexual uncertainty. Nuns have often relished intellectual argument and have sought most strenuously to acquire knowledge and understanding. Often, they have been inspiring teachers. Yet, like all women who teach, they have represented confusing possibilities for their pupils. They have often stood for lives lived in obedience to men as well as for particular kinds of rebelliousness. And teaching itself, as a kind of work, has come to embody some of that ambivalence.

I want to end this chapter with a glimpse of another kind of school, of the group of women teachers who taught there, and of the schooling and destination of the working-class East London girls who attended the school. This is to be found in the daily handwritten log-book kept by Miss Ketcher, the Head Teacher of the Girls' Department of the Kensington Avenue Schools in London's East Ham (part of what is now the London Borough of Newham), from its foundation in August 1901 to the last day of the summer term in 1929.[38] It is a record of women teaching and of a school producing teachers, and its regime and its curriculum exactly mirror the tensions within education for working-class girls at the beginning of this century. For what is on offer can be seen to expand during the more than twenty years of Miss Ketcher's tenure. Yet it is always carefully designed to contain the minds and energies of the girls, and to direct them towards lives of circumscribed service to family and community. Probably the school's most celebrated alumna was Edith Thompson, who was hanged with her lover for the murder of her husband in 1923, and about whom we shall hear more in Chapter 6. As Edith Graydon, she attended the Infants Department of the school from 1903, and the new school from April 1905 until April 1909, when she was fifteen, earning at least two medals for 'perfect attendance' throughout the year.

The school operated as what was sometimes called a 'central school' at that time, which might be thought of as a middle elementary school, cohorts of eleven-year-old girls arriving from infant schools at the beginning of each school term and staying until they were fourteen or fifteen. The Head Teacher's log is a concise and formal record, written in a clear, round hand and regularly checked by the Clerk of the local education board and by Inspectors. It contains information about the numbers of students and teachers and pupil-teachers; about curriculum innovations; about public occasions and successes; about celebrations and outings; and, more mundanely, about teacher absences and the reasons for them. It also provides detailed information about changes in the training of certificated teachers and in the slow expansion of secondary-school provision for girls.

The school grew fast from the beginning. Indeed, steps were regularly taken to limit its intake and control the numbers of girls staying on after the statutory leaving age. From a Head Teacher, 2 certificated assistant teachers and 205 children, the school quite quickly acquired a staff of at least 11 class teachers and something like 500 children on roll. No married women are employed as permanent teachers, though several appear from time to time as supply teachers, and at the end of the First World War, one of the teachers who has married her soldier fiancé, is, unusually, kept on at the school.

From the beginning the school was involved in both using and training pupil-teachers, and clearly this was a central responsibility for the Head Teacher and, indeed, something like a *raison d'être* for the school. Before long, the pupil-teachers become 'student teachers', and we hear more about the training they begin to receive outside the school: at local centres and later at training colleges, mostly in the London area, and usually on scholarships. Particular students may spend half their week at Kensington Avenue, one day or one half-day 'observing' in either an infant or a secondary school, as well as four or five half-days in a local centre. By the 1920s, girls are going for interviews at colleges like Furzedown and Goldsmiths and the London Day Training College. There are more and more public examinations, organised by the school. Some are for the Civil Service, for positions as 'sorters' and telegraphers. Others are for commercial or secretarial posts. By the beginning of the First World War, a handful of girls are taking scholarship examinations for what were then called 'higher elementary schools' or to high schools. By the twenties, girls who sat the scholarship examination for local high schools and failed them might take up fee-paying places in the same schools. Others would go on courses in technical colleges or at other central schools.

Kensington Avenue School itself changed gradually during these years too. It soon became the most popular school in the area, though this did not mean that the usual problems presented by poverty and disease were avoided. By 1920, the teachers began to offer specialisms or groups of subjects, rather than operating as class teachers, and by 1924, streaming had been introduced, with the promise that the B classes, containing 'Girls of Slow Development' will have the advantage of 'working in small classes'. In 1925, the school employed its first graduate teacher, and there were to be one or two more recruited by the end of the decade.

One particularly interesting change is recorded here: this is the slow opening up of secondary schooling for girls, produced in response to gathering demand. The Head Teacher quotes a local report she has been sent in May 1908. This explains the recent setting-up of classes for older children in twenty of the borough's existing schools.

> The object of the classes has been to provide special instruction for scholars who can remain at school beyond the completion of their fourteenth year; to prepare boys for commercial or trade life, and the girls for commercial or domestic life. The general curriculum has been carefully drawn up and in each case a skilful class teacher has been chosen. The curriculum includes commercial correspondence, office routine, shorthand, book-keeping, mensuration and higher arithmetic, history and geography with special reference to trade, besides an extension of the ordinary course in English, drawing, elementary physics for boys and of English and domestic subjects for girls . . .

It is doubtful whether the division into two sections, office and trade, or domestic, is sufficiently marked to necessitate a separate curriculum for each. Further experience will probably suggest modifications in some of the classes. It is also to be regretted that there is no provision for handicraft teaching for boys, corresponding to the extended cookery course provided for the girls.[39]

By the end of the log-book – in the late 1920s – most of the girls are going on to secondary schools. The school is regularly praised by the inspectors, with only the repeated reservation that arithmetic is not well enough taught and must improve. The girls go to a cookery centre down the road and to swimming at the nearby baths, and these visits are logged, as are class outings to Wanstead and other local parks for nature study, and also to the zoo, to Downing Street and the Houses of Parliament, to the Crystal Palace and Westminster Abbey. Shakespeare and St George are commemorated on the same day with recitations. King George V's coronation is marked in 1911 by hymns and patriotic songs, and Empire Day is enthusiastically celebrated each year, with feverish additional lessons during the worst days of the war on Nelson, 'Our Navy' and tableaux scenes from Tennyson, *Ivanhoe*, *The Faerie Queene* and *Hiawatha*. Enemy planes fly overhead in 1917, 'aircraft drill was practised: the children were kept happy by singing' and more than one young teacher is allowed time off to see a fiancé on leave from France. The Head Teacher is appointed East Ham's representative on the Juvenile Employment Sub-Committee, which entails regular absences, while assistant teachers take time off for sick parents, funerals, bilious attacks, the usual flu and toothache and so on, and (as I remember a doctor once writing rather aptly on a certificate he made out for me in the 1970s) 'general debility'.

Strangely, the school's intake began to shrink in the late

1920s, and the number of classroom teachers was reduced. Presumably this was due to the growth of alternative forms of post-11 provision for girls in the borough. It was common for teachers to be transferred to other local schools, and such moves are recorded. Pupil-teachers might start at the school at fifteen, and certificated teachers in their early twenties. Ethel Bewley, for instance, who joined the school as a pupil-teacher in 1901, when she was seventeen, resigned from the school at the end of 1924 when she was forty. By then she was Mrs Burrows, having married her soldier fiancé and been allowed, exceptionally, to stay at the school after the war. We know that she collided with a pupil and came off worst, badly damaging her thumb, that she frequently suffered from abdominal pains, that she looked after a seriously ailing sister and that when the school resorted to 'specialist teaching' she concentrated on geography and literature. We hear nothing of children or husband, of course, and can only imagine how she managed her particular working and family life.

In 1930, volume 1 of *Forty Years of Change* was published, as an appendix to Booth's *New Survey of London Life and Labour*, and it is worth reading Sir Hugh Llewellyn-Smith's triumphant account of the successes achieved in London education during a period which ends with the twenty-eight years covered by Miss Ketcher's log. He writes,

> It is however impossible to understand the changes which have taken place in the past 50 or 60 years in the conditions of life and labour in London without taking account of what is perhaps the most profound change of all, viz. the transformation of the London working population from a semi-educated to an educated community.[40]

In many respects a most enlightened survey of the expansion of elementary, secondary and of what was already thought of as 'vocational' provision up to the late twenties, Llewellyn-Smith's chapter also connects demand for more education with the social and economic position of families and with improved staff/pupil ratios and a modernising of the curriculum. He does not, unsurprisingly, refer to the fact that this huge growth in educational provision depended on the massive, continued recruitment and training of women teachers.

4

Teaching as Work

Women have sometimes sheltered behind the notion that teaching is not so much work as a sort of religious calling or service to the community. And even amongst those North American feminist educationalists who have written most penetratingly about the contradictory character of the work women do as teachers, there has been a tendency to claim the maternal relation to children as the organising metaphor of women's contribution to teaching, however ambiguously valued that relation may be.[1] Both the image of the woman teacher and the conditions under which women work in schools have suffered from the peculiarly diffuse manipulations of this idea that women who work with children do so out of 'natural' inclinations and needs, of a kind men are unlikely to share. These 'natural' inclinations will include the biological, but also the inculcated capacity to serve others. The uncertainty as to what sort of work teaching is, and whether it should be regarded as a profession, derives, I think, from women's overwhelming presence within it and from the confusions inherent in the way most women are expected to perform paid and unpaid work simultaneously, usually for 'greedy institutions', as the sociologist, Sandra Acker, has put it,[2] which if they are not families are inclined to behave as if they were.

There exist polarised versions of what teaching is, what

kind of work it is. At one end is the scholar, gnarled by strength of character and intellect and a passionate interest in his subject. He may – but additionally, as it were – teach what he knows to the young and teach them by his own example. He is likely, however, to regard scholarship and research as more important work than teaching, and he will not have been taught to teach. Rather, his right to teach and his talent for doing so will be won out of his own long, rigorous study and his acquisition of knowledge. From his position on the frontiers of knowledge, as the Canadian critic, Northrop Frye, once put it, 'the teacher imparts the knowledge that has already been established to less advanced students'.[3] He has 'a trained mind' and will know how to train other younger minds, through a kind of pragmatic, retrospective unravelling of the stages of his own education, rather than from any perception or theory of how learners learn. The material itself (the texts, the ideas and the procedures) and the process of encountering it will be what the student learns. That image derives, of course, from teachers in the ancient universities, and probably from Socrates, and is likely to take the form of a man teaching younger men; although – and significantly – it has also been a model of teaching aspired to and achieved by some women in secondary schools and in higher education. At its most abstract, that version of teaching entails 'reading off' the student's learning, or inferring it, from the text, whether spoken or written, which is offered by the teacher. As a pedagogy, it requires no psychology of learning, and only the most rudimentary knowledge of the learner, since it can rely confidently on the value and the efficacy of what is being taught.

At the other extreme is the teacher who, as an idealised and indefatigably loving mother, watches over 'her' children in order to bring out their latent talents. Tender, loving care will nourish the bodies and the minds of the young, which are braced to unfurl anyway, like healthy plants in a good soil and sunlight. The teacher of young children has been thought of as 'the mother made conscious' within an educational philosophy that probably originates in the work of the early nineteenth-century founder of the kindergarten movement, Friedrich Froebel.[4] Her concern is with teaching and learning, rather than with knowledge, and with creating the social conditions that may make those things possible. Like the mother, this teacher is engaged in the ostensibly contradictory business of fostering nature while also intervening to improve on nature, in ways which have a good deal less to do with nature in the end than with social and cultural conventions. As Cathy Urwin[5] and other social psychologists have shown, mothers are encouraged to believe that they have a primarily pedagogic relation to their children, in the sense that they, like teachers, are relied on to support and further the 'normal development' of children.

Between those extremes – and they are gendered, of course – lie more delicately inflected versions of what teachers do and are. In fact, most teachers will testify to some degree of oscillation between those extremes. But ever since the middle of the nineteenth century, when teaching became something more commonly done by women than by men, the very notion of teaching as work has been a confused one. For if the qualities and the duties of the teacher approximate to what the good mother does naturally for her own children, there can be no need for a training, nor indeed for any of the paraphernalia of professionalism. Besides, as Geraldine Clifford, writing about the issue of training in America in the 1850s, has expressed it,

> since teaching was not expected to be a career for most of its incumbents, bound as they were for *homemaking*, society's limited investment in teacher training 'made sense' to most teachers, to public officials, to public opinion.[6]

Nor should such activity be regarded or rewarded as real work, for it is only a step away from what mothers do willingly for nothing, simply because it is in their nature and their interests to do so.

There was always at least one major flaw in such arguments. Rich mothers did not spend all that much time with their children, and working-class mothers were known to have more children than they were always capable of nourishing physically or mentally. So the teacher was not only an idealised mother but a compensatory mother, a mother designed to make up for the pretty serious shortcomings of most real mothers.

An additional paradox in the nineteenth century was that virtually no teachers in this country actually were mothers. The erratic but widespread use of the 'marriage bar' saw to that. And so did the fact that many young women saw teaching as a way out of family life and marriage. So, it was not women's own experience as mothers that was invoked or relied on, but a flickering set of beliefs in women's 'natures', which were just as likely to be held against them as not. Their 'physical weakness', for instance (which became 'mental weakness' at the drop of a hat), could produce a handy 'gentleness', but it could just as easily disqualify them in a variety of ways. Clara Collet suggested the absurdity of one of those ways:

> their youth and inexperience are facts constantly brought before them up to the age of thirty or thereabouts, and then with hardly an interval they find themselves confronted by this theory of sudden decay of faculties in women.[7]

Their bizarre ageing habits, like their maternal inclinations, could be used as positive or negative attributes. More importantly, such attributes could function to control and limit women's working lives and careers, for as Clara Collet went on to write, most advertisements for headmistresses included the sentence, 'No one over 35 need apply.' She continued,

During the second five years of teaching there is a constant agitation among young mistresses in the endeavour to secure a headship, and then amongst those who fail in the lottery – for it is a lottery – comes the deadening prospect of, perhaps, a quarter of a century's work to be carried on without hope of promotion.[8]

In 1990 the Department of Education and Science (the DES, as it still was), issued a recruitment poster containing the caption, 'The reason you left teaching is the reason you should return', which accompanies what Sabrina Broadbent, who is a teacher educator, has described as

appropriately enough, a double image of a woman; both pregnant woman and working mother. In the first image, her floral maternity dress connotes the unthreatening conventionality of pregnant women constructed as natural nurturers. Its proximity to the second image, where she stands in an ambiguous posture of concern and protectiveness beside a small boy who could be her son or one of the pupils in her care, signals both her suitability for such a job as teaching and her responsibility to return.[9]

Broadbent goes on to recount the anger and frustration this poster produced in a group of women teachers with whom she discussed it. 'They felt it misrepresented the nature of their job, which at the time was becoming a battle over the curriculum and a struggle to defend the profession's working conditions and developments of good practice in various subject areas.'[10] The slippage implied by the poster and experienced constantly by teachers is made even less tolerable by the appalling and deteriorating child-care provision now available for those women who do return to the classroom after having children. Yet as Broadbent points out, the poster's arch allusion to the condition Simone de Beauvoir once warned women against, as 'the nurturers of the knowers', fits those assumptions that have made teaching a seductive calling – irrespective of its other imperatives – women have found it hard to resist.

Still largely absent from policy on, and discussion of, women's recruitment to teaching and their progress within it are women's own motives for pursuing their education and for returning to the classroom as a teacher – particularly to classrooms filled with young, working-class children. Something called a training is simply to be inserted between a girl's own schooling and her adult life (or between her years of child-rearing and the fifteen or twenty years left of her working life) when she will be responsible all day for as many as thirty children or more and for important aspects of their future lives. Understandings about how children learn, and learn differently, it seems, are not required. Indeed, 'theory' in this scenario becomes the culprit, distracting and irrelevant – other people's theory, that is – dryly dealt out to these young women against their better judgement and in the teeth of their own apparently clamorous demands for foolproof, or at least practical and child-proof, tactics for survival. Such teachers will have no ideas of their own, no politics and no interest beyond the most rudimentarily instrumental in what happens to the children they teach.

Even if the main reason for encouraging women into teaching has always, in fact, been economic, and even if women's own motives for becoming teachers have also been economic, that is neither the whole story, nor is it something that is ever adequately acknowledged. Expectations of teachers were, as Carolyn Steedman points out, always linked to changing attitudes to the family and to child-rearing generally,

> it has recently become clear that the job changed from being a predominantly masculine one not only because of the obvious economic reckoning of various local authorities faced with recruiting teachers on a large scale,

but also because of certain societal shifts in the idea of family government, and the decreasing status of the father as a patriarch. In the early nineteenth century overt reasons for selecting men as instructors of infants had to do with assumptions about the ordering and disciplining of families, with the practice of judicious tenderness that such domestic practice helped acquaint men with, and that was seen as so vital an experience for the successful management of large numbers of small children. Towards the end of the century women could be seen to occupy this position of authoritative watchfulness.[11]

It is possible to see those changes as part of the new gentility of the early nineteenth century, when middle-class women were encouraged to devote themselves to their own households rather than to paid or unpaid work outside the home. Working-class women were expected to do the same. Yet those changes – to which I return in Chapter 8 – may also have made teaching attractive to women who needed to earn a living. For if schools were often grim and daunting places, work with children *did* appeal to women as something they expected to be good at. And just as there have been changes in the demands made on teachers, in terms of class size and classroom organisation, which have affected pedagogic approaches, but also procedures of control, in ways which may have been felt to favour women, so too, those going into teaching have sought and found different versions of what teaching could offer them.[12]

All teachers now, men and women, in secondary as well as primary schools, are administrators *in loco parentis*, as well as trained professionals with specialist or more general kinds of expertise. All teachers can expect to intervene in fights; organise outings; supervise meals and sports or playtime; perform 'first aid'; mediate with parents, welfare agencies, the police; administer examinations and tests; serve on after-school committees and working parties; plan time-tables and draw up class lists; raise funds and negotiate publicity; represent their colleagues in unions; attend courses and professional conferences; prepare for and undergo inspections. The list could go on and on. Teachers rarely have access to secretaries, so that all of them need good secretarial skills. It would be difficult nowadays for any teacher to spend less than an hour a week reading government orders, guidelines, directives, circulars on the curriculum. Nor could they keep their records up to date in much less than another hour a week. Those activities are simply part of the job of being a teacher. Then more and more teachers are finding themselves responsible for student teachers on teaching practice. Interaction with a classroom full of children learning to do Maths or English, say, and all the preparation and follow-up work that entails, is part of the job too. But public discussion of teaching tends to focus on these aspects of the job at the expense of all the others. This is paradoxical. For if teachers are not to be thought of as intellectual workers, they are also not to be given help with those aspects of the job which deflect from a concentration on the subject-matter of what they teach. And that denial rings with the kinds of contempt meted out to the job of running families. As if the flexibility, the knowledge and the judgement required to plan and carry out that job were the outcome of instinctive, innate capacities in women, rather than the result of thought, planning, experience, discussion with others and – very importantly – a collection of competencies which must be capable of developing productively over time.

So what sort of work is teaching? Whatever the answer to that question, there has been a long history of evasion in most descriptions of the processes that teachers set going in classrooms with children over time in the interests of learning and development. Instead, there has been a focus on all the other things that go on. In fact, most accounts of the good teacher exceed the notion of professionalism at both ends of the spectrum: the scholar, because his calling is based on his own gifts and passion for his subject; the mother/teacher, because in her own way she is doing what comes naturally. Mothers themselves are caught on this dilemma, for the idealising rhetoric of motherhood expressly rules out any account of caring for one's own children which allows it to be seriously hard work, let alone a chore. It is also remarkable, I think, that both extremes of the 'good teacher' make any sort of training appear unnecessary.

Professions were in some sense a nineteenth-century invention, the institutionalising of areas of work through the control of recruitment and training, and an extension of the self-regulating structures already developed by doctors and lawyers to other areas of work like the civil service. This was in the interests of creating hierarchies and career structures for middle-class men, whose work had hitherto been performed outside strictly class boundaries and independently of agricultural and commercial activity. Even now, the image of the 'professional woman' has to contend with the contradictions inherent in a woman belonging as a man might to what is specifically a male way of life and work. Professions have not adapted to the increasing presence within them of women, because their *raison d'être* has been to support and give shape to a type of male working life. Men 'join' professions, and belong to them, while women perform the work professions have been designed to protect. And the word 'career' assumes its more sinister meanings (with echoes of 'careerism' and even of the wild careering of the joy-rider), in relation to the notion of a 'career woman', who is no longer simply a worker, but someone who is married to her job and has replaced the 'natural' patterns and expectations of a woman's life with hectic ambition, in ways that men may do, but women do at their peril. She may also have chosen to work in what is thought of as a male world rather than a female one.

In fact, as Sandra Acker has shown, the concept of a career in teaching has little in common with most uses of the word, and is marked above all by absolute differences and divisions between teachers, according to the age-levels they teach, subject specialisms and size of school. Using DES figures for 1987, Acker sets out some aspects of the situation like this,

> The majority of nursery and primary teachers, 78.1 per cent, are women ... Nearly all teachers and head-teachers in nursery and separate infant schools ... are women. Combined infant/junior schools ... and separate junior schools ... have higher percentages of men teachers (25 per cent and 34 per cent respectively) and are likely to be managed by men, who hold 69.4 per cent of the infant/junior headships and 79.6 per cent of the junior headships. In secondary schools 54 per cent of teachers, and 83.8 per cent of headteachers, are men.[13]

Then, as Acker comments, if we are to consider the 'career chances' of each sex, we would see that they are 'exceedingly good' for men in primary education. While in secondary schools, men are four times more likely than women to become heads, and at least twice as likely to rise to positions of middle management. 'Career', at the very least, means quite different things for men and women going into teaching, for the vast majority of women, in primary as well as secondary schools, are to be found on the bottom two pay scales. It is not surprising, therefore, that the woman who breaks through such barriers will be seen by many to have 'unnatural' kinds of drive and ambition and to have competed with men and succeeded on their terms.

Given such unequal career possibilities, it is also not surprising that the notion of professionalism has meant many contradictory things. I used often to feel that it meant not much more in the end than the establishment and mainten-ance of standards of probity and discretion and the wearing of unsightly clothes. No bad thing in itself, even if it boiled down in the end to not shopping your colleagues to children or their parents, and being prepared to heed the irrational edicts of the Head Teacher on the subject of women teachers' dress. Teachers and the teaching unions have been divided for a long time as to whether teaching should be regarded as a profession at all, and there are analyses which cast the spasmodic drive towards 'professionalisation' amongst some teachers as having played into the hands of those who have been intent on controlling education and teachers. From this point of view, women teachers are often blamed for such a drive and for a history of conciliatory and complaisant responses to attempts to regulate teachers and ultimately to reduce their sphere of influence and expertise. It is likely, after all, that women have in some cases been less exercised than their male colleagues about improvements in pay and career structures, since they have often expected to remain at the same level within both for most of their working lives.

Michael Apple, the American sociologist, has portrayed teachers as especially vulnerable to such uncertainties about their status as professionals or workers; and he appears to link what he regards as a necessarily doomed impetus towards professionalisation with women teachers and with their presumed malleability. It is women's majority presence, in his view, that underlies teachers' particular susceptibility to the proliferating demands for more and more testing and for other paperwork. Teachers who accept such extra work, in Apple's view, do so in confirmation of their already shaky sense of themselves as professionals. And this works to remove them further still from the solid ground of their own expertise.

Apple's analysis is a complex and subtle one, sympathetic to the complexities faced by women teachers as workers and anxious to acknowledge the dilemmas implicit in considering any area of work from a broadly Marxist point of view, when that work has been performed by women more often than by men. Yet, like earlier work in this area, by the British sociologist, Gerald Grace,[14] for instance, it cannot escape from the in-built suspicion that women are the problem with teaching. It is worth quoting Apple here,

> We cannot understand why teachers interpreted what was happening to them as the professionalization of their jobs unless we see how the ideology of professionalism works as part of both a class and gender dynamic in education. For example, while reliance on experts to create curricular and teaching goals and procedures grew in this kind of situation, a wider range of technical skills had to be mastered by these teachers. Becoming adept at grading all those tests and worksheets quickly, deciding on which specific skill group to put a student in, learning how to 'efficiently manage' the many different groups based on the tests, and more, all became important skills. As responsibility for designing one's own curricula and one's own teaching decreased, responsibility over technical and management concerns came to the fore.
>
> Professionalism and increased responsibility tend to go hand in hand here. The situation is more than a little paradoxical. There is so much responsibility placed on teachers for technical decisions that they actually work harder. They feel that since they constantly make decisions based on the outcomes of these multiple pre- and post-tests, the longer hours are evidence of their enlarged professional status.[15]

It *is* paradoxical, and it is true that a visitor to a school will be struck by all the 'housekeeping' tasks a teacher must perform in addition to teaching. Administering and marking tests, yes, but also the collection of money for this and that, the organising of swimming lessons, visits from the dentist, and from foot and head inspectors, collections for local charities. Yet, because that image of the bearded scholar interrogating his eager student sits so improbably with the life of a contemporary teacher in a state school, or indeed of a village schoolmistress at the end of the nineteenth century, it seems to me unhelpful to suppose that what she is actually doing is therefore *not* intellectual work at all, but extended housework, a kind of mopping up, interspersed with moments of concentrated lecturing on her part, or organised reading or writing by the class. And all mediated by unquenchable flowings of love and hope.

What makes teaching both difficult and demanding as work, requiring very high levels of intelligence and judgement, is that the day-to-day pressures of the job must always be subordinated to the longer perspective. Teachers must always have their eye on two quite different time-scales at the same time: on children's lives and development between, say, five and eighteen, but also on what may have happened before those years, and, most significantly, what will follow them. Yet in trying to characterise my own time as an English teacher in a large London comprehensive school during the seventies, I am struck by how hard it is to focus on myself as a teacher at all, and how even harder it is to be clear about what is 'professional' and what is produced by the power structures of the school, the local authority, government policy, and so on. This is by no means because teaching encourages some kind of selflessness – though curiously the peculiar loss of self testified to by some actors and allied, I daresay, to a performer's particular vanities, suggests something of what teachers may experience – but because the relation between actual days, lessons, children, moments and the scale of the whole enterprise is simply not available to me imaginatively as I tangle with the day's immediate demands. It would be as difficult to present oneself as a good teacher as it would be to present oneself as a good mother. The role I occupied, I now think, was inherently anomalous, quite outside any equivalence with scholar, mother, administrator; yet involving all those possibilities, and also more and less than any of them. To some extent – and this was, after all, the early seventies – I did have freedoms in my classroom. I had choices about what to read and how to read. I had choices about the activities I engaged the children in. And I had choices about what the relations between children and between teacher and children would be like and the ways in which they might be realised. Those freedoms were both circumscribed and supported by a male management, male head, male heads of houses and departments, a system of budgeting and of 'governing' schools, which left me to do 'my' job. And what exactly was my job?

I see myself now, restlessly moving between tables, squatting down to look at a child's writing. Always visible and always alert to trouble. I once ripped a bright red circular skirt from top to bottom as I whirled round the corner of my own desk and got caught by a splinter of wood. Thirteen-year-old Patrick Heany, the only child I've ever known who wrote phonetically, accused me of doing it on purpose to distract them all. I was aware that I did distract them, and there were certainly quieter and less disruptive ways of energising classrooms. And then, even when I find myself congratulating the children I taught for their directness and good sense, I wonder whether I may not be deflecting attention from my own activities. And if I offer myself up as the 'good egg' teacher, absurd but resilient, I wonder whether that is to deflect criticism too. There are few models of the woman worker which depend on her own account of it, and which ignore the disparaging as well as the celebratory images of women doing 'what comes naturally' out of a nature they are usually quite unable to recognise in themselves.

Clara Collet assembled her diary entries from 1878 to 1885 (presumably for publication) as the 'Diary of a Young Assistant Mistress'.[16] She left school in London to become a teacher in a brand-new high school for girls in Leicester at the age of 17. There is a good deal in her diaries about her own studies. She was working for an external London BA. Miss

Buss, her old headmistress at the North London Collegiate School, wrote to her in November 1880, congratulating her on her success in the examination and on being the school's first graduate.[17] She writes about walks and friends and tennis and holidays and other teachers. There are incipient love affairs which come to nothing, and an offer of marriage she rejects and suffers over. There are regular entries about her pupils' examination results, and a moment of terror and subsequent depression as she contemplates humiliating public failure when she teaches a test lesson at her old school as part of the 'Teacher's exam', watched by Miss Buss. This exam, incidentally, was probably taken under the aegis of the Council of the College of Preceptors. Miss Buss, as the Council's first woman member, had, in 1870, persuaded them to start training classes for secondary-school teachers.[18] Clara writes of inspections, staff meetings, disagreements and outings. She mentions her salary when she starts at 17 (£80) and the fact that it has risen to £160 after seven years. She writes about sermons and Unitarianism, and her reading, which takes an uncharacteristic nose-dive as she makes her way through writers on education like Bain and Arnold and Fitch. But we never see her in the classroom with her pupils, and the sense that her role there is oddly uncomfortable is conveyed by several allusions to 'the worry of school', and, not long before she left teaching to study for an MA in Moral and Political Philosophy at University College London (where she was the first woman to do so) – by her comment that:

> my views on every subject are growing more and more unpopularly unorthodox and I doubt very much whether I shall be able to teach children much longer; what I care about no one wants taught and I do not know other subjects well enough to hold my own as a first class teacher.

Clara had enjoyed her own schooling at North London Collegiate School, and had appreciated the teaching of Miss

Buss herself and her staff of clever and committed women teachers; but she was already aware that she needed to develop her own intellectual interests, and that this might distance her from the classroom rather than strengthen her work in it. Her studies, undertaken while she was teaching, had widened beyond the scope of what seemed at the time the only possible way in which she could earn a living for herself.

Most accounts of the history of women's training simply allude to the inferior provision for women, as H.C. Dent does:

> Women suffered more than men. They had, in general, poorer buildings, poorer amenities, a poorer staff-student ratio, and heavier domestic duties. And they were more conscientious and compliant than the men.[19]

There is little sense in Dent's careful history of teacher training that many women came to teaching as their only way of getting more education for themselves. When, for instance, Queen's Scholarships for training colleges were abolished in 1863 as part of a large-scale cost-cutting exercise (masquerading as an attempt to raise standards), the men's colleges were hard hit. However, as Dent writes,

> The women's colleges were little affected; there were few other occupations open to educated women, the colleges were cheaper to run, and the demand for women teachers strong: they accepted lower salaries than men.[20]

The teacher training and the test lesson that Clara undertook alongside her London BA degree, and while she was actually teaching, were parts of a scheme to train secondary teachers which had little impact on men going into teaching until the end of the nineteenth century, though it was taken up enthusiastically by women. And it was women's commitment to secondary training – partly, as I have suggested, as a way of getting an education for themselves – which transformed entry into teaching, for good as well as ill. So that from the early years of this century, patterns of training – a degree plus an additional year, or three-year or four-year certificates or degrees – became accepted, as did the more problematic division within such courses between what came to be thought of as the 'academic' aspects of teaching and the 'professional'. It is this division, still enshrined in all teacher-training programmes and policy documents, which has contributed so disastrously to the misdescription and the undermining of the work of teachers, and to the doubt cast in the public mind on the intellectual character of teachers' work.[21]

It is a Monday morning in mid-May 1973. Eight forty-five. I hurtle through the technical block to the staffroom to collect my register and barely stop before running on to the west block, through crowds of children and teachers surging both ways, to my classroom on the corner overlooking the park. The ILEA[22] is building a high wall to deter intruders as well as escapees, and its designer has – marvellously – decorated it with tiny steps, bricks set in endways, so that both ingress and escape are made markedly easier than they were in the old days of black, spiked London railings.

My room has huge plate-glass windows. One of them has had a giant spider's-web crack across it for months. A crazy man, with lacquered hair and leather gloves and backed by a posse of less audacious henchmen, arrived one afternoon and simply punched the window and left. For a second I pictured thirty children cut and bleeding, but the window did not quite shatter. Inside, we were too stunned to react, except for one resourceful eleven-year-old, who asked for permission to tell the Head and did so.

I fumble for my key, one of twelve I hang on a cord round my neck. We all pour into the room, my class, me, bags, two other teachers who want books from my cupboard as well as paper and chalk and keys for other rooms. I open two windows, and Arti and Sharon shiver a bit showily and huddle into their coats. A bell rings and the tannoy sputters into action. Hard to hear it all, but something about £200 in cash, gone missing from the Deputy-Head's desk in her office. Somebody must have picked up – quite accidentally – the collection box with their books. Obviously a mistake. Could people just look in their bags . . . return it as soon as possible. It's for the local housing trust. Graham asks me whether *I* think it's a mistake. I nod in a non-committal way.

'Two hundred pounds. Go on, Miss!' says David.

Most of them are here. Graham and David are elbowing each other with rhythmical, if perfunctory, jabs. Betty looks worn out and is sitting on her own again. Tracy is late and so are Carlton, Prince, Byron and Ephraim. I do the register and notice a letter in it. Beautiful italic script from the head of the art department. I skim through it. The usual thing: sorry to tell you that your class . . . mayhem again on Friday . . . a whole set of felt tips missing and two pairs of scissors. David and Eddie locked themselves in the paper cupboard, and Stephen actually hung from the window, outside, and had to be hauled in. The girls tried to work, but gave up in the end. Detention. In future no . . .

I start to roar. This must be the tenth time this year I've had these humiliating notes left in the register about 'my' class, who seem unable to behave themselves the moment my back is turned. Graham puts his hand up and says 'Miss, but Miss'. I roar on. No, Graham, I am not to be interrupted. This won't do. It isn't fair on those who behave themselves perfectly well in the art department. Graham is becoming red in the face, with one arm stretched imploringly upwards and the other one propping it up. But on I go. I hear my voice bellowing quite gracefully now . . . fed up, end of tether, maddened beyond endurance . . . having to field these endless complaints about a class which is thoroughly capable of working hard and playing well together and . . .

'O.K. Graham, but make it quick, please.'
'Miss, if you read that note carefully you'd see that it isn't about us at all. It's about Fox Ia.'

I look again. He's right. So I start the week eating humble pie, and amazingly they don't rub my nose in it.

They have diaries to write while I deal with beginning-of-the-day business. A message that Tracy's mother rang and she won't be in. Byron arrives late again, and I'm worn out with roaring so I don't and he goes quietly to his seat by the window, the hood of his anorak obscuring ears, mouth, eyes, everything but his nose. Norma calls me over and I go. She is writing this terrible story she writes all the time about a dad killing a mum and being put inside. Norma is small and bleached, with delicate lilac veins and sharp elbows. Often, as we make our way to the other side of the school, she puts her arm in mine and tells me more of this terrible story, which is too unnerving to comment on. I have to stoop painfully to hear what she says and keep our arms linked at the same time.

Today, I've decided to read Aesop's fable, 'The Belly and the Members'. I'm not quite sure what I want them to do with it, so I've got a few other fables we'll read if they're not interested. But they are, amazingly. They pull their desks together round mine, because I've got a tape recorder and they want to speak into it. Several of them explain at some length what they think the fable means. Every sentence is punctuated with a 'Miss', but they seem to want the others to hear too. Analogies abound. Schools need teachers, but teachers wouldn't be much good without kids. Football teams need managers, players, a ball, a crowd. And so on. Some of them become earnest and moralistic. They have understood quite a lot about what sort of stories fables are and are going to try one of their own for homework. It's one of those mornings when you'd almost be grateful for a visitor, you're so proud of them. You've hardly needed to speak and they're talking so well, listening to each other, comforted, I think slyly, by having come so well out of our fracas at registration.

I marvel at the volatility of this group of eleven-year-old London children. Three-quarters of them have endured difficulties which would floor me. The class can run rings round a lot of their teachers. Me too, though my being their class teacher may have spared me their worst excesses. But at lunch-time the boys organise themselves (and no one is left out) to play cricket, and they've started to accept the girls too. Though that's Bella's doing, really. Their organising ability was used, on one disastrous occasion, to fleece the local supermarket of about a dozen packets of crisps. And I heard about that from Wei, a Vietnamese boy, who'd found himself innocently implicated and came to tell me, terrified that his parents might hear about it. We kept the whole thing dark, I'm afraid, and Wei and Ky offered to collect enough money from the class to leave at the till on their way out the next day. I'm embarrassed not to have done something more punitive.

Just before the bell goes a man puts his head round the door to tell me he's the plumber come to mend the pipes in the stock room. I worry for a moment that he has three teeth in front, where most of us have two. This and a strange green hat make him look like a sinister Pied Piper. Ashamed of my beady intolerance, I give him my keys and tell him where to go. The boys' lavatories have been leaking into the piles of *The Rover* and *The Silver Sword* and the bowdlerised Temple Shakespeares in the corner of the stock room I look after. It smells awful. At dinner-time, another member of the English department puts her head round the door to tell me that all the tape recorders and record players, and the new video camera, have gone from the stock room and the door has been left open. The smell is unchanged. I spend the dinner hour explaining things to the Head and filling in an insurance claim. Each of my twelve keys must be replaced.

I'm never sure whether I know too much or too little about the children in my class. Byron, for instance, lives in a residential home, but spends the weekends with his grandmother. Bella lives with her father and his elderly lover, and David's father died last year of leukaemia. Carlton has frightening asthma, and lives with his father and brother. His mother killed herself when the boys were still at primary school. Debbie, who is clever and unkind, has a mother known to be on the game. And there's Norma. And so on. I know these things, and often wish I didn't. There is a move to capitalise on all the information we may possess individually and develop more systematic banks and lines of communication amongst the staff. This was before the school had a computer. So my knowing that Dennis already had a police record in primary school is meant to be written in his file and shared with all his teachers. I'm not sure about this. Most of what I know helps me not to say grossly insensitive things to the class or to particular children, and certainly not to assume that they live in two-up/two-down families, but it doesn't help the children much. Some of the older boys say they hate the thought of what may be written on their files that are kept in the offices of the heads of year. It makes them distrust teachers, who may know all kinds of disparaging things about them, though the boys don't know what they are, so they can't explain them or answer back. Last year, one such office stuffed with files was burned to the ground, presumably by one of the children. Yet I've often enough needed someone else to talk to about the problems I was having with particular children. With Barry, for instance, who carefully placed slivers of broken glass between the pages of *The Grapes of Wrath* and then, pale and stiff in his unspeakable rage, held the remains of his broken bottle half an inch from Becky's cheek.

After break I have my upper-sixth A-level class. I tear across the bald, hummocky lawn in front of the school (sometimes I have the sense of myself as nearly horizontal and only an inch or two off the ground as I manoeuvre my way round the spread-eagled buildings, always at the double). This time it's to the Lodge, once the bizarrely adorned home of a famous financier – peacock tiles and exotic hardwoods – now both the library and the home of the sixth form. We're reading Hazlitt, which, perhaps oddly, we all like: maybe because he is simultaneously ingratiating and endearing. All too easy to mimic the 'scholar' teacher in such a lesson, so instead, I ask beautiful Jessica, whose father is Indian, what she thinks it would have been interesting to talk about with Hazlitt. She says she'd have been far too tongue-tied to speak. I tell her that the author of *Liber Amoris* would have been only too interested in talking to her. Perhaps I should rephrase my question. What could you have said to him to fend him off and yet keep the conversation going?

It's a long day. I have my O-level class after lunch and it's that difficult bit at the end of *For Whom the Bell Tolls* when they're in the mountains. My witheringly superior student will be 'observing' me. He doesn't seem anxious to get going himself. He is, temporarily, I imagine, an Althusserian; and I am no 'hero' teacher in his eyes, but a culpably female and liberal one, who is doing my working-class students no favours. I think I'll get them to make a map of the terrain so that I can understand what's going on. Then it's my fourth year CSE[23] group. They're doing editing today, reworking and choosing their best bits of writing to put in their exam folders for next year. I need to warn them that a journalist friend of mine has asked if he can come to their lesson tomorrow. I think he wants to write about the effect of ROSLA[24] on schools like mine. The members of my fourth-year class are not given to affecting good behaviour just for visitors.

At half past three I speed off again, this time to the staff-room. There's no meeting after school today. Instead, I have to parcel up over a 150 coursework folders to send to the CSE examinations board. I do it fast and badly, sitting on the floor of the staffroom, with brittle grey sugar-paper and cheap, furry string. The parcels, it later turns out, collapse by the time they reach the local post office. Luckily, nothing is lost, but it could have been a disaster of the sort the *Evening Standard*[25] would enjoy. I should have taken more time and trouble, but it's my turn to collect my daughter and two of her friends for tea and I'm already late for them.

When I left school-teaching for the university in 1976 I marvelled especially at having my own desk and my own telephone, and at the fact that I sat down to teach. There can't be many teachers of children in schools who sit down, though I have sometimes looked into classrooms in schools where I was visiting students, and seen teachers reading *The Times* with their feet on the desk while the pupils wrote or read. But those were usually selective schools for boys, of the kind politicians send their sons to. There was never much point in sitting down in my school. You'd have had to get up as soon as you did.

As I remember days like that one I can see ways in which it might be offered to student teachers as an object lesson in what not to do. There were incidents I should have reported. There were some parents, then as now, who would have disapproved of my mentioning *Liber Amoris*.[26] I should certainly not have handed over my keys to a total stranger. I should have read the note in my register before indulging in histrionic rage. I should have prepared all my lessons more carefully and I should have learned to make proper parcels. I should most certainly not have decided to allow my journalist friend into the school. The class, as it turned out, and quite predictably, played to his obvious horror at their language and their reluctance to work; though at least he did not write an indignant article about it. The scope for small and larger errors of judgement seems, and indeed I remember it as being, almost infinite. Certainly, as a 'professional', I score low marks. Yet many English teachers in large urban schools like mine would recognise that day as one of the better ones: enjoyable, interesting, relatively productive, with good-tempered relations amongst the children and between them and me and most of their other teachers. I was often exhilarated by days like that, and exhausted too, of course. And there were even days when I might have a really good idea or might adapt the really good idea someone else had given me in the lunch hour.

But I am also aware that this is just one way of telling my story. There are certainly others. Some of my friends saw my late entry into teaching as masochistic and even a bit priggish and do-gooding. Though most of them sent their own children to such schools they saw teaching in one as zealous and excessive; no doubt necessary and difficult, but also intellectually low-level and embarrassingly unglamorous. The account I have written of my day seems to me to be addressed to them, and its oddly androgynous 'cool' and its emphasis on the chaos out of which good things might come – as if by magic – is probably uncharacteristic of how most women would tell their story. A serio-comic genre was developed in the late sixties and early seventies as a way of writing about working-class children's education, which aspired to account for the possible romance, at once radical and transfiguring, of teaching in a difficult school. My own voice hears and echoes what was undoubtedly a male romance.[27] One teacher friend describes her own tendency to offer her students' achievements as if they had nothing to do with her teaching, as one strategy for countering the contempt that is publicly expressed for working-class children and for their teachers. Others will focus on the minutiae of their preparation and the discrepancies between this and what eventually transpires in the classroom. A kind of modesty, almost certainly suspect, is enjoined on us all, I think: due to fear of exposure and mockery, and the difficulty of being seen to take yourself and the work you do too seriously.

Margaret Littlewood, in her study of the National Association of Schoolmasters (NAS), the union which broke away from the NUT in 1922 in order to defend the interests of male teachers, shows how versions of sexual difference have evolved as justifying chorus to economic arguments as well as determining the arguments themselves. She argues that the 1944 McNair Report on the supply of teachers, for instance, embodies the assumption that:

> teaching attracted emotionally immature individuals, who preferred the sheltering body of the school rather than facing the demands of a full adult adjustment in the outside world. What was wanted were people who had a mature and wide experience of life. But what constituted this maturity was crucially dependent on gender. For men, it was defined as experience of employment in other occupations; for 'wise married women' maturity meant fulfilment in marriage and motherhood. While the report implied rather than stated that women who rejected marriage were unsuitable to be trained as teachers, others were not as reticent. John Newsom in his book *The Education of Girls* argued that single women teachers suffered from emotional problems, arising from sexual repression or homosexuality.[28]

Yet the use of the marriage bar in many parts of the country was also defended on a whole range of implausible grounds: from the belief that married women had, necessarily, no need of money, to the drawbacks inherent in encouraging women to neglect their own families. And even those who argued for women's special bent for teaching – their patience,

gentleness, sympathy for and understanding of young children
– were caught by the opposition such arguments drew on
themselves: that this was work better performed by real
mothers within the family, and that what women teachers
provided was not education but delegated child care. When
I was promoted in 1972 to responsibility for the plumbing
in the book cupboard, amongst other things, I was charged
by my Head with doing it for 'pin money', when there were
others who needed the money more than I did. I had been a
mature married woman with three children when I began to
teach, too wise and mature, as it turned out, to qualify for a
grant for training. Over the Christmas holidays, I had gone
from a job in publishing to a London classroom. Mothering
was no help in itself, though my interest in my own school-age
children and their sometimes uneasy passage through school
undoubtedly contributed to my interest in teaching as work.
I soon learned that I would not be much helped either by
approximating to the tactics of the bluff military man, for
example, who had been the last person to teach me, fourteen
years earlier, in an ancient university. He had taught me
Russian, along with 200 National Servicemen, whom he
regularly and – as I felt it – savagely ordered to their feet as I
tumbled in, late and dishevelled, to his nine o'clock lectures.

Most societies have resorted to explanations based on
women's natures when they have wished, for whatever
reason, to control that half of the potential workforce that
women represent. Their natures have been invoked to explain
what they could not study as well as what they could not do,
though as Clara Collet so neatly put it,

> The futility of forbidding women to do what they were
> incapable of doing was never perceived by the opponents
> of the movement for the higher education of women,
> who based their opposition on this ground:[29]

Forty-six years later, in his *The Education of Girls*, Sir John
Newsom was recommending that girls might take the same

examinations as boys – but later. A commonly held view, as it happens, despite the fact that current beliefs incline to the somewhat different view that the problem with *boys* is that they mature more slowly and later. Moreover, while admitting that 5.5 million women were currently in paid employment outside the home (this was in 1948), Newsom was also prepared to remind his readers that since 300,000 of them were employed as teachers and nurses, an education preparing girls for a life in the home would for all practical purposes do just as well – double duty, as it were – since these professions are 'traditionally supposed to require by transference the qualities and capacities normally associated with the home'.[30] 'Nature' acquires a wonderful elasticity within such wholly irrational plans to solve the 'problem' of women and the 'problems' of education simultaneously.

It is only recently that historians and sociologists of education have identified the presence of women within the teaching force as significant. Gerald Grace's study of teachers of urban working-class children in London during the second half of the nineteenth century and until the 1970s, for instance, barely mentions women teachers. Even though many of the teachers he talked to were women, nothing is made of the possibility that they had become teachers for different reasons, and had experienced teaching and actually done their work differently from their male colleagues. Nor does he consider the impact on state education, and on teaching as work, of the overwhelming presence of women in schools and classrooms. Though one reference to women does suggest that their 'dominance' amongst teachers may explain why 'the intentions of a section of the Victorian middle class to keep the teachers of the people apolitical and ideologically bland, were largely successful'.[31] The 'compliance' of teachers, that is, was at least partly due to the numbers of women amongst them.

Yet Grace's analysis of the tension between teachers' struggles towards 'professionalism', and the uses made of those struggles by people with powerful interests in controlling teachers and schools, becomes even more revealing when considered in terms of the numbers of women entering teaching in the middle of the nineteenth century:

> control through professionalism cannot be seen as an unproblematic part of a 'conspiracy theory' of the working of society. While some middle-class writers saw in professionalism the means to keep the teachers loyal to the existing order and strategically separated from the rest of their class, others were concerned that it generated discontent, over-confidence in relation to superiors and dangerous aspirations towards autonomy. There co-existed, therefore, with an impulse towards the 'embourgeoisement' of the teachers, an impulse to keep them in their place and these contradictions were perceived by the teachers who were ready to advance their own constructions of what professionalism should involve.[32]

When that double dynamic is considered in relation to women it looks rather different. Grace ignores the complex political and professional formation of women teachers, who were still fighting for the vote, while being required to conduct themselves both as state employees and as loyal members of professional associations, which, in their turn, often strenuously resisted their presence. Hilda Kean has written about the involvement of women teachers in teachers' unions during the period before 1918, and her account of their relation to the state needs to be inserted here, I think.

> In some ways women teachers, as state employees, were in an anomalous position. On the one hand they were worse paid than their male colleagues, yet better qualified than other women workers. The function they provided in relation to state education was the same as that of their male colleagues but their treatment at the

hands of the state was different. It was not that they were the same as other women workers but that their position as women performing a function within the state was treated differently to that performed by men ... This consciousness of the particular role of women in relation to the state was elaborated in their explanation of their own 'civic consciousness'. They believed that because they were denied full citizenship, as voters, yet were nevertheless employed to teach the state's future citizens, they were more conscious of their own role as citizens and of that which would be played by the girls they taught.[33]

That notion of women's potentially greater consciousness of the class contradictions lived by teachers and, differently, by their pupils, particularly the girls, is an important insight. Kean's analysis also reminds us that it has been too easy to theorise social and cultural relations and leave women out of them, and that once the peculiar position of women teachers is entered into the history told in different ways by Gerald Grace and Michael Apple, the expectation or hope of some uniformly macho resistance to the coercions and reductions of the state education system become much harder to envisage.

Far more has been done and is being done in this area of research in North America and Australia than here, though writers like Grace have made some amends in this country by returning to issues of professionalism and careers, with gender at the heart of the questions to be addressed.[34] Indeed, there is coming to be a small industry in the historical unearthing of examples of early women teachers and the conditions under which they worked.[35] Tales of the solitude, the dangers and the adventure experienced, for instance, by young women teachers in the more remote parts of British Columbia in Canada or of Australia or New Zealand in the early years of this century return us to the appeal and the hardship of such lives, as well as to the wilful ignoring or misreading of them. Even today, large numbers of Canadian women teachers go north to teach in those Inuit communities which live 'above the tree line', descending in the summer to renew their skills as teachers and to acquire higher degrees and undertake research at the universities of Ontario and Quebec and Alberta.[36]

I suspect that there have been many young women entering teaching during the last thirty years who have hoped, in some more or less utopian way, that teaching working-class children would make 'organic intellectuals' of both teachers and taught, in the distinctive sense of 'intellectual' that Antonio Gramsci proposed.[37] Teachers would be intellectuals and perform intellectual work by virtue of their relation to the community, to the school, to families and children and to the wider set of relations linking those families to the work place, to government and unions and the church and so on. We would call ourselves intellectuals, not because of 'what' we taught, not because of what Gramsci emphatically warned against in any definition of 'intellectual' – that is, 'the intrinsic nature of intellectual activities'[38] – but because we worked with working-class children and for them. We would be involved in the processes and realities of their lives and in the possibilities for understanding and changing those realities, so that children would learn to understand and control their own destinies. It has not been easy to keep to that vision, even as a hope, not least because Gramsci – and most of his followers – do not regard women as intellectual workers of any kind or even as potential agents (except inadvertently) in the processes of change and renewal. The refusal of the left to think of women as workers whose experience has been significantly different from men's, and to consider the effect of that on institutions and practice and power relations, has been as damaging in the end as many of the onslaughts on teachers delivered by the right.

5

Boys and Girls

Raymond Williams remembered the year when he won a scholarship to the grammar school in Abergavenny:

> It happened that the village had its golden year when I sat for the scholarship – seven pupils won County scholarships. There was a group photograph taken because it was such an exceptional event: six girls and me. But the girls – several of them were farmers' daughters – would usually go only as far as the fifth form and would then leave. The other boys from the village also went to the fifth form, where they then often had difficulties in passing the matric. So by the time I got to the sixth form I was the only one from Pandy.[1]

The story I have been telling is full of contradictions: momentum and growth, but also waste and disappointment, or what has sometimes been envisaged as inflation followed by deflation. And there are quite different ways of telling the story. Williams does not ask what happened to those girls who left in the fifth form (the ones who were farmers' daughters and the ones who were not), though in one of his novels, *Second Generation*, he has a character, a clever and unhappy woman, who might have gone to university had her father not died. Her moral dilemma is played out in terms of loyalty to men, to her union-leader husband, to her clever, wayward son, to the Oxford don who is briefly her lover, rather than as a matter of choices and decisions she might have made on her own behalf.

In another conversation included in *Politics and Letters*, Williams recalls somewhat ruefully that the WEA[2] classes he had taught in his youth were more likely to be attended by 'commuter housewives at Haywards Heath who wanted to read some literature' than the working-class men he would have preferred to teach. Housewives who wanted to read literature were not, apparently, what adult education was really for. Yet he was also willing to see that his mother's politics could have been formed by quite different experiences from his father's, even if those experiences are seen to be ones on which she is incapable of reflecting except in entirely *ad hominem* terms.

> It was the classic situation of a Labour Party woman. She makes the tea, she addresses the envelopes, she takes them round – she does not have very many political activities in her own right. But my mother had her own opinions. She actually felt much more hostile to the farmers than did my father, who was mixing with them all the time. She still makes very hostile remarks about farmers as a class, whom she conceives as the ultimate in exploiters! But then these were about the only social relations she ever directly experienced. Her mother had been a dairy maid on a larger farm, and she had worked on one as a girl, so there was a sense of farmers as employers.[3]

In the early 1970s there were still many LEAs[4] who were adjusting boys' 11+ scores upwards by as much as 10 per cent because there were so many more grammar-school places for boys than for girls and (inconveniently) more girls passing the exam. There are the stories of lost confidence told by those women – usually, though not always, from working-class families – who did get into grammar school, only to find themselves cast there as 'average', 'capable but mediocre', a 'steady, reliable worker', even a 'plodder', who were later directed towards teacher training or other 'useful' careers, rather than to the kinds of further study they knew were accorded a higher value in the world.[5] In Carol Dyhouse's study of working-class and middle-class girls growing up at the end of the nineteenth century and the early years of this century, it is girls' sense of deprivation in comparison with their brothers that they remember. Dyhouse quotes Hannah Mitchell, who grew up on a Derbyshire farm in the 1870s and who resented above all the freedom enjoyed by the boys compared with the endless domestic tasks required of the girls, and 'the fact that the boys could read if they wished filled my cup of bitterness to the brim'.[6]

No one has written more ringingly, I suppose, of the deflation experienced by many girls than George Eliot in *The Mill on the Floss*, when Maggie visits her brother, Tom, who is staying with the schoolmaster Mr Stelling and his family. Flown with her own cleverness and her success with Mr Stelling, and too fond of her brother to realise how puncturing of him her cleverness can be, she insists on confronting the teacher.

> 'Mr Stelling,' she said, that same evening, when they were in the drawing-room, 'couldn't I do Euclid, and all Tom's lessons, if you were to teach me instead of him?'
>
> 'No; you couldn't,' said Tom, indignantly. 'Girls can't do Euclid: can they, sir?'
>
> 'They can pick up a little of everything, I daresay,' said Mr Stelling. 'They've a great deal of superficial cleverness: but they couldn't go far into anything. They're quick and shallow.'
>
> Tom, delighted with this verdict, telegraphed his triumph by wagging his head at Maggie behind Mr Stelling's chair. As for Maggie, she had hardly ever been so mortified: she had been so proud to be called 'quick'

all her little life, and now it appeared that this quickness was the brand of inferiority. It would have been better to be slow, like Tom.[7]

George Eliot's affectionate allusion to Maggie as 'this small apparatus of shallow quickness' rescues the scene from undue pathos. But the moment has been registered.

As I am writing this, and in just one week, there has been a *Panorama* programme called 'The Future is Female' and several long articles devoted to the surprisingly recent public discovery that girls do better than boys in examinations and are, therefore, better qualified to run the world. There have been several well-publicised research reports;[8] and a full-width headline across a page of my newspaper reads *The Trouble with Boys*[9] accompanies a photograph of some boys smoking and an article about whether or not boys really are doing worse in examinations than girls. The writer of the article spoke only to sixth formers in an independent co-educational boarding school, so her conclusions can hardly be read as applying to young people generally. However, she links her findings with one or two pieces of research, so that, beneath her suggestions that these boys have become complacent (they believe they'll get good jobs whether they do well in exams or not) and that they don't work as hard as girls, together with some reassurances that if men are getting more third-class degrees they are also getting more firsts (at least in some universities) lurks the hinted-at proposition that boys have become the sacrificial victims of 'equal opportunities'. And the advertising slogan for the *Panorama* programme, 'The education system is favouring girls and failing boys', somewhat belied the programme's other message, which was that girls are inherently 'better at' language and therefore have an advantage. There is no evidence, it should be said, for any discrimination against boys in schools, and a fair amount of evidence that they still demand, and get, more attention from teachers than girls do. But there is no doubt that anxieties about boys – and most particularly working-class boys – are growing and that in one way or another they inspire most of the criticisms levelled at schools these days.

The divided character of universal and compulsory secondary schooling since its real beginnings between the wars (that is as opposed to its official 1902 beginnings) always entailed selection, with those who passed the 11+ going to grammar schools and those who failed going to secondary-modern schools or their forerunners. This was validated by the useful belief that 'there *are* sheep and goats',[10] and that since we have simple tests for discovering children's natures (and there are luckily only two varieties of these) we can perfectly easily tailor the schooling they get to suit these natures. Such a position accords a pretty self-fulfilling, indeed pessimistic, function to education; and the fact that this process of division has always produced a high correlation with children from middle-class and working-class families simply serves to confirm the appropriateness of the division in the first place.

However, parallels between gender and class are complicated by their overlap. Girls – it should not need saying – belong to classes too. But when researchers have demonstrated the disappointing overall effect of comprehensivisation on the take-up of post-compulsory education by working-class children, they have rarely studied the issue of how girls have fared in relation to this. For girls have continued to do better; in part, of course, because they had so much ground to make up, given their history of impoverished provision and a second-rate curriculum. It is, therefore, unhelpful to see their current statistical superiority over boys in terms of examination results as somehow attributable to innate female advantages. We have been here before, after all, with bigger male brains to explain greater male intelligence, and both then confidently profferred as the reason for superior male educational performance.

It would also be foolish to be complacent about all this.

There are still, for instance, huge differences between the educational achievement of working-class and middle-class girls. Yet it seems probable that we are seeing now, and have been seeing for nearly twenty years, the consequences of having in the past denied all girls the possibility of going as far as they wanted to go in developing their educational potential. Or, put differently, we are seeing the results of girls emerging from beliefs, their own and others, which depressed their confidence. There is a strong interest amongst girls from most ethnic-minority groups, for instance, in staying on at school. They often have a confidence in their abilities which exceeds their schools' confidence in them. We are also seeing very radical shifts in employment patterns, with a decline in manufacturing industry and the growth of precisely those service industries which have traditionally employed girls and women. At the very least it seems important to consider how girls – and particularly working-class girls – have been affected by increased educational opportunity and transformed employment patterns.

It is not, of course, that working-class boys fared so much better than their sisters in the past, but that before the move towards comprehensive schools, it was easier for a boy to get a grammar-school place than a girl, and easier too for boys to get apprenticeships and other kinds of training. In the past, girls have been expected to fill their timetables with 'domestic' subjects or 'secretarial' ones, which were always marginalised within the curriculum, discounted by the assessment system and liable to downgrade in the public eye girls' achievements and qualifications. It is certainly worth calculating the effect on girls' academic performance generally of the reduction in typing, needlework and cookery.

Brian Jackson and Dennis Marsden did their research for *Education and the Working Class* in the late fifties, nearly forty years ago. It is extraordinary to consider, from the vantage point of current anxieties about girls doing better at school than boys, how easily they could accept that the girls in their sample of 88 'successful' working-class children in Huddersfield would do so much *less* well than the boys. Not only would none of them get into Oxbridge, when a quarter of the boys did, only 16 girls (as opposed to 38 boys) would go to university. And while several of the girls had no higher education at all, 20 girls and just 1 boy went on to training college. What is also striking, viewed from here, is the authors' contempt for those of their sample who went into teaching. These were 'drifters' for the most part, or those wanting only a 'safe career'.[11] And, of course, they were most of them women, whose ambitions, like their careers, are seen to be circumscribed from the beginning by parents, the expectations of schools and teachers, and by the wavering confidence of the girls themselves.

A general improvement in education provision for girls, changes in job opportunities, the foregrounding and making problematic of gender: these are amongst the explanations on offer for what can look like an astonishing reversal. However, they are almost certainly inadequate as explanations for the relatively poor showing of working-class boys in recent years compared with girls. A central theme of the new anxiety is also, of course, the feminisation of schooling: all the ways in which the increasing presence of women in teaching may have led to the sense of education itself being somehow an unmasculine business, inimical to a majority of working-class boys.

Paul Willis, in *Learning to Labour*, which was published in 1977, looked at the post-ROSLA offer for teenage boys from the vantage point of some of 'the lads'. These were the boys who, by rejecting school and the culture of the 'ear'oles' (their name for those boys who accept the school's values), were preparing themselves quite adequately for the least skilled and worst paid work in the manufacturing industries available to them in one part of the Midlands. Willis is explicit about the connections between the culture of such work, the culture of 'the lads', who express their hostility to school by 'having a laff' and managing to avoid putting pen to paper throughout a school year, and masculinity.

> The credentials for entry into shopfloor culture proper, as into the counter-school culture, are far from being merely one of the defeated. They are credentials of skill, dexterity and confidence and, above all, a kind of presence which adds to, more than it subtracts from, a living social force. A force which is *on the move*, not supported, structured and organised by a formal named institution, to which one may apply by written application.
>
> The masculinity and toughness of counter-school culture reflects one of the central locating themes of shopfloor culture – a form of masculine chauvinism. The pin-ups with their enormous soft breasts plastered over hard, oily machinery are examples of a direct sexism but the shopfloor is suffused with masculinity in more generalised and symbolic ways too.[12]

It is significant, I think, that Willis should oppose literacy to life, in this way, and femininity to masculinity. Such a head-and-heart antithesis would have been thought Lawrentian in the fifties. The difficulty with Willis's analysis is not simply that girls are excluded from discussion of the school/work misalliance (indeed their role is understood as a wholly sexual one), but that masculinity is presented as an idea or an experience which is learned amongst males and outside family relations. That is not the only difficulty, of course; for since that book was published, heavy manual work has become almost impossible to find in that part of the world, and the heroic 'lads' of Willis' research will, in most cases, have lived through at least a decade of unemployment. The need now is for an understanding of the possible counter-cultures produced by unemployment, or by non-traditional kinds of employment, and of how gender differences figure within them.

Learning to Labour blames teachers from a position on the left for the 'irrelevance' of school to these boys. Paradoxically, the governments of the eighties and nineties have also been blaming teachers for the defection of working-class boys and even for their unemployment (and, therefore, for their anti-social, even riotous potential), and on much the same grounds that Willis did: new, more open ways of teaching, new examination syllabuses, more time spent on the arts and design, on English and social studies and humanities, more preparation for a lifetime of family as well as work relations. Such moves have been castigated by both left and right as inappropriate for working-class boys.

In 1981, Michael Hamerston investigated one of the courses offered by a further education college to school leavers who were in training as plumbers.[13] The young men worked four days of the week on the job and spent one day in college, during which they spent four hours doing practical work in the workshop, two hours on the Theory of Plumbing, one hour doing Calculations, and a final hour on General Studies. The students' evaluation of the course was emphatically in that order too, with the practical work as the most relevant to the job, as they saw it, receiving their whole-hearted approval, particularly as it was taught by a man who had spent many years of his life as a practising plumber. For the General Studies, on the other hand, taught by a woman teacher and covering subjects like economics, the financial world, and contraception, they expressed nothing but contempt. Hamerston sat in on many of their classes, and he contrasts their absorption in the workshop, and even in the Theory and Calculations classes, with their 'irreverent marauding behaviour' (a phrase borrowed, in fact, from Willis) in their General Studies class. They regarded these classes as a waste of time. They treated the woman teacher (who was certainly to the left of the students politically) to sexist and racist and, indeed, extreme right-wing opinions. As Hamerston puts it, they cast her as the 'representative of the thousands of "helpless housewives" whose sinks they will be called upon professionally to unblock'.[14] General Studies involves the students in no examinations, and it appears to them to have no link with the world of either practical or theoretical plumbing. It is worth quoting Hamerston's account of how the students manage to subvert the classes and undermine their teacher:

> Opposition manifests itself at a variety of levels. The most basic of these is simple misbehaviour, anything to disturb the social harmony which is vital for sustained conversation. Thus, the students lounge about the room slumped in their chairs, engage in sporadic chatter at high volume, and exercise a mobility not seen in Theory and Calculations classes. From the outset, the intention is to do as little as possible, and, while most of the opposition is in no way malicious, it is nevertheless deliberately subversive. Individual acts might even be seen as good-natured, but the cumulative effect is profoundly destructive, and may be compared with 'the laff' described by Willis . . .
>
> I have observed at least five different methods of incitement to disorder, invitations to subvert the formal purposes of the class. The first is an attempt to relate to the teacher in an informal way. S1, for example, tags many of his remarks with 'girl': 'How much tax you pay on that, then, girl?' and 'See you later, Miss. Thanks very much for that, girl'. The second is to propose questions of related content at inappropriate moments, disrupting the flow of the lesson. In one lesson dealing with stockmarket shares, the teacher wanted to discuss the role of brokers in buying and selling. But her question 'Do you know the name of the man who sells your shares for you?' was cut across by a loud demand

to know which is the better credit card – American Express or Barclaycard. The third method of subversion is humour played invitingly to the gallery:

T   They're talking about a Pill for men now.
S1 Yeah, it's called a reef knot!

The fourth is to turn the recognized structure of the classroom against itself. By this means, the right to ask questions, any question to anyone at any time, is turned into an indignant defence of disorderly conduct. If reprimanded, the student replies, 'I want to ask him a question!' The fifth is the exaggerated retort. After a questionnaire-type test paper was returned, some students were puzzled about what to do with their copies:

S   What do we do with these?
T   Put them in your files.
S   Files! What are files?

This last example begins to suggest the way in which cultural differences between teacher and taught may be exploited. The keeping of files is something done by academic students and professional people, not by apprentices. Academic training also bestows a different language, which can itself become the subject of exaggerated response:

T   Now we can't have all this levity, Mr S1!
S1 This what?

And if all else fails, reasoned opinion may be abusively denied with cries of 'Balls!'[15]

Perhaps the most shocking aspect of Hamerston's evidence, which will not, sadly, surprise most teachers, is that it too comes to us from what can seem like a lost and golden age, when at least it was possible to get apprenticeships and to follow well-structured courses, which spanned college and workplace and were seen by young men as genuinely useful preparation for a working life. In addition, the notion that masculinity can only thrive by undermining all female claims to knowledge or relevance or practical usefulness has back-fired most hideously, with men and boys emerging all too often, in the end, as the underdogs.

An example like Hamerston's reveals the need for conceptions of class and gender which, far from being fixed and absolute categories, function as metaphors and flexibly across a range of relative and comparative kinds of self-definition. Terry Lovell attempts just such a move, and she makes it within the sphere of education and culture:

> One motif which runs through cultural images of class locates the male working class as absolutely masculine, to uncivilized excess, while on the other hand, images of the effete and decadent upper-class male abound. The bourgeois male appears as relatively civilized and 'softened' when compared to his working-class counter-part, refreshingly 'manly' when viewed in relation to the other end of the class spectrum. In bourgeois culture the bourgeois male marks the position of human normality . . .
>
> The arts, and English literary study in particular, have laid claim to a certain moral and cultural superiority which is at the same time a subtle and covert mark of inferiority. The logic is identical to that which structured nineteenth-century domestic ideology. Women were seen as both physically and intellectually inferiors to men but morally superior . . . An identical 'civilizing power' is attributed to literature and to women.[16]

There seems no question that little girls take to school more easily than little boys, and there has never been a shortage of explanations for this. Valerie Walkerdine argues that it is the relation between the domestic and the pedagogic and the way in which women signify as mothers and teachers, taking positions of power within those practices, which provides the space for the early success of girls. This success is achieved precisely because successful school performance requires them to take up such positions in pedagogic discourses. On the other hand, this is equally a site of struggle for the boys, a struggle in which they must work to redefine the situation as one in which the women and girls are powerless subjects of other discourses. It could well be this very resistance to that quasi-domestic power which explains boys' failure to do well in early education.[17]

Walkerdine has grounded her research in an analysis of classroom behaviour, in this case a by now famous example of two four-year-old boys turning on their teacher with jokes and improvised rhymes, which impale her suddenly and improbably on their infant command of astonishingly effective and, of course, conventional sexist language.

> 'Shit Miss Baxter, shit Miss Baxter,' says one.
> 'Miss Baxter, show your knickers your bum off,' chimes the other.
> 'Take all your clothes off, your bra off.
> 'Yeah, and take your bum off, take your wee-wee off, take your clothes, your mouth off.'[18]

And so on. The transcribed tape all too vividly enacts Miss Baxter's predicament, as she wrestles with the need to protect herself against what must feel like an unbearable and embarrassing onslaught, while just managing to maintain her teacherly humour or poise with interventions like 'That's enough, you're being silly,' and remembering that these are small boys in her charge, for whose 'normal' development she is currently responsible.

Walkerdine sets her moment and its analysis within a larger historical account of the ways in which such research is likely to be interpreted. So that, for instance, it is rare, at least in my experience, for her brief scatological classroom drama to be read without Miss Baxter being multiply blamed for it; just as Hamerston's General Studies teacher is blamed, if only implicitly. Most head teachers admit that they expect young women to have difficulty with boys, yet few of them raise the issue at interview and fewer still offer young women teachers any advice or support on the matter when they start their careers.

Similarly, Walkerdine shows how most examples of girls' successes are 'explained' within a whole assembly of disparagements. So, for instance, girls' early successes are produced by the culpably 'feminine' character of early schooling and are achieved at the expense of boys, who are adventurous rather than neat, and, quite properly, later developers. And those early and 'immature' successes are anyway to be contrasted with boys' 'real' and later success at secondary school, even though girls are now seen to be doing better than boys at GCSE and at A level as well. Then, girls' successes are understood to be the result of hard work rather than the 'brilliance' which boys are presumed to possess, though no evidence is likely to be adduced for this. Furthermore, the subjects at which girls succeed are construed inevitably as 'soft' ones, requiring care and superficial kinds of competence, while Maths and Science, at which boys are presumed to do better, are seen as rigorous and demanding of the more valued forms of reasoning and abstract intelligence.

And then, as Walkerdine has recently pointed out in a newspaper article written in response to what is by now the well-established fact that girls' examination results are better than boys', it is anyway middle-class girls in independent schools or well-funded state schools who are doing so well.[19] Though working-class girls are certainly doing better than working-class boys. So that the overall successes of some girls and the relative successes of all girls are allowed to be at the expense not only of middle-class boys but of all their working-class contemporaries. The threat then is not just femininity, but middle-class and educated femininity, perhaps even politicised and articulate femininity, a category personified for many otherwise politically disparate groups by the woman teacher. In Chapter 7 I shall focus on English as a school subject and on the way in which it has come to be seen as a subject taught by women and preferred by girls, and therefore in particular need of reform. Now, however, I want to return to the ways in which women, as mothers and as teachers, and girls, as successful students, are seen as the reason for the failure of working-class boys in school.

In D.H. Lawrence's extraordinary account of young Ursula Brangwen's first weeks as an elementary-school teacher at the end of *The Rainbow*, her ordeal is seen throughout in terms of an impossible struggle between feminine and masculine attitudes to discipline and teaching: attitudes which are arbitrated by means of enlisting children's own responses to them. The chapter itself is called 'The Man's World' and it begins with Ursula's initial and lyrical dreams of what teaching might be for her.

> She dreamed how she would make the little, ugly children love her. She would be so *personal*. Teachers were always so hard and impersonal. There was no vivid relationship. She would make everything personal and vivid, she would give herself, she would give, give, give all her great stores of wealth to her children, she would make them *so* happy, and they would prefer her to any teacher on the face of the earth.[20]

It is possible to hear in that passage not only the scorn of the neophyte for the experienced teacher, but the scorn of those educational theorists on the Left, who so pilloried what they saw as the sweetly meretricious manipulations of 'progressive' women primary teachers in the seventies and early eighties. Yet Lawrence's achievement in the chapter is to allow us to understand the tension and the oscillations Ursula experiences between absolutely antagonistic views of what teaching working-class children should be. Untrained and seventeen, Ursula has so few actual resources in the classroom that she is bound before long to capitulate with desperation to the brutal regime of the school.

Though there are one or two other women teaching in the school, the ethos is masculine, personified in the hateful figure of Mr Harby, the Headmaster; and the school, grimly acquiescent in the poverty and despondency of the children who attend it, is run along regimented and even violent lines. In her utter dismay at what is being asked of her and what she finds so impossible to do, Ursula is wholly – if provisionally – susceptible to the philosophy that tells her she must be wrong, since she can't get the children to do as she asks. At one point she even comes to see herself as responsible in certain ways for the terrifying anarchy of the school.

> The first great task was to reduce sixty children to one state of mind, or being. This state must be produced automatically, through the will of the teacher, and the will of the whole school authority, imposed upon the will of the children. The point was that the headmaster and the teachers should have one will in authority, which should bring the will of the children into accord. But the headmaster was narrow and exclusive. The will of the teachers could not agree with his, their separate wills refused to be so subordinated. So there was a state of anarchy, leaving the final judgement to the children themselves, which authority should exist.[21]

Her sense of terror and failure are sharp, for 'it was agony to the impulsive, bright girl of seventeen to become distant and official, having no personal relationship with the children'.

And it comes to be the boys, particular boys, she most dreads, and one especially, Williams, a 'rat-like boy' all teachers will recognise, whose insolence to her drives her to beat him horribly, in a way she knows to be unforgivable, and which serves to alienate all the other boys in the class.

> So the battle went on till her heart was sick. She had several more boys to subjugate before she could establish herself. And Mr Harby hated her almost as if she were a man. She knew now that nothing but a thrashing would settle some of the big louts who wanted to play cat and mouse with her. Mr Harby would not give them the thrashing if he could help it. For he hated the teacher, the stuck-up, insolent high-school miss with her independence.[22]

Ursula eventually becomes 'broken in' to teaching, even finding some pleasure in its 'sheer oblivion', so that though she still sometimes hates school she is ready to embark on her three years teacher training in a college where she has a place. And when Lawrence returns to Ursula in the classroom in *Women in Love*, she has made her peace and is getting on with the children, teaching them well, almost as she had wanted to from the beginning.

The chapter from *The Rainbow* is a passionate evocation of the terrors of teaching, and of the raw power struggle that Lawrence plainly experienced himself at the beginning of his own few years as a teacher. What makes it unusual is that he should write of these struggles as inevitably determined by sexual antagonisms, and that he should have exposed so brilliantly the rage and impotence a woman may feel when confronted by the absolute and public contempt expressed by young boys for a pretty young woman attempting to assert some authority over them.

> As she went along the street, clattering on the granite pavement, she was aware of boys dodging behind her.

> Something struck her hand that was carrying her bag,
> bruising her. As it rolled away she saw that it was a
> potato. Her hand was hurt, but she gave no sign.[23]

A 'rat-like boy' I once quarrelled with found out where
I lived and lobbed a small pebble at my large front window.
I left the small crack he made in it for over twenty years, as
a kind of memento.

Kate Pugh, the Head of English in a large mixed comprehensive school in London, has recently studied the relative
failure of boys at English in her own school. She writes of
them with honesty and sympathy.

> The educational, and economic, prospects of these boys
> are bleak, their relationship with staff, particularly
> female staff, at best uneasy and often embattled. We
> are shocked, angered and distressed by the racist and
> sexist behaviour of some of this group and often driven
> into expressions of our contempt for them by their
> challenge to our authority in the classroom. All of us,
> however, come from working-class backgrounds our-
> selves and feel some bewilderment at the contradictions
> our dismissive attitudes to this group of pupils imply.[24]

But dismay and sympathy hardly meet the character of the
struggle women teachers may have with boys in classrooms,
nor the anomalous and contradictory positions both groups
occupy in relation to forms of authority. Kate Pugh continues,

> What is most often totally missing from these accounts
> is any sense of classrooms in which both women teachers
> and students are engaged in conflict and struggle. The
> very phrase I have chosen, 'engaged in', is indicative
> of the difficulty. What I mean is that women teachers
> are often angered and hurt by their experiences in
> classrooms, but, although this is hardly a secret, it is
> difficult to say in professional or academic contexts. The
> admission is haunted by the spectral stereotypes of the

teacher who can't control the class, the over-emotional woman, the embittered feminist, and is rendered gauche by loftily donnish voices politely concealing embarrassment at the failure to understand what is appropriate. To maintain their self-respect and to be respectably professional or academic, women teachers have to remain silent.[25]

That this should be such a courageous admission is part of the explanation we need. These are contradictory attitudes because they are held by women who are teachers, people whose work depends on their wielding a certain kind of control in the classroom. Yet those same teachers also have a complex interest in their boy students doing well, and their own class experience tells them that the public opprobrium heaped on such youngsters is a large part of the problem, producing a culture of violence and antagonism, which is all too easily reinforced and inflamed by the real poverty and exclusion experienced by many young working-class men. That teachers should be, or should be seen to be, part of the problem for these boys is a painful paradox for many women teachers.

In a powerful critique of the current tendency to fasten on 'the yob' as a terrifying and emblematic bogey of the nineties, the journalist and academic, Rosalind Coward, has written,

The language in which such young men are described – louts, scum, beasts – can be heard across the political spectrum. It appears in an extreme form in *Sun* editorials and in a modified version in sombre discussions of youth crime, as well as in some feminist writings on contemporary masculinity. Individual men disappear in this language into a faceless mob, or appear only as thuggish stereotypes.[26]

She is right in her emphasis, and certainly right to wish to counter some absolute or, indeed, essential opposition between the masculine and the feminine, and the useless simplicities of that. Yet seen in the context of schools and women teachers it is important to go further. For mothers and teachers are implicated in the production of 'yobs', and while the media may whip up terrors at the potential of this new 'underclass', there is also an insidious tenderness expressed by the media and reflective of an underlying view of families and school and sexual relations: for it is women who have somehow failed working-class boys. And in that scenario a curious nostalgia remembers working-class boys and men as potentially the salt of the earth, betrayed not by capitalism or exploitative modernisation, but by their teenage mothers, their working mothers, their over-indulgent mothers, their out-of-touch women teachers and by the feminists who have impugned their sexuality and good faith.

Let us take our distance for a moment from those boys and their teachers in the 1990s and repair to the past and its arcadia. It is rare to find records of schools attended by working-class children before 1870 and the establishment of education for all children. Pamela and Harold Silver discovered the log-books and other records of St Mark's voluntary aided primary school in South London, going back to its foundation in 1824 as a National school. There were schools for girls in the area earlier than that, and from the beginning the new school was in fact comprised of two schools, one for boys and one for girls. It was clear from that moment, of course, that the schools would be different. The girls would follow a separate curriculum, for instance, and while the newly appointed Head of the boys' school was to be paid £120 a year, the Head of the girls' school was paid £50 a year. Both schools were designed to take 200 children, but the boys' school recruited much better than the girls' school. A public statement about the school in 1825 spoke about the 'progress of all the children in useful knowledge, and that of the girls in industrious work'. Whenever the girls' curriculum is mentioned, the focus is on needlework, which earned the school much needed money, a little of which went on clothes for the girls to wear to church on Sundays. Also, as the Silvers write 'The teaching of reading, writing and arithmetic are only occasionally mentioned, but moral and religious training is inferred or explicit in everything related to the school.'[27] The Silvers also quote from an Inspector's report of 1840 on schools in the north of England. They suggest that it is typical of reports of the time on both British and National schools:

> In some of the girls' schools very few of the children could write, and the writing was very bad; while even in the boys' schools, where more attention is paid to this important art, there were very few boys, and in very few schools, who had attained to a good running-hand without the aid of lines. In several of the girls' schools the children do not learn arithmetic at all.[28]

In general, then, it is assumed that girls are taught less and achieve less, and that fewer of them are sent to school in the first place. There is an interesting comment from a teacher at the school in 1867: 'Commenced work this afternoon with a large attendance in consequence of having told the girls we were going to have a lesson instead of needlework.'[29] It is the only moment when there is a sense of girls wanting to learn and truanting because they were not given enough.

Throughout this period it was always publicly acknowledged that male literacy was higher than female. The Silvers put it at two-thirds of the population for males and a half for females in 1840, and by 1870 something like 80 per cent for males and less than 75 per cent for females. It was easy enough to attribute this discrepancy to girls' inferior capacity, to suppose that they were always as 'dull and inert' as one LCC Inspector found them in 1912. And when, in 1927, the boys were congratulated for being 'intelligent and responsive' in their English lessons, it was noted without comment that the girls of the same age were doing infant-school work while 'senior school work is expected' of the boys.[30]

When the first Head of the girls' school, Rebecca Marchant, retired in 1848, she was succeeded by her niece, Miriam. Rebecca's salary never increased during her twenty-four years as Head of the school, perhaps because in 1829 a report charged her with being 'intemperate and violent in her conduct towards the children in the exercise of her duties' and, more seriously, that

> she was frequently absent from her house in the evening, not returning home until a late hour, – and on some occasions was absent the whole night, leaving the house in the charge of little girls, who are too young for such a trust, and who, for obvious reasons, ought not to be left in such a situation by themselves at night.[31]

The worst of the charges was that,

> on a recent occasion, she had staid out until a late hour, when on her return home she found the outer gates locked (as is the order of the committee) and that she had recourse to getting over the railing or wall, in order to gain admittance to her house.

Things were, in fact, settled amicably in the end, with Rebecca promising the committee that she would always leave 'a proper person in the temporary charge of her house'. It is hard to imagine that the private lives of male head teachers were investigated quite so thoroughly. Her niece, Miriam, suffered from poor health and, criticised for weakness in methodical teaching, was advised to 'study a good manual'. She was replaced in 1853 by the wife of the boys' school Headmaster. At this stage, the question of qualifications for the job seems to have been treated cavalierly. However, the Silvers quote an interesting story from the much later records of 1922.

> When the head resigned in 1922 the committee inter-viewed eleven candidates, including Mrs Pratt – who

was highly recommended by the head. The committee selected Mrs Pratt as 'the most suitable candidate for the position notwithstanding the fact that Mrs. Pratt has had no college training'. They believed her to be a 'well educated woman', and – again indicating the prevailing educational atmosphere – recorded that 'her personal charm, her refined attitude, her up-to-date and progressive methods and her kind and inspiring manner commended themselves most highly to the managers and warranted her appointment'. The L.C.C., however, were not impressed by Mrs Pratt's qualifications – or lack of them – for the post, and its Teaching Staff Sub-Committee recommended 'that on educational grounds consent should not be given'.[32]

Mrs Pratt did not get the job, marking a moment perhaps in a continuous struggle since about 1905 to establish elementary-school teaching as a profession, with respectable training and educational requirements, indeed with the beginnings of graduate status. That women were at the forefront of such moves and anxious to improve their knowledge and their practice is illustrated by other moments in the Silvers' findings, when infant teachers are recorded as visiting other schools and training colleges 'to keep abreast of new ideas'.

These are only glimpses of the inequality that was institutionally maintained between boys and girls in elementary schools until relatively recently, and of the ways in which women teachers were appointed, employed and controlled. They help, I think, to redress the balance somewhat, and to remind us just how briefly girls have enjoyed equality with boys, let alone any advantage over them. It is worth recalling the conviction with which Rousseau pronounced in his hugely influential *Emile*, first published in 1762, that

Little girls always dislike learning to read and write, but they are always ready to learn to sew. They think they are grown up, and in imagination they are using their knowledge for their own adornment.[33]

There can be no single or simple explanation for the reversal in expectations as to who will do well at school. It has been characteristic of some journalists' interest in the topic that biological explanations have been sought so strenuously, alongside reasons for a malaise amongst boys which might be caused by aspects of the education system itself. Of course, there may turn out to be explanations of both sorts, though they seem to me to rely on an entirely ahistorical version of the past, denying the fact that until quite recently girls were assumed (and all too often by themselves) to be intellectually, emotionally and physically inferior to boys.

It may be that, historically, those who have done well at school have been the ones who have been able to see most clearly what the connections might turn out to be between the practices of education and their future lives. They were children who could understand from their own perceptions of adult life that literacy, for instance, might be useful and even pleasurable. They were able to see continuities between the material of the school curriculum, the procedures and skills encouraged by school, and the ways in which certain adults go about their lives in the world. For many children these were not easily perceptible connections, and for many they are still not easily perceptible. Not only that. It can be difficult for children from poor families living in inequitable societies like ours to maintain a sense of their own worth. And sexual identity is a crucial part of how individuals come to feel and express confidence in who they are; especially if they are subject to disparagements based on class and race.

I believe that masculinity – in itself a vital aspect of a boy's developing sense of his worth in the world – has become entangled with the rampant individualism of the last fifteen years, with its aggression and philistinism and competitiveness. So that, even for boys at the very beginning of their schooling, success as a boy, social success, depends on exhibiting no signs of weakness, admitting to neither failure nor difficulty. My seven-year-old Londoner grandson's favourite terms of approval are 'cool' and 'wicked'. To work hard at school is, for some boys, to admit that you need to work, that you are not 'brilliant', that you may find school work harder than some other children, even girls. Indeed, one small boy on the *Panorama* programme insisted that boys who worked hard weren't boys. There is so much in the acquisition of femininity in our culture that prepares girls for their future marginality. They learn quickly that a secure identity is not for them, and that a culture presented as universal and for everyone is not for them either. From a position on the margins it may be easier to try hard, to admit to difficulty and to the possibility that you are not the best; and that not being best does not in itself spell total disenfranchisement.

For upper- and middle-class men, schooling, as it diversified from the Middle Ages onwards, could be seen to offer useful skills and knowledge, but also, of course, accomplishments which marked them as gentlemen and as superior to other people. For several centuries, many women from the same classes embraced literacy as a way of enlarging their experience and of maximising their competences in the family setting; eventually even, by the eighteenth century, using writing (if only in a few cases) to earn a living. Many paintings and accounts of childhood up to and during the nineteenth century contain representations of mothers or nursemaids reading to children or teaching children to read. The home could house schooling, could even contain a schoolroom, so that schools were not in themselves alien places for the children of such families.

It is possible that too much trust has been put in the benefits of schooling, or at least in its inevitable pay-off in terms of future adult employment, profitability or happiness.

We have entered into a period of mass unemployment, particularly affecting men. We may never emerge from it, or at least, never to return to what have come to be seen as traditional patterns in men's working lives, though most of these are actually of pretty recent origin. An era of techno-logical advance and a managerial revolution have – if only provisionally – proved an advantage to women, and from their position of expecting less for themselves than men did, they have leapt at these possibilities and developed new capacities and ambitions.

If it is the case that girls' successes in education in this country have been won at the expense of boys – and there may even be some truth in that – this is due to policies of constraint and reduction, where genuine expansion is in order. A comparison with France during the eighties makes the point. The government's policy in France has been to increase the proportion of young people taking the *bacca-lauréat* (the examination entitling successful candidates to a university place) to 80 per cent of the population by the year 2000. In 1991 50 per cent of the age group had actually reached that level![34] The government target in this country for entry to higher education in the year 2000 is 30 per cent of school leavers. Similarly, just 27 per cent of the population in this country achieved two or more A levels (the minimum requirement for entry to any kind of degree course) in the same year, 1991. And we know that four years of improving, as well as record A-level results, from 1991 to 1994 (indeed, the claim is that 32 per cent of the age group studied for A levels in 1994) have meant that many students who are qualified will in fact be denied a place of their choice, and in some cases will be denied entry to higher education altogether. Moreover, those students' A-level studies, usually pursued in two or at most three subjects, will leave them with a narrow base of purely academic qualifications, which is not as a rule very helpful if they are hoping to go straight into employment. Yet higher education has expanded during the

1990s in this country, in the sense of offering access to more people, if not in funding or in the quality of provision.[35]

Two final examples make their own case, I think, and put the education of girls into historical and geographical contexts. Harriet Martineau wrote with passionate enthusiasm in her autobiography of the two years she spent in school when she was eleven and twelve in the early years of the nineteenth century. They remained for her, as she put it, 'a lifetime to look back upon: and to this day it fills a disproportionate space in the retrospect of my existence, – so inestimable was its importance'. She follows this memory with a somewhat less ecstatic allusion to the difficulties placed in the way of women like her, who had serious intellectual interests,

> When I was young, it was not thought proper for young ladies to study very conspicuously; and especially with pen in hand. Young ladies (at least in provincial towns) were expected to sit down in the parlour to sew, – during which reading aloud was permitted, – or to practise their music; but so as to be fit to receive callers, without any signs of blue-stockingism which could be reported abroad. Jane Austen herself, the Queen of novelists, the immortal creator of Anne Elliot, Mr Knightley, and a score or two more of unrivalled intimate friends of the whole public, was compelled by the feelings of her family to cover up her manuscripts with a large piece of muslin work, kept on the table for the purpose, whenever any genteel people came in.[36]

She was remembering what it had been like to be eighteen in 1820, thirty years or more before the first day schools for girls were opened. And for the majority of girls there was no schooling whatever until 1870, and that was only elementary and confined to the most basic skills, as we have seen.

Then, in the South Indian state of Kerala, which has

achieved the highest levels of literacy in the whole of India, research has shown that it is women's acquisition of literacy that has borne most fruit. When the men become literate, it seems, they put this to good use in furthering their own earning power and gathering qualifications for more lucrative work. When the women become literate they use their new skills to improve their families' health and diet and to encourage their children to do well at school. Whole communities benefit, and the fabric of society is changed. So that, inevitably, the women themselves will demand more: more education, more training, greater possibilities of useful and interesting work, more control over child-bearing and more efficient and effective forms of child-rearing and child care. It may well be that policies based on the Kerala phenomenon still neglect the possibilities that literacy and education might open up for the women themselves. Yet strategically, it may be that such communal benefits will, in the end, be the most effective evidence to adduce in favour of educating girls. Certainly, one of the more horrifying aspects of natural and man-made disasters in parts of the third world has been the revelation that sending tins of powdered milk to a community in which, by and large, the women cannot read means that thousands of babies will die unnecessarily, because their mothers will be unable to read instructions about boiling the water to make up the feeds.[37]

We have come a long way; and if some of the victories have been achieved inadvertently – the consequence of cynical or cheese-paring education policies – there are victories, nonetheless, which women themselves have fought for and earned and which some men have supported staunchly. So that it is extraordinary to witness the disparagement of the single most impressive gain in the public provision of education during the last 150 years: the achievements of girls and women. For there is no question that the education of women has profoundly changed all social arrangements and relations throughout the world. We should not allow those achievements to be seen as merely the flipside of the failures of boys. An understanding of why some boys have done so well and why some girls are now doing even better is our only hope for building a more useful and productive and comprehensive education system.

My own view is that the effects of unemployment on educational achievement are not only incalculable, but likely to worsen. For many, the expectation that there will be no work at the end of their schooling and no chance of either higher education or serious and directed training has made much of the education on offer seem irrelevant or worse. Indeed, the connection between schooling and adult work has always been a more tenuous one for young people who anticipated a future which was not a professional one. This country still has the lowest number of school-leavers entering higher education of any country in the developed world. So that girls' successes relatively to boys' are bound to be read as threatening so long as a static system of higher education is required to absorb changes and even expansion without increased investment.

Since 1991, more women than men have been applying to universities. What is in some lights a momentous achievement may also be read as menacing, for there is no accompanying policy of general expansion for these institutions, and if more girls are applying it may also be that fewer boys are. The Prime Minister, John Major's, expressed contempt for higher education may in this context be construed as rather more than sour grapes; indeed, it can sound like a timely reminder that 'real men', men who do well in the world, can do so without the kind of education which – since it appeals more to women than to men – is probably too liberal and wishy-washy and out of touch with the tough demands of a modern technological world, anyway. We are back to what Ken Jones, in his analysis of current Conservative education policy, has characterised as its 'Janus-headed' linking of tradition with modernity in a strategy which 'fuses the archaic and the modern, mixes nostalgia with technology, evokes community and promotes entrepreneurialism'.[38] Education for a man's world these days appears to mean 'basic skills' and Shakespeare, spellmasters and spelling, computers and your twelve-times table.

The lesson to be learned is not after all an impossibly difficult one. It is simply not feasible to offer access to the whole population, even in principle – when that population emphatically includes women as one half of it – while maintaining those structures which were put in place when education was meant to serve only a carefully strained and sieved minority, reduced 'naturally' by exclusions based on class, gender, race and intelligence.

6

Literacy

The very different ways in which boys and girls read – both at home and at school – have become the focus for much of the anxiety about boys' relative failure in examinations in recent years. There is even research going on into the possibility that girls' language capacities develop much faster during the first year of life, and that this prepares them for conversation, for the peculiarities of written language and for the forms of metalanguage which are useful for discussing texts in the classroom.[1] Yet such findings, if they emerge and are persuasive, will not be able to ignore the overwhelming evidence that in this country in the past, and in most of the third world today, girls were and are less likely to read and write than boys are. It seems clear that even the most clinching evidence of biological difference will have a hard time countering the realities of particular historical manifestations of social inequality. In this chapter I consider how such inequalities have combined with experiences of literacy to influence our attitudes and our behaviour as readers and writers, and how these attitudes are likely to rely on the dualities and conflicts embodied in family life and the uses of literacy in actual communities. I shall start from the particular and the idiosyncratic, in my own childhood.

There was a time when more than almost anything else I liked my mother to read me the stories of Joseph or Isaac or

Moses from that great plum-coloured door-stopper, *The Bible Designed to be Read as Literature*. She read beautifully, knew most of the stories of the Old Testament by heart and has illustrated hundreds of their moments of strangeness and drama in paintings and lino-cuts throughout her life. I was always a little sad – though usually, I hope, politely so – when my father offered to read to me in her place. His boredom was palpable. He read stiffly and even, occasionally, against the sense.

My mother still writes letters. She is left-handed, although nearly ambidextrous, and still writes in a flowing, curly, flamboyant style, with an uncertain grasp of spelling though never of idiom. She wrote letters and poems and stories for us as children, and she illustrated everything she wrote. My father wrote painfully, tightly, unidiomatically and with no pleasure, though he had sailed triumphantly through a battery of examinations, so must once have been able to write fast and to the point, and he also wrote professionally and for publication from time to time.

My mother has never really thought of herself as a reader, though she has always read novels. She has hated newspapers all her life, feeling that they contained hard, serious knowledge, of the kind she should want to possess, but couldn't. She has in her time read novels written in the past, but more recently she has read detective novels and other fiction by respected contemporary writers of the kind often thought of as 'middle-brow'. She is irritated by the beginnings of novels which are weighed down by names, and she used to like poetry when it rhymed. She rarely reads novels by men, though she would certainly not regard this as significant or principled. I believe that all her reading has been done in or on her bed, usually as a prelude or an encouragement to sleep.

I don't think my father read a novel during all the years I knew him, though he sometimes mentioned having read *Wilhelm Meister* and several of the less well-known novels of Balzac. He must once have read the Russian novelists and

Dickens and Thackeray, I suppose, but if so he had only the most general things to say about them. He read newspapers fast and carefully every day and, during the Second World War, books on military manoeuvres. He had a nearly phenomenal memory for the detail of such things. Ordinarily he read poetry and philosophy in languages other than English. He was a pianist and a piano teacher, and, he practised arpeggios on the piano from six o'clock in the morning he also read, and always (as it seemed to me) the same things: Alexander Blok's poetry in Russian, Victor Hugo's poetry in French, Goethe's *Faust* Part 2 and Heine's poems in German. He also returned again and again to Collingwood's *The Principles of Art*. A huge mug of strong, black, unsugared tea steamed at his side on its platform of books, and once he had drunk it, he would proceed to the bathroom and the stropping of his cut-throat razor, where he read from an edition of Dante which he kept on the shelf there, bound in studded, chocolate-coloured leather and dusted with mildew.

I write of these habits and tendencies not at all in the spirit of someone definitively sorting out the male from the female, but in order to suggest that for each of us these practices and their meanings are learned as both gendered and opposed. At its simplest, I have inherited a sense of reading and writing as pleasurable, so long as there is no question of my being tested or judged in relation to them. Yet I almost always have paper and pen available as I read, in the expectation that I shall want to make notes. The anticipation of pleasure is marked by the absence of those things, though I usually find in fact that I want to make notes about almost everything I read. My father stood for serious reading and its ambiguous purposes, but he did not make notes. In fact, I have no idea at all why he read as he did, and have always wondered about it. For his purposes, which were implicit, were also somehow thought of by him as too obvious to inquire into. He made no bones, however, about learning new languages through reading their literatures, a method he much preferred to travel or conversation: believing, as many have, that you get a better class of language in books than on the street. He almost never read anything by a woman or, indeed, by anyone alive, unless they were writing in a newspaper or a literary weekly (though I remember teasing him about this not long before he died, and he was clearly surprised to be told it). He had spent his life amongst women, but I think he felt most comfortable in the romantic and idealised male company his reading offered him: European, mostly nineteenth-century, fenced off from the local, the female, the modern, possibly even the American.

The books he read again and again, or sipped or dipped into throughout his life, have been hard for me to love, though I attribute value of a particular kind to them, requiring a commitment and a sense of their history which is beyond my powers. Even as I write of my father's reading, I am bowed down by its weight, its gravity and density and inaccessibility. He certainly read more poetry than prose, for instance, and I am a nervous and inhibited reader of poetry. I avoided reading with him as I grew up, and even kept from him some of the reading I was doing on my own or at school that would have pleased him: Goethe, Racine, La Fontaine, Dostoevsky. If I inadvertently mentioned that we were reading *Le Rouge et le Noir* at school, he would be sure to tell me that *La Chartreuse de Parme* was a better book. I felt my father's reading as an accumulation, an impenetrable thicket, beyond emulation or equivalence. Now I marvel that such a reader was never tempted by anything written much after the 1940s, and I wonder whether fear or satiation prompted such a lack of interest in the things I read.

However, even as I associated comfort and creativity with my mother's reading and writing, and dry difficulty with my father's, I also grew up to look askance at my mother's frivolity and self-indulgence as a reader and writer: at her refusal – as it seemed to me – to struggle with the rebarbative and the dull; at her need to 'like' the characters in a novel, even to be 'cheered up' by them. I also harboured a secret pride in my father's grim incursions into the literatures of Poland and Czechoslovakia, for instance. This was reading I thought of as most unlikely to make him either laugh or cry, but on which he made himself a kind of expert, if only by virtue of his solitude and his knowing scarcely anyone who knew as much as he did about these writers, and certainly no one likely to challenge his view of their interest, their meaning or their value.

I also, of course, associated my parents' different approaches to reading with education, though – as it happened – they had been at the same school. I thought of my father as 'highly educated', and as I write that in my sixties it rings with falseness and denial. A very particular kind of 'educated', I want to add, rarer each day and none the better (or perhaps, the worse) for that. He was born in 1905, and grew up in a household of 'highly educated' aunts (Clara Collet, whom we have met in earlier chapters, was one of them) and an uncle. They were Nonconformists, teachers and civil servants. At eleven my father could write competent and wholly derivative sonnets, in French as well as English. The family's literacy was also unusual in some respects, in that whole correspondences between sisters and between brothers and between future husbands and wives had been preserved intact in small beribboned packages since the early eighteenth century, though I don't think my father read any of them. He does seem to have inherited an appetite for reading from his aunts and a confidence about what was worth reading. He was, for instance, rather given to talking about major and minor writers and works. I have the sense of his turning his reading into something resembling the beard and whiskers sported by his father but not his grandfather: intimate attributes of his person, which were, nonetheless, susceptible to cultivation.

My mother's reading had an opposite quality: chancy, surprising, informed by what I think of (probably patronisingly)

as excellent instincts but very little knowledge. Reading was
to be measured in terms of the comfort it afforded, and when
we were in bed with colds she bought us copies of *Woman*
and *Woman's Own*: a treat shot through with the disapproval
my father was expected to express for such reading matter,
had he taken the slightest interest in what it consisted of. He
was, in fact, far too grandly out of touch with his daughters'
tastes for that. The exuberance of my mother's reading, as
I remember it, was also circumscribed by her own sense of
its inadequacy. Brought up in a Jewish family, in which
men were rational, and scientists or historians, while women
might go in for the arts, write poetry, paint, sing, and so on,
she has suffered all her life from a sometimes hobbling self-
consciousness: the outcome perhaps of a split between a belief
in her talent and despair at her ignorance. Yet it was what she
told me about *War and Peace* and *Anna Karenina* that made
me want to read them. My father gave me the sense that
the first of these was probably about military strategy and
diplomacy, should anyway be read in Russian, but also that I
mightn't amount to much in the world if I hadn't read them
both. Yet that too is rather a caricature. Because I also learned
from him that when you read a book you know something you couldn't know if you hadn't read it, and that
became important, like wanting to visit places you'd heard
about in order to know and somehow possess their substance,
consistency, light, sound for yourself.

Here is another woman, older than I am, writing in 1936
about her experience of how men and women treated books.

> It is still, I greatly fear, one of the outstanding differ-
> ences between men and women that men care for books
> more than we do. How often does a man inwardly
> (sometimes also outwardly) quiver with annoyance at
> the careless way in which a woman handles a book,
> lays it face downward, dog-ears it unthinkingly to keep

her place, even sets down her cup of tea on it as it lies beside her table? Even men whom we number among the non-readers are, on the whole, respectful towards a book, as if having some inborn sense of all that has gone to its making, but women too often, when they do read, are intent chiefly upon the mere contents of the book they read or are attracted by fancy bindings.

The other day the proprietor of an old-established bookstall in London gave it as his mature opinion that no woman loved books. 'They will give half a guinea for a hat,' he said, 'as soon as look at you. But they grudge half a crown for a book worth a guinea.' Also, he finds women untidy about the handling of books. One woman stood her cup of tea on one of his books. When he told her that a man liked to have his books nice and clean just as much as she might want her clothes or children to be, she was thoroughly cross with him. 'Men,' he sighed, 'are the only true book-lovers.'

It is interesting that this authority should find that, of all books, those most popular with his working-class customers are on world religions and politics. Workmen in the neighbourhood spend, many of them, their entire lunch hour every day reading books at his stall which they cannot always afford to buy, and most of what they read is 'hard, intense, philosophical stuff.' But a girl among such readers is rare. When will working-class woman and her middle-class sisters read anything but novels? Women in Russia do. But has anyone ever seen a charwoman with a 'hard intense philosophical work' under arm to con when she has done her scrubbing? Not in England, I fear.[2]

Catherine Carswell was a Scottish novelist, and hers is a light-hearted approach to the gendering of reading, this time from the point of view of bibliophiles, collectors, booksellers, book 'lovers'. The actual physical act of reading books is set within conflicting assessments of their public value. Yet there is surely a hint of approval for women's disrespectful appetite for reading what they like, for preferring the 'contents' of books to their covers, and for their wholesale domestication of books as objects, whether disposable or ornamental. As it happens, neither my mother nor my father looked after their books very well. You could say that it was one of the few things to do with reading that they shared. Indeed, books were usually to be found in disreputable piles rather than on shelves – and usually with cups of tea and even apple cores upon them – and very few paperbacks, in French or English, retained their covers. Guessing the author of a book from internal evidence became a kind of challenge. We acquired several copies of certain books, simply because it hadn't been possible to lay hands on the first one when it was wanted.

I always gave my father books as birthday presents; ones he asked for and which were usually very difficult to find. Occasionally, I added a book I wanted him to read. After his death, I found most of them looking untypically pristine. He would have agreed with Carswell, though, that serious reading hardly went on in the British Isles, and if you wanted to find readers of the kind he liked you would do well to visit Russia. He was interested in what certain famous men liked to read, and could tell you who Goethe most admired or Denis Healey. And André Gide's 'Victor Hugo, hélas!' – Gide's nominee, when asked for France's greatest poet – particularly delighted my father, for some reason. He rather enjoyed league tables, I'm afraid. He would, perhaps, have been more squeamish than Carswell is about commenting on the reading habits of women, let alone, 'charwomen' and other women of the working class. I should think that Carswell's double view of women as either readers too buried in books to look after them or as non-readers, would have been more common in the thirties than it is now. But my father would have been capable of making some kind of jocular allusion to the relation of the cost of a book to the cost of, if not a hat, certainly a pair of shoes; and I assumed that he derived some sort of masculine comfort from such thoughts. He was by no means an extravagant man, but he much preferred buying us books to buying us shoes, and would usually pay quite willingly for anything that seemed to him to be incontrovertibly educational.

My father's reading, of course, differed from other people's besides my mother's. Not only was he no bibliophile, he was also in important respects no professional. He read neither to write about books, nor to publish them, nor to teach them. He did not even read in order to discuss what he read. His relation to texts was, I suppose, meditative, almost religious (although he was not at all a religious man), but without the exegetical leanings of most traditional readers of sacred texts. His reading belonged, though, with the discipline and the habitual practice that informed his piano-playing and his learning of languages. So that it could not quite be equated with the gentlemanly or even the cultivated, but equally, was untouched – perhaps he thought, untainted – by the professional or the academic, both of which were to make dire demands on my reading time, in his eyes. Yet he also liked to believe that I had read far more than I was ever likely to divulge; and that was meant, I think, as a sort of compliment. He was surprisingly uninterested in recent theoretical debates about both language and literature (surprising to me, who have been interested in both). He read about languages as world history rather than as linguistics; and literary criticism, rather as we were encouraged to read the Bible: as literature.

I want to stress this difference in his reading from what I have called 'professional' or 'academic' reading and writing – a difference of motivation and of actual conduct – because I think the two kinds of practice are usually blurred and invoked in muddled ways to justify conservative and reductive views of what English teaching in schools should be. There may be, for instance, areas of agreement between Prince Charles's enthusiasm for reading plays about his ancestors and the curriculum in many university English departments, which aim at varieties of coverage of famous and admired English writers. Yet it also seems important to say that practitioners of literary scholarship, criticism and theorising use texts and create new ones which are in fact a long way from current exhortations to deliver 'their' heritage to schoolchildren. The idea, for instance, that 'English' should be equivalent to the study of literature, but exclude all literature translated from other languages – or even literature written in varieties of English which are not home-based, let alone texts in other media – comes from an educational tradition rather than a literary one. It is distinctive for its reductive rather than its expansive approach to the development of literacy in the younger generation. Most writers and readers of literature have, after all, looked to other cultures for interest and inspiration, at the very least.

Historically, education and literacy have been perceived as almost interchangeable. This has often separated off the teaching and learning of reading and writing and of literature from the multiplicity of ways in which these activities are performed in the world. We are not helped, it seems to me, by refusing to distinguish between the very different ways in which adults use and value literacy. These days, too much discussion of English and of literature teaching concentrates on punitive and uncritical versions of a 'common culture', based on fudged and gimcrack notions of English-ness, which few people recognise as their own and which is peddled as what everyone wants and should have. And schools have been to blame; but not through narrowing the range of texts and the ways of reading them that they introduce children to. They have fought hard for a broadening of the literature curriculum. Where they have been to blame is in oversimplifying and finally confusing young people and their parents, I think, by operating with too bland and uncritical a view of reading as being principally about pleasure.

An interest in reading and a need to read is not equivalent

to pleasure. Many of the confusions in current discussions of literacy stem from a refusal to acknowledge how diverse readers' purposes are always likely to be and how far removed, for the most part, from anything they would describe as pleasure. And whatever pleasure is, there is no reason why it should resemble my mother's, or my father's, or mine. Pleasure in reading is not contagious or prescribable or constant or effortlessly repeatable. Nor is it easy for the rookie or apprentice reader to believe that the close and rigorous scrutiny of texts is valuable because of the heightened pleasure it is bound, in the end, to deliver.

Certainly, my experience of contrast and conflict as intrinsic to the practices of literacy is both peculiar to me and produced within a particular class and generation in England. Far from wishing to generalise from those practices, I want to make the quite different point that a child's developing sense of the values and purposes of literacy is always related to class and is always idiosyncratic. And it is this, the class context and the peculiar division of labour in particular families, that is centrally implicated in what is sometimes called 'the literacy debate', and in the disputes about the teaching of early reading and writing and later, literature. Inevitably, this debate is organised, both openly and covertly, around gender difference. Perhaps I should also add – as a cadenza for my father – that I studied French and Russian literature at university in response to his injunction to do something at once difficult and useful. However, I escaped to the consolations of English, as a reader and a teacher, at the first opportunity.

Judith Solsken, an American writer on literacy, has studied the acquisition of literacy in a number of young children. She talked to them in their homes, interviewed their parents and watched them during their first days at school. In wanting to build on the work of anthropologists of literacy like Shirley Brice Heath,[3] whose studies differentiate *between* the literacy practices of different communities, Solsken takes the notion of difference and conflict further, into the learning of literacy *within* communities, and, indeed, within families and their particular gender negotiations. She is not out to isolate these early experiences from the social relations in the wider world which bear on family relations, but, on the contrary, to suggest the ways in which they connect. For instance, taking the example of a particular boy, she writes,

> literacy learning was embedded in an interplay of tensions around gender identification, tensions that are certainly connected to ideologies in the larger society that associate literacy, or at least certain varieties of it, with femaleness. Even though males dominate within the territory of literacy (e.g. literary, legal, academic, and other hierarchies are male dominated), the territory itself is regarded as relatively female and, in at least some social groups, as impotent. Moreover, the responsibility for children's literacy within families is generally assumed by females as part of mothering. Even in families where fathers work in highly literate domains . . . it is most often mothers who read to children, oversee homework, and attend parent-teacher conferences.[4]

A particular point that emerges from Solsken's study is that current pedagogy in early schooling, and the theories of language development on which it relies, may hold too unthinkingly to a view of literacy as offering primarily its own intrinsic satisfactions rather than as instrumental. Such a view accords neither with dominant work-oriented views of literacy, nor with what are thought of by many as the highest and most prestigious kinds of literacy in the culture. Since most teaching of early literacy is done by women, and upheld and furthered by mothers, such divisions come to be seen as gendered ones.

> Sharp divisions between manual and mental labor often intersect with gender divisions so that mental labor,

especially school-like tasks as opposed to practical problem solving, is seen as 'effeminate,' the pejorative connotation of the adjective showing the devaluation of activities assigned to women.[5]

And within those divisions, women teachers themselves may be torn between the pragmatism which tells them that children need immediate satisfaction if they are to be persuaded that reading is worthwhile and the sense that they must also value, as Solsken puts it, 'the male behaviors that will also ultimately win boys greater social status and power'.[6]

Solsken's scenario relies on a contrast between literacy seen as work and literacy seen as play. She does not – as I had hoped she might – connect the valuing of literacy within families to the particular work of the parents or the kinds of employment children may expect to enter themselves. She does, though, suggest the ways in which work may be transformed into play, and vice versa, in an easily exploitable slippage of meanings, as these meanings move between men and women. She gives examples: of a woman whose husband commented, when she reported that she was rarely without a book, 'Never a good book'; and she alludes to Janice Radway's work on women's reading of popular romances, which 'is often regarded, by husbands and even by themselves, as an illegitimate escape from their domestic work, whereas male forms of play are rarely so regarded'.[7]

The value women attach to reading for pleasure becomes the rationale for the reading and literature curriculum in school, while also furnishing an explanation for the suspicion cast on 'English' as a school subject and on the ways in which reading is taught in infant-school classrooms. Pleasure in reading is at once the highest and best reason for having literature on the curriculum, but it is also regarded as something like an excuse for escape from real work: a private self-indulgence. Pleasure deflects attention from reading as a set of instrumental skills, which are necessary to forms of public achievement or shared entertainment. That clash of views has a long history and important implications, I think, and needs at the very least to be understood.

Flora Thompson, in her *Lark Rise to Candleford*, has given us an extraordinarily rich account of how literacy was come by and used in a small English village in the 1880s. Not only does she tell us how reading was taught and learned, she gives us an insight into what certain kinds of popular text meant, particularly to women.

There is a doubleness to her account of reading as she remembered it from school. Her sense of the school's underlying policy, 'Once teach them to read and they will hold the key to all knowledge' is that it didn't work. The children resisted it. 'Their interest was not in books, but in life, and especially the life that lay immediately about them.'[8] Similarly, the reading lessons themselves are remembered by her stand-in self, Laura, as both tedious and eye-opening.

> Once a day, at whatever hour the poor, overworked mistress could find time, a class would be called out to toe the chalked semicircle on the floor for a reading lesson. This lesson, which should have been pleasant, for the reading matter was good, was tedious in the extreme. Many of the children read so slowly and haltingly that Laura, who was impatient by nature, longed to take hold of their words and drag them out of their mouths, and it often seemed to her that her own turn to read would never come.[9]

Yet there were strange treasures in her Royal Reader, snippets from Scott and Fenimore Cooper, descriptions of far-away places: Greenland, the Pacific islands, the Himalayas. And there were poems: 'Young Lochinvar', Hogg's 'Skylark', all the most anthologised poems of Byron and Tennyson. The selection in the Royal Readers, then, was an education in itself for those who took to it kindly, but the majority of the children would have none of it, saying that the prose was 'dry old stuff' and they hated 'portry'. With vast classes made up of all ages between five and eleven or twelve, it is not surprising that teachers made use of choral recitation at both ends of the reading process, as it were: reciting the alphabet forwards and backwards in the 'babies' class; reciting by heart almost everything encountered in their Readers for the older children. Laura declares herself from the beginning of school a dunce at arithmetic and needlework and good at reading and writing. We see her relative enthusiasm for reading in school as continuous in the early stages with what happened to some of the other girls, but not to the boys. I shall quote at some length from *Lark Rise*, for the pages contain, if not historical data or generalisable fact, a wonderfully clear and detailed account of how one young girl became a reader (and later a writer) within the specific texts and attitudes to those texts which she encountered in childhood.

Most of the younger women and some of the older ones were fond of what they called 'a bit of a read', and their mental fare consisted almost exclusively of the novelette. Several of the hamlet women took in one of these weekly, as published, for the price was but a penny, and these were handed round until the pages were thin and frayed with use. Copies of others found their way there from neighbouring villages, or from daughters in service, and there was always quite a library of them in circulation.

The novelette of the 'eighties was a romantic love story, in which the poor governess always married the duke, or the lady of title the gamekeeper, who always turned out to be a duke or an earl in disguise. Midway through the story there had to be a description of a ball, at which the heroine in her simple white gown attracted all the men in the room; or the gamekeeper, commandeered to help serve, made love to the daughter of the house in the conservatory. The stories were often prettily written, and as innocent as sugared milk and water; but, although they devoured them, the women looked upon novelette reading as a vice, to be hidden from their menfolk and only discussed with fellow devotees.

The novelettes were as carefully kept out of the children's way as the advanced modern novel is, or should be, today; but children who wanted to read them knew where to find them, on the top shelf of the cupboard or under the bed, and managed to read them in secret. An ordinarily intelligent child of eight or nine found them cloying, but they did the women good, for as they said, they took them out of themselves.

There had been a time when the hamlet readers had fed on stronger food, and Biblical words and imagery still coloured the speech of some of the older people. Though unread, every well-kept cottage had still its little row of books, neatly arranged on the side table with the lamp, the clothes brush and the family photographs. Some of these collections consisted solely of the family Bible and a prayer-book or two; others had a few extra volumes which had either belonged to parents or been bought with other oddments for a few pence at a sale – *The Pilgrim's Progress*, *Drelincourt on Death*, Richardson's *Pamela*, *Anna Lee: The Maiden Wife and Mother*, and old books of travel and sermons. Laura's greatest find was a battered old copy of Belzoni's *Travels* propping open somebody's pantry window. When she asked for the loan of it, it was generously given to her, and she had the, to her, intense pleasure of exploring the burial chambers of the pyramids with her author.

Some of the imported books had their original owner's book-plate, or an inscription in faded copper-plate handwriting inside the covers, while the family ones, in a ruder hand, would proclaim:

George Welby, his book:
Give me grace therein to look,
And not only to look, but to understand,
For learning is better than houses and land
When land is lost and money spent
Then learning is most excellent . . .

All or any of these books were freely lent, for none of the owners wanted to read them. The women had their novelettes, and it took the men all their time to get through their Sunday newspapers, one of which came into almost every house, either by purchase or borrowing. The *Weekly Despatch*, *Reynold's News*, and *Lloyd's News* were their favourites, though a few remained faithful to that fine old local newspaper, the *Bicester Herald*.

Laura's father, as well as his *Weekly Despatch*, took the *Carpenter and Builder*, through which the children got their first introduction to Shakespeare, for there was a controversy in it as to Hamlet's words, 'I know a hawk from a handsaw'. It appeared that some scholar had suggested that it should read, 'I know a hawk from a heron, pshaw!' and the carpenters and builders were up in arms. *Of course*, the hawk was the mason's and plasterer's tool of that time, and the handsaw was *just* a handsaw. Although that line and a few extracts that she afterwards found in the school readers were all that Laura was to know of Shakespeare's works for some time, she sided warmly with the carpenters and builders, and her mother, when appealed to, agreed, for she said that 'heron, pshaw!' certainly sounded a bit left-handed.[10]

Not only is there a perceived opposition between the reading done by women and the reading Laura sees men doing, her own attitude is seen to shift as she describes the difference. The women's reading is play, escapist, even improper, and to be undertaken secretly and away from the children. It also, and characteristically, represents a falling off from the higher standards of the past. And though at one point Thompson suggests that these women may find a particular pleasure in stories which elaborate on the kinds of flirtation they may well, as young servant girls, have indulged in with the young masters of the houses where they worked, she also condemns this reading, as unrealistic, formulaic, literally useless. Men read less in her experience, but the newspapers and trade magazines she associates with her father and other men of her childhood are seen to be useful and serious and even to touch on areas of high culture, if only inadvertently.

Reading is a constant theme of the book. Laura remembers the stories about children from city 'slums' that they brought home from Sunday school. She is lent copies of *Pilgrim's Progress* and *Cranford* and *Pamela*, for she and her friends speedily exhaust the resources of the school library, 'which, though better than nothing to read, made little impression upon them, for they were all of the goody-goody, Sunday-school prize type'.[11] Her father had a few of the *Waverley Novels*, and she delighted in these. It is significant that the chief champion of Laura's 'bookworminess' should be a man, her Uncle Tom, who articulates for her in yet another way the idea that what she is reading is better and different from the magazines and romances read by most of the women in her family.

Her hunger for reading matter comes to be seen by some as a problem. She is thought by her mother, for instance, to be 'outgrowing her strength', and there is open conflict when Laura is found reading while holding her baby brother.

> The situation came to a head one day when Laura was nursing the baby with a book in her hand and, absent-mindedly, put down the little hand which was trying to clutch her long hair.[12]

Her mother is disappointed in her. Laura shows none of the

qualities needed to become a nurse, let alone a mother. She lacks the knack, the heart, the nature. So nursing as future work is forgotten.

When she starts work at Candleford post office at fourteen, she thinks of herself as having two principal assets: a large book in which she will write her journal; and 'a curious assortment of scraps of knowledge she had picked up in the course of her reading'. As it happens, her landlady and employer, the postmistress in Candleford, is also a reader, and guiltily Laura removes from her elegant glass-fronted bookcase, Byron's *Don Juan* and volumes of Shakespeare and Darwin: forbidden texts, as she sees it. The more she reads the more she is able to differentiate between kinds of reader. For though she owned no books of her own, 'there were always books to borrow', from the library of the Mechanics' Institute in the town, for instance.

And there were also 'penny readings', occasions attended by whole families, at which there would be readings aloud from Dickens and Scott and Harriet Beecher Stowe. Yet she is clear that though these occasions were popular, and people liked to listen, most of them were not readers quite as she was a reader. What she has also taken in with her reading is the sense that there is something meretricious about female reading. And to read better books, let alone to do so voraciously as she does, is somehow unfeminine. What her novel's heroine, Charity, takes into her life as a teacher is this dilemma, and it is a dilemma which women teachers could be said to have fashioned into a pedagogy, a belief in 'English teaching' and a faith in the humanising effects of literacy and of encounters with literature. It is a faith born of class difference and the articulations of class manifested in education. And it is a faith sustained but also challenged by traditions of male adjudication.

It seems to me unsurprising that the proselytising fervour sometimes to be found amongst teachers of reading in primary schools, but also amongst literature teachers of older children, should so often have met with resistance from boys and contempt from certain professional and academic men (and by now, of course, women: particularly those who want to distance themselves from schoolteachers). It is also clear that literacy cannot possibly be thought of as equivalent to the experiences children have of it in schools. Yet for most people in the world, the ways in which they are taught to read and write in school, and even the practices surrounding the reading of particular texts, remain, at the very least, influential. Recent research on literacy by anthropologists has rightly reminded us of the ways in which reading and writing are differently learned and used and valued in different cultures, and of how remote these ways often are from what goes on in schools.[13] They have also seen as unhelpful the tendency for classroom pedagogies to become a naturalised ingredient of common-sense notions about reading and learning to read outside school. It would be a pity, however, if the practices developed in classrooms were excluded (as they have sometimes been) from the same kind of critical attention by anthropologists. For it is the discrepancies between those schooled practices and the values placed on experiences of literacy outside school which are at the heart of many people's actual use of reading and writing in their lives.

Edith Thompson and her young lover, Frederick Bywaters, were hanged in 1923 for the murder of Edith's husband, Percy. Their story has been told and retold, and recently, René Weis has written a version of it called *Criminal Justice: The True Story of Edith Thompson*, which is particularly illuminating for its insights into the part played in their lives, as well as their deaths, by reading and writing.[14] Nor is it irrelevant to point out that most of their adult lives were lived against a background which led to the 'Newbolt Report' into the teaching of English in England, which was published less than two years before their trial, provoking its own kind of discussion about schooling and literacy.[15] Their story – lived by the nation through the daily newspaper accounts which reported on their trial, as the trial itself reported on the letters written by the lovers (for they were thought to prefigure the crime) – has been constantly written and rewritten, before, during and after its brief unfolding, in an early version of that two-way mimicry of life and literature, which has become a central motif of the post-modern narrative.

The three protagonists were formed as readers and writers within a world whose historical and geographical specificity is lovingly mapped by Weis. Edith, her husband Percy and her lover Freddy all grew up in the Manor Park area of East London, in 'respectable' and comfortably off working-class families which

> furnished the crews, sailors, pursers, stewards, writers and other non-commissioned personnel of the ocean giant companies like the Peninsular and Oriental (P & O), the White Star, Red Star, and Cunard Lines. While their men were at sea, the women were anxiously following the shipping news which every local paper carried.[16]

This was an outcome of the Empire, it might be said, which produced new uses for literacy and a newly skilled workforce.

Between her tenth and her fifteenth years (1903–9), Edith went to Kensington Avenue School near her home, the school we glimpsed from its Head Teacher's handwritten log during its first twenty-eight years of existence in Chapter 3. Edith liked school, and remembered with affection the reading and writing she did there.

> I remember at school we used to have what was called a 'Reading Circle'. A Dickens book was chosen by our teacher, we read it at home, not at school, and then we each chose a character from the book and wrote a little

essay on him or her, as the case might be. These essays
we would all take to Wanstead Park on a Saturday afternoon: we would each read our own out loud, and then
it was discussed in general.

We usually took our tea to the park and made a little
picnic party of it. I remember an essay I was highly
commended on by the teacher. It was on 'Quilp'.[17]

She also appeared in at least two 'recitative performances', as
Hippolyta in *A Midsummer Night's Dream* and as Portia
in *The Merchant of Venice*. After school, when she had
started work in the City at a wholesale milliners, where she
was rapidly promoted to buyer for the firm, she also became
an enthusiastic member of an amateur theatrical group in
Stepney, where she attended elocution lessons and took
part in one or two Shakespeare productions. She learned
early to share her reading and to think about novels and
plays primarily in terms of characters to be considered as
more or less likely 'real' people: a way of thinking about
literary works sanctified by long practice, A-level examinations and the current National Curriculum. Her sense of
the importance of literature could not be faulted. A year or
two before she was hanged, she wrote that 'We ourselves die
& live in the books we read while we are reading them & then
when we have finished, the books die and we live':[18] a properly robust (reader's) alternative to

> So long as men can breathe or eyes can see,
> So long lives this, and this gives life to thee.

Freddy, who was nine years younger than Edith, later went
to the same school, though to the separate Boys' Department
of it. He was also commended for his essays, in particular for
one on 'Kindness to Dumb Animals', and his favourite novel
was *Tom Brown's Schooldays*, by no means the choice of a
'school refuser', one might think. He left school in 1916, when
he was thirteen, to work as an office boy with a shipping firm

in Leadenhall Street. After narrowly missing a direct hit on his office from a fleet of airships, he tried to get into the merchant navy and finally succeeded, when he was still only fifteen, in getting a job as a ship's writer on the P & O troop carrier *Nellore*, which was bound for India. As a clerk, writing was a basic activity for Freddy in his work, as it was for Edith, a successful business woman, and for Percy in his city shipping office.

Meanwhile, Edith had married Percy Thompson, and they seem to have been fairly happy together at this stage. Both of them were doing well in their jobs, and they shared an interest in amateur theatricals and, indeed, in going to the theatre. Freddy and Edith had known each other slightly before the war, through her brother. When they met again in January 1920, Freddy was seventeen and she was twenty-six. They became lovers shortly after they met, conducting their affair as much through letters winging their way across the world as in beds or even on a few occasions in a carriage of the train that daily transported all three of them back and forth between the stations of Fenchurch Street and Ilford.

In October 1922, Freddy savaged Percy Thompson in a manner which was clearly out of character and which implicated Edith, who can have had nothing to do with the murder. The trial that followed from that night exposed the lovers and their affair to an eager world. And what was revealed and reviled was a sexual liaison which somehow thrived on and expressed itself in terms of the literature the lovers read and, in consequence, wrote. The dozens of letters, sent between Aldersgate and Bombay, or Aden, or Sydney, so participating, as Weis puts it, 'in the rhythms of the imperial trading routes',[19] are the stuff of the trial and its attendant commentaries, and their targets and moral judgements come vastly to exceed the finally pretty meagre facts of the murder itself.

These 'nauseous' letters, as one juror described them, impaled their authors as inescapably on the disparaging snobberies of the time as on their guilt. Their affair is 'a squalid and rather indecent one of lust and adultery'.[20] Edith's 'letters are a deplorable correspondence of the most mischievous and venomous kind'.[21] Margery Fry sat with Edith in Holloway Prison during the last hours of her life and reported that she was 'a rather foolish girl who had romanticised her sordid little love affair'.[22] 'Ordinariness' was, in Mrs Fry's view, Edith's principal shortcoming.

On the night Freddy killed Percy Thompson, Percy and Edith had been to the theatre with another couple to see Ben Travers' *The Dippers*. They often went to the theatre, particularly to melodrama and vaudeville, as Freddy did too when he was at home. At one moment in the trial Freddy used the word 'melodrama', and was picked up instantly by the Solicitor General, who asked him to define the word, clearly expecting such an uneducated boy to be ignorant of its meaning. Freddy, however, acquitted himself better than most of us would. There was a long and crucial passage of the trial in which discussion of Robert Hichens' novel, *Bella Donna*, and Edith's comments on it in a letter to Freddy, were allowed to implicate her in plans to poison her husband. The judge and the lawyers managed to misread her letter because they had jumped to false conclusions about the novel's plot. But the judge insisted that there could be no need for anyone actually to read the novel in order to check Edith's account of it. As Weis writes, 'A human life was at stake, but the judge preferred for the jury not to be over-burdened with the additional task of reading an entire novel.'[23]

In fact, discussion of literature formed the substance of the letters Edith and Freddy wrote to one another during the long months of their less than two-year affair when he was away. They recommended novels to one another, but they also conducted written arguments about the novels they had both read; and this became a bashful and somewhat constrained way of communicating their thoughts about their own relationship, but also of interrogating the novels for their truth to human behaviour as they knew it. They quite often disagreed. Freddy recommended a war story to her by W.J. Locke, for instance, but she was 'not very keen'. Edith, in particular, used some of the women characters in the novels they had both read to press Freddy for his views about women, and for his approval, or disapproval, of their 'sensual natures': their capacity for love. There is a subtext to her letters: questions about her age and his, an anxious desire to know whether he thinks her too generous or not generous enough in her love-making.

Edith read *If Winter Comes* by A.S.M. Hutchinson soon after it was published to mostly admiring reviews. This was one of the middle-brow novels Queenie Leavis later excoriated in her *Fiction and the Reading Public*, which was first published in 1932. It was her recommendation, I remember, that moved me to buy it and several others like it in an Edinburgh junk shop called Madame Doubtfire. Though the novel would strike most contemporary readers as woodenly heroic and sentimental, Edith was by no means alone in finding the book interesting, though she also wrote to Freddy that 'none of the characters strike me as live men and women'.[24] Not only were Edith and Freddy avid readers of novels which Weis characterises as 'Edwardian middle-brow fiction' (Jeffrey Farnol and Robert Hichens and W.J. Locke, for example, are favourite writers who also make an appearance in Queenie Leavis's list of inexcusably popular novelists), both of them used the romanticism of current songs – for instance, 'One Little Hour of Happiness Divine' – and of some of the novels they read, to express and reflect on their feeling for each other and their times together. Many of the novels they read and the plays they saw dealt with subjects like adultery and bigamy, and clearly Edith was interested in what Weis sees as the 'erotic charge' of some of the novels she read, particularly those by Robert Hichens, whose novel was praised in *The Times* 'as though it were the equivalent of a Graham Greene novel'.[25]

On some occasions Edith used the plots of novels they were reading to touch on painful anxieties of her own. Hichens' *The Fruitful Vine* was her favourite novel, Weis tells us, and in asking Freddy what he thought of it she was also covertly referring to the fact that she had twice been impregnated by him, while constantly fending off her husband and his desire for a child. What, she appears to be asking, does Freddy think about that?

Edith left school at fourteen and Freddy at thirteen. Both of them were intelligent, well-read young people, conscientious and capable in their jobs, who used their literacy skills effectively as part of their working and private lives. They read books which were read and reviewed widely at the time, by authors (almost all of them men) who have for the most part slipped since then from popular or middle-brow canons, in the way, as Raymond Williams has reminded us in his discussion of what he calls 'the selective tradition',[26] that the vast majority of authors always have. Given a different scenario, it is possible to imagine Edith being congratulated for her copious reading and writing, and for her enthusiastic response to the teaching of those things in the school she went to. Yet Edith's reading and her letters actually worked to condemn her.

Freddy never denied his own guilt, and he showed the most admirable – indeed, 'romantic' – loyalty to Edith throughout the trial. When all seemed already lost he actually wrote to the Home Secretary, in an attempt to explain his lover's letters and her absolute innocence of plans or intentions to kill her husband. The central quarter of his letter reads,

> She is a hysterical & highly strung woman & when writing letters to me she did not study sentences and phrases before transferring them to paper, but, as different thoughts, no matter what, momentarily flashed through her mind, so they were committed to paper. Sometimes, even I, could not understand her. Now sir, if

I had, for one moment, thought or imagined, that there
was anything contained in Mrs Thompson's letters to
me, that could at any time, harm her, would I not have
destroyed them? I was astounded when I heard the
sinister translation the prosecution had put to certain
phrases, which were written quite innocently. Those
letters were the outpourings of a hysterical woman's
mind, to relieve the tension & strain caused by
the agony she was suffering. If you like sir, merely
melodrama.[27]

This may be read as in part the tactical performance of a
brave and clever twenty-year-old man speaking to his 'betters'
(he had learned how to placate Flashman from his reading,
after all) about a woman's love-letters to him. Even stylistic-
ally, there is little to complain of, beyond an over-anxious
attraction to commas. It also sets up for me some interesting
questions about the relation between schooled literacy and
the uses men and women make of their developed language
skills in the world. Freddy's 'knowledge about language'
(a recent National Curriculum requirement) enabled him to
understand that those in authority would have preferred Edith
to be sucking her pencil stub and planning her paragraphs,
rather than letting her feelings spill out into a prose which was
in any way adequate to the strength of those feelings.

Both Edith and Freddy won prizes for their writing at
school, and one can see why. Indeed, it is possible to envisage
Edith as in some ways the ideal school student of English:
keen, conscientious, careful; taking to reading and to the
theatre in exactly the ways in which working-class children
are too often expected not to. She 'lives' in the books she
reads: not foolishly identifying with the characters of plays
and novels, but interrogating texts for versions of what
is thought 'normal' behaviour, what is to be expected, or
regarded as extreme or improbable. It could well be claimed
that a discussion of novels and plays which treats their plots

and characters as if they actually existed in the world is sanctioned to this day by most literature examinations, whatever more sophisticated theorists have maintained.

Edith looks to texts for information and instruction about other women and about men; about people's sexual interests and needs and desires; and about conflicting moralities round issues of marriage and sex, adultery and divorce. She may at times 'read into' these texts concerns which chime with her own concerns – unwanted pregnancy; the difficulty of being involved sexually with two men, only one of whom she finds sexually attractive; and so on – yet such 'reading into' texts is what, under other circumstances, is thought of as 'personal response' or even 'interpretation'. It certainly looks harmless when compared with the cavalier and contemptuous reading of her letters by lawyers and judge, let alone their refusal to read the novels which determined the outcome of the trial, on the grounds that it is easy enough to predict the plot and the ingredients of formulaic and meretricious novels like these, which are intended for women, and which professional men would never ordinarily read for themselves.

Edith had taken the injunctions of many a good English teacher to heart. She never discussed books she had not read, and when writing about the books she had read, she always accompanied her arguments – which were usually tentatively offered – with textual reference and example. To read Queenie Leavis, writing eight or nine years later, on the terrors of this new literacy, is to glimpse something of the resistance there has been from more quarters than the judiciary to spreading education and literacy to the whole population; and something of the perennial ambivalence that exists in attitudes towards women's reading.

No one who has made a point of frequenting London and provincial branches of the book-clubs for the past few years can avoid concluding that the book-borrowing public has acquired the reading habit while somehow failing to exercise any critical intelligence about its reading. It is significant that the proportion of fiction to non-fiction borrowed is overwhelmingly great, that women rather than men change the books (that is, determine the family reading), and that many subscribers call daily to change their novels . . . In suburban side-streets and even village shops it is common to find a stock of worn and greasy novels let out at 2d. or 3d. a volume; and it is surprising that a clientele drawn from the poorest class can afford to change the books several times a week, or even daily; but so strong is the reading habit that they do.[28]

In the following chapter I will be alluding to recent battles over the National Curriculum in English especially, and to a recent HMI report which worries somewhat ineffectually at the superior examination results in English of girls to boys.[29] If Edith and Freddy had been born fifty years later they would probably have stayed on at school until the age of sixteen, and, given their intelligence and their interests, the chances are good that they would have taken some A levels and proceeded to university, perhaps to read English. Yet their reading and their writing were disparaged as 'uneducated', undiscriminating, even though their brief schooling clearly 'took' in ways which must have had something to do with their confidence that they would get jobs after school and that the education they were getting would be useful in such jobs.

There is still a quite widely held faith in the transcendant virtues of schooled literacy and in the socially binding character of English literature. Such faith sits oddly with some of the examples we have been considering, in which claims for the virtues of English and of language and literature rest so squarely on simple class predilections. English as a school subject has, in recent years, become the battleground on which such questions have been fought out.

7

A Civilising Influence

I have suggested in earlier chapters that women occupied an ambiguous position in state schooling as it developed during the nineteenth century and into the twentieth. Teaching afforded them the possibility of some sort of education for themselves; scope for relatively interesting work; greater independence than most middle- and working-class women enjoyed, and a sense of participating, if in limited ways, in public life and even in politics. This included an involvement in the culture and in an important area of expanding provision, which could be seen to allow for emancipatory, modern, even progressive aims and practices. Yet schooling, particularly the schooling of poor children, was also coercive and narrow in its purposes. Schools were to provide a curriculum which was reductive and often contemptuous of the children themselves, based as it was on the assumption that the school's duty was to assert a spurious national cultural unity, in order to bind together disparate social groups. In addition, women who went into teaching were often subject themselves, as we have seen, to severe regulation in their private and professional lives.

Within that history, no aspect of the curriculum stands more exactly for the inherent contradictions of the role of women teachers than the evolution of all those activities and values which were to become 'English'. English could even be seen to *be* and to have been the curriculum. It was certainly equivalent to a good deal of what was prescribed for the new elementary schools. Even now, the English part of the National Curriculum (with the History syllabus, which, incidentally, was always thought of as part of English or the 'English Subjects', as they were called) has provoked more argument and passion than all the other subjects. There are indeed ways in which the history of English as a subject (and it is not a long history, any more than the presence of women in education has a very long history) embodies the tensions and contradictions inherent in a national education system designed to promote ideals of English maleness, but dependant on women for its delivery.

Brian Doyle's recent history of English is one of a number which have been undertaken in the interests of theorising literature and the study of literature. He tells the story of the development of English as a subject, particularly a university subject, and his version of it is unusual in that it makes pivotal the transformation of English from a female sphere of influence into a male profession; though the slippage between 'female' as metaphor and women working as teachers of literacy and English is not investigated. 'Before 1880,' he writes,

> most teaching of languages and literature was either associated with women, or allied to the utilitarian pursuit of functional literacy; and therefore occupied a dramatically lower cultural status than the upper-class masculine studies of Classics and Mathematics.[1]

It may be that Doyle makes too much of this absolute division between 'functional literacy' and Classical studies. We will meet with examples in the next chapter of a sturdily middle-class and securely anti-aristocratic insistence on an English rather than a Classical education from the middle of the eighteenth century. This is unlikely to be exceptional. However, Doyle also rightly sets this opposition within the ambiguities of women's position in a developing state system of schooling.

> In the course of the nineteenth century a fully national system of schooling with predominantly female staff was established throughout Britain. The role given to women within this new national context was itself novel and embodied a conflict of cultural status. There was an unbridgeable gulf between the role of women as homemakers and any professional practice.[2]

Again, he goes too far. The gulf was far from unbridgeable. Indeed, much of the testimony I have already offered suggests the ways in which teaching children in school was often perceived as continuous in certain respects with women's traditional relations with children in families. Doyle's interest, though, is in showing how English had, by the 1930s,

> become fully established as a professional activity within higher education on terms very different from the semi-professional practice of nineteenth-century women teachers. Instead . . . it became a distinctively male domain, having its own professional modes of research and teaching and ways of controlling admission.[3]

Thereafter, Doyle's purpose becomes the charting of a struggle between powerful groups in the society to lay claim to and regulate English as a subject: the universities, professional associations, publishers and government are all implicated. And all have clear-cut interests in arguing for English as a relatively fixed and containable body of knowledge – of texts, of ways of reading them and writing about them – which could have the potential to disguise and soothe bitter conflicts of interest between social classes, by proposing 'Standard English' and standards of literary excellence, as bench-marks of unassailable validity. The establishing of 'great works', of a 'broader culture' – from Matthew Arnold through the Newbolt Report to F.R. Leavis – and even of pleasure and of morality itself as the somehow natural ingredients of this part of the curriculum and as values capable of transcending difference, inequality and conflict, was intended both to justify the expense of a national system of education and to announce the forms of its monitoring.

Even today, as the writer and teacher, Ken Jones, has pointed out,[4] the so-called 'Cox Report', published in 1989 and embodying the proposals of the Subject Working Group on English chaired by Professor Brian Cox, offered prescriptions for 'bridging' and 'narrowing' gaps between classes and between boys and girls, so that notions of class and gender or race are comfortingly emptied of inequality or conflict, and need only to be entered and then reconciled. An irony there is that 'Cox' politely advised teachers to attend to the difficulties that might be experienced by girls and by children from minority groups at a time when girls' far better performance in English, like the performance of many children from minority groups, was encouraging teachers to feel that perhaps they needed to worry more about boys, and certainly about boys from white working-class backgrounds.

Brian Doyle's version of the history of English concentrates on the professionalising of English teaching through the universities; and through the English Association, which was founded in 1906 to promote the teaching and advanced study of the English language and of English literature. His analysis of where power has been located and how it has been exercised relies on his understanding of how the professors of English at University College London, at Oxford and Cambridge and then, increasingly, in the provincial universities, managed to assert a gathering jurisdiction over English as a school subject, partly through flooding the membership of the Newbolt Committee, which reported on the teaching of English in England in 1921.

Doyle's story is persuasive, as far as it goes. But its focus and its analysis move firmly from the top down, revealing an ideological (and, of course, material) struggle on the edges of the existing higher-education establishment to resist or let in new institutions, some modernisation and reform, and some modification of the dominion of Oxford and Cambridge. Within, or behind that struggle, a rather different struggle was going on. This was the struggle to let women into universities to take degrees: a struggle which took a quite different form in the London colleges, and the new colleges and universities in the provinces, from what went on in Oxford and Cambridge. For, as we have seen in the case of Nottingham University College, in Chapter 2, many of these new institutions accepted women without demur from the beginning (tolerance for women usually accompanying, rather bizarrely, tolerance for most forms of religion), though they were not always pleased by what became women's instant preponderance amongst certain sections of the students. Oxford and Cambridge put up longer, harder fights against full acceptance. Indeed, when I went to Cambridge in 1952, the women's colleges had only had full membership of the university for four years.

English as a university-degree subject could scarcely have taken off, in fact, without the virtually endless supply of women students wishing to study it.[5] So the 'femaleness' of English lies partly in its uncertain status, its association with women, its potential as 'a civilising influence' rather than a rigorous course of study or an established body of knowledge. More than that, there has always been some suspicion cast on moves to academicise the teaching of reading and writing and the reading of literature, when these were so obviously domestic activities, undertaken by women, particularly mothers, in the home. For if English as a subject has a relatively short history (even though there were English schools from the Reformation onwards) its character may also be read from ancient traditions of iconography and fairy tale, which picture the acquisition and the practices of early literacy as a wholly female terrain: domestic, parochial, consolatory and unthreatening.

But its 'femaleness' also derived from its position in a curriculum which challenged the traditions embodied in the Classics and in Oxford and Cambridge: a challenge from the margins, from the new colleges and university colleges of provincial cities. Therefore, gender plays an even more tangled role in all this than at first appears. For the struggle of the universities outside Oxford and Cambridge to establish themselves, and the struggle of English to establish itself as the central discipline of the Humanities, relied in some respects on the understood virtues of feminine refinement and sensitivity; but they were also struggles of dissociation from the 'feminine', and of counter-assertions of the properly masculine character of this new discipline and these new institutions. One example may illustrate what I mean.

I have already written about my great-aunt Clara in earlier chapters, of her studying for a London BA and a teaching qualification while teaching at Wyggeston Girls' School in Leicester in the late 1870s and early 1880s. From there she went on to take an MA (the first woman to do so) at University College London. She returned to teaching for only a few months after getting her MA, before moving into the new and developing profession of social researcher as an assistant to Charles Booth, who was producing his monumental study of London, *Labour and Life of the People*. From there she went on to found and develop the department in the Board of Trade which dealt specifically with changing legislation on women's work and women's pay, and to write about this and other connected topics. I have written about her life and work elsewhere, so I will not expand on these here. However, Clara became a close friend of George Gissing, the novelist, during the last ten years of his life. They could also be said to have shared an experience of the newly opened colleges and universities, which made it possible for the first time for a few women and a few men from poor or Nonconformist families to have some kind of formal higher education. Yet what they shared was also shot through with the peculiarly negative ways in which gender difference was habitually invoked in the storming of established citadels.

Gissing was thirteen when his father died, leaving a widow and five children with almost nothing to live on and nowhere to live, since they had at once to leave the flat over the chemist shop which Thomas Gissing had owned.[6] A local collection in Wakefield made it possible for George and his two younger brothers to go to a Quaker school. In 1872, when Gissing was fifteen, he won a scholarship to Owens College in Manchester, which, at that time, was still principally an institution preparing students for entry to Oxford, Cambridge and London. Gissing was a star student there until the moment in his third year when he was caught stealing money, and was expelled and then gaoled for a month. He had fallen in love with a young prostitute called Marianne Helen Harrison, known as Nell, and had been stealing money for her to buy drink. This effectively put paid to his formal education, though not to his interest in the subject or his determination to get his younger brothers an education that might allow them to become professional men.

There is an early correspondence with the older of his two brothers.[7] William won prizes at school, but no scholarship, so he went to work in a bank near Manchester at sixteen for seventeen shillings a week. The hours were grim; his lodgings cost more than he earned; and he too often felt lonely and outcast. He is an endearing presence in his letters to the worldly George in London, as he plucks up courage to leave the bank and set himself up as a music teacher; and as he gently mediates between members of the family; and studies and reads and keeps his counsel about his brother's first, and apparently awful, attempt at a novel. Then suddenly, at twenty, he died of a ruptured blood vessel in the lung, having suffered from congestion of the lungs for some time: a condition he made light of. Gissing's letters to his remaining brother and his sisters overflow with fortitude for a week or so, and are followed swiftly by letters about William's clothes, which are sent to George in London to be sold. This takes a bit of time as they are shabby. Eventually, however, George reports getting ten shillings for them, which he duly sends home to Wakefield.

William was no man of destiny, as George was, but his letters show him to have been afloat on his interests in music, drawing, reading, walking. He includes in a letter to George a page from his diary: one week. The main events are letters arriving. His days are routine and exhausting, and he has no money for books or music or other pleasures. Yet he is humorous, affectionate, and encouraging to his brothers. His poverty and the exiguousness of his prospects oppress him, yet he manages always to entertain himself. He plays the organ locally and hangs back from agreement with some of his metropolitan brother's more advanced ideas. When he is melancholy he sounds like his brother: he has no friends who are his intellectual equals: his poverty cuts him off from those who might be; and the rest are 'mere louts devoid of nearly any ennobling sentiments'.

As Raymond Williams pointed out when writing about George Eliot, Hardy and Lawrence, it is unhelpful to think of such people (or, indeed, of William Gissing) as autodidacts, since they had reached a level of education that was 'higher, absolutely, than those of four out of five people in mid-twentieth-century Britain'.[8] Yet William Gissing and his brothers were half inclined to see their educational experience from that point of view which assumes that 'the pattern of boarding school and Oxford' represents what education really is, rather than what 2 per cent of the population actually receives, while the rest of the population come to be 'seen as uneducated' or else as 'autodidacts'. Only half inclined, however, since they were able to experience in their own lives the beginnings of an alternative.

However, such views of a 'real' education prevailed for a long time. For instance, John Buchan wrote in his autobiography of his growing-up during the 1880s,

> I never went to school in the conventional sense, for a boarding school was beyond the narrow means of my family. But I had many academies. The first was a dame's school, where I learned to knit, and was expelled for upsetting a broth pot on the kitchen fire. The next was a board school in the same Fife village. Then came the burgh school of the neighbouring town, which meant a daily tramp of six miles. There followed the high school of the same town, a famous institution in which I believe Thomas Carlyle once taught. When we migrated to Glasgow I attended for several years an ancient grammar school on the south side of the river, from which, at the age of seventeen I passed to Glasgow University.[9]

When my husband was still an undergraduate at Cambridge in the early 1950s, he was asked by Sacheverell Sitwell when he had been at Eton, to which he replied that he had not been there at all. Later that evening, Sitwell was overheard saying, 'Remarkable fellow that Miller, totally self-educated.' My husband had 'attended for several years an ancient grammar school' as John Buchan had, though one in Edinburgh rather than Glasgow. Unlike Buchan, he knew his luck.

After William's death in 1880, George turned his attention to the younger Algernon, who was tussling with matriculation and then with the London law examinations. The correspondence between these Gissing brothers offers valuable glimpses of the new arrangements made by London University for examining external degrees in 'English subjects' as well as in law. These syllabuses, emanating from Burlington House, must have had an immense influence on how and what many young men (and, from 1878, young women too) studied all over England, and eventually in many parts of the Empire.

George sends Algernon his old notes and books. He tells him often and exactly what a liberal education and a well-trained mind consist of. He tells him what to read, and how much trouble to take with parts of his reading. He should, for instance, become a fluent reader of German; and George has suggestions for what may sensibly be read in translation from Latin and Greek and what may not. His advice about the London syllabus comes from his Owens days, and the syllabus itself comes to assume an equivalence with all that is required by a modern man of parts.

It is possible to see in his recommendations, and in his references to texts to be studied for the examination, a version of culture which encompasses an accommodation with some of the patrician expectations of Oxford and Cambridge, while significantly exceeding them in certain ways. The breadth is different and new: not just Classics and History and Mathematics, but German as well as French, and the Philosophy of Science. Gissing recommends Marsh's *Lectures on the English Language* to his sister, Margaret, and suggests she study the notes of the Clarendon Shakespeare 'thorough', for 'a woman is a mere duffer if she is not able to read Shakspere with perfect intelligence of his vocabulary'.[10] More is expected of Algernon. He should read Morris's *Outlines of English Accidence* and Adams' *Elements of the English Language*[11] for the 'English' part of the course, and George takes it for granted that his brother will have read all of Shakespeare, Dickens, George Eliot and the Brontës. He also alerts him to what Tennyson is up to, rather in the spirit of handing out useful literary gossip. The profuse educational detail of his advice is often compounded by the editors of the letters, who see it as their task to correct his Latin, insert a dozen or so *sic*s and 'place' his Shakespeare quotations, as if to suggest that they and we know that we are better educated than this unconventionally schooled writer.

Gissing was reading Comte and meeting German socialists in London during the late 1870s, and William and Algernon thought of their older brother as a thoroughly modern man, in favour of science, not God. They are impressed and a little wary. In fact, Gissing became rather disillusioned with science and socialism in later years and a little less dogmatic. My point is this, though: the challenge to the centre from men like Gissing and from the institutions which developed in the second half of the nineteenth century to support that challenge, were based on an attempt to discover values, ideas, a culture which would expand on and alter the narrow base of high bourgeois and aristocratic culture. But it was vitally important for them to assert the masculinity of all this, the absolutely non-female character of this version of the modern: Gissing's words in a letter to his brother, written when he was twenty-two, become an essential part of the case he is making for the new educated man:

> This matter of girls' exams. depends entirely upon what is likely to be the girls' future life. If a girl is to be made a teacher, it is certainly right that she should pass examinations; but, as a mere feature in education, I see little could to be (*sic*) effected by these tests. A girl's education should be of a very general and liberal character, adapted rather to expand the intelligence as a whole than to impart very thorough knowledge on any subject. General reading is what I should advise a girl to undertake; and that reading should certainly *not* lie in the direction of the Higher Mathematics or Political Economy.[12]

The idea of a general education, in which nothing is actually known about anything in particular, has a long and dishonourable history, unfortunately, and has come to stand for the contents as well as the capabilities of the female mind. The paradox is that Gissing was offering this as advice to his two young sisters, and that he was prepared to except from his proscription women who might be going to become teachers. Yet his own passion for enlarging his own and his brothers' education needed this proviso to buttress its rationale and definition. His friend Clara Collet is unlikely to have read this letter. She would have been grimly amused, I assume, by its certainties. She and her sisters were especially good at mathematics and she was to specialise in the study of political philosophy, economics and statistics.

John Dixon has done well to propose an alternative history of English to those, of Doyle and others, which focus on the determinations on school English from above, as it were, in the form of policy statements, the views of professional associations and developments within universities. Dixon's emphasis is on the constant stream of innovations from the 1860s onwards which came from 'below', even from teachers, and quite often from women. He considers, for instance, university extension work and cultural and educational organisations set up by groups of workers and by women teachers. He also discusses new approaches to spoken and written language and to the reading of literature, developed by teachers in mixed-ability classrooms and in further and adult education during the sixties and seventies.[13]

Dixon's recent *A Schooling in English* may also be read as something of a *mea culpa* for his earlier *Growth Through English*,[14] which was first published in 1967 as a record of an international conference on English held in Dartmouth, New Hampshire in 1966. This stood for many years as a reference point for progress in research and teaching in English across the English-speaking world, and its definitions and proposals were deservedly influential. A later 1975 edition of the book carried a kind of apology from James Britton and James Squire for the failure of both conference and book to pay adequate attention to social class and race, and to the always problematic relations between schools and working-class children. Yet – and by no means uniquely – the book offers to account for the excited construction of something like a 'new' English without referring to, or apparently involving, women teachers of English, except as occasional providers of classroom data and in relation to the unglossed statistical likelihood that they left their jobs in secondary-modern schools even more readily than their male colleagues.

For all its exclusions, *Growth through English* remained a seminal work on English teaching for many years, and it heralded some of the most influential writing and research into English teaching of the century. I am thinking of James Britton's *Language and Learning*, the Bullock Report, *Language, the Learner and the School*, by Douglas Barnes, James Britton and Harold Rosen, and Peter Medway's *Finding a Language*, amongst others.[15] These in their turn inspired teachers to develop materials and ways of working with children which transformed classrooms from places in which children might be found – if not rendered – incompetent (and, of course, definitively assessed as such) through their presumed lack of a culture or a language, to places where their voices and experience were able to teach teachers how and what to teach them. English teachers during those years learned to listen to children, in ways which some have even seen as learned from the ways mothers must listen to and interpret their own children: as, therefore, peculiarly feminine. I have already stressed the danger of generalising in this way from mothers to teachers (or vice versa). Yet I also think it likely that it *is* easier for women to listen to children than it is for men, who even in their passionate advocacy of the virtues of 'talk in the classroom', of dialogue and of 'language across the curriculum' have been inclined to retain the posture and monologic speech style of the lecturer.[16]

That movement, like others before it and since, acknowledged neither the predominance of women as English teachers nor the difference that predominance might have made to these new developments in English. It would be unfair to single out one particular generation of 'heroic' English teachers for their refusal to recognise what women teachers were doing, both in primary schools and in English lessons, whilst constructing a muscular pedagogic theory of language and learning on the back of that practice. That has been the story of so much writing about English teaching; and from both sides, as it were.[17] For if programmes of progressive practice have been mounted without recognising women teachers' central contribution to that practice, it has also to be said that the many women teachers who have delighted and excelled in traditional approaches to the teaching of language and literature have also been thought to need spokesmen.

In the recent furore about girls' successes at school, English has starred: as the subject, above all, at which girls excel; and as the subject which is most in need of a return to conventional ways of teaching children and assessing their achievement. The connection between the two has not had much attention. In fact, the numbers of students of both sexes achieving pass grades in English has steadily increased since the introduction of more course-work-assessed syllabuses. Though I believe that 1994 registered a down-turn in line with changes back to a weighting in favour of timed papers. However, within that general improvement, girls have been doing better than boys in English for some time. Indeed, they were doing better even before the introduction of course-work examining. Subsequent research has shown that after the first year of GCSE (1988), this gap between girls and boys widened substantially. In one local education authority, where a detailed comparison of figures has been carried out, the gap between girls and boys widened from a 5.7 per cent difference in 1987, the last year of the combined O level/CSE examinations, to 16.5 per cent in 1988, the first year of the new GCSE. It should also be said that the numbers of boys with pass grades increased too, though less dramatically, and that the figures for the girls can be broken down to show that Afro-Caribbean and Asian girls shared in the improved grades equally with white girls.[18] Any interpretation of these figures, therefore, must take into account this difference between girls' grades and boys'.

Either these improved grades will be taken to indicate a softening of standards, due, perhaps, to course-work modes of assessment and teacher involvement, and even to complicitous marking by teachers – in which case it becomes necessary to explain why these changes should favour girls – or this new opportunity for matching assessment to curriculum practices and to the in-service training this has afforded teachers, must straightforwardly be taken to produce better overall results. And so long as there are improvements in curriculum and assessment, and therefore better results, we need to understand why it should be that girls still seem able to exploit these possibilities more easily than boys.

A recent HMI report, *Boys and English*, based on visits to 51 secondary or middle schools and 1 sixth-form college between 1988 and 1991, set out 'to identify teaching approaches which improved boys' attitudes towards English and their performance in the subject'.[19] It may be worth summarising the facts and figures from which the report starts. These are drawn from recent surveys which show that girls are already doing better than boys in reading, writing and spelling by age seven, and that what the HMI call 'these contrasts' persist through the ages of eleven and fifteen; produce huge discrepancies in English GCSE results; are manifested after sixteen by the fact that more than twice as many girls as boys embark on English A level; and have significantly widened since 1989.

With a determined refusal to consider or even mention class (we hear, instead, about conditions like 'disadvantage' and their potential for encouraging 'low expectations' and 'unwarranted assumptions' about boys disliking poetry), the report's principal focus is on a somewhat frustrated search for examples of 'sensitive teaching', which will lead pupils to 'an understanding of the qualities of good literature'. Teachers make all the difference to boys, apparently, in the texts they choose and the approaches to them that they initiate. It is not, it seems, that boys reject 'good literature', but that teachers expect them to. It is not made clear whether teachers also make all the difference to girls, or whether girls are just naturally good at 'doing English': able to write from birth 'with conviction about personal feelings',[20] for instance; and to respond appropriately to whatever poetry is put before them. They also, it turns out, are thought by their teachers to be neater writers, more accurate 'and more likely to do thorough work; girls were better at spelling; girls were more fluent, although less likely than boys to use technical terms'.[21] And who are the teachers? They are women predominantly, though there were more than twice as many men as women in Head of Department posts.[22]

This is not a very useful report. It tells teachers and probably almost everybody else what they already know, and it avoids contentious questions about schooling and class and gender. Its view of English is untheorised and contradictory, as is any sense of who these teachers are and who the boys and girls in their classrooms are, and what kinds of cultural activities and values English may have to compete with in the outside world. The 'affective' is left as a central category of experience at the heart of English, without definition or context. Indeed, it appears from this that girls are good at English because they are good at 'emotion', and boys are not. The only interesting thing about the report is that it was produced at all; that it recognises, if confusedly, that there are problems with English and how it is perceived by some boys; and that these problems are associated in some way with sexual difference. The report's non-committal blandness fails to disguise its damaging denial of the distance between much that is enshrined in the English curriculum and the culture of most boys (and a good many girls) in a period of mass culture and high unemployment.

I have already quoted Kate Pugh, the Head of an English department in a mixed, London comprehensive school, on the problem posed for teachers like her by some of the working-class boys in her classes. In a glimpse of one moment from her classroom, she offers a dramatically different expression of the dilemma from any postulated by Her Majesty's Inspectors.

Recently I took photographs of my classroom for a display on open day. The girls, without being told, understood the part they had to play in the fiction I was creating. They did not look at the camera, they posed themselves as good workers, intent on their books and their writing. Some of the boys, on the other hand, refused these positions, even after I had explained that the photographs were 'supposed to show them learning'. It was not that they did not understand the story the photographs were designed to tell. They understood as well as the girls and because they understood they were determined/compelled to subvert my story. They looked directly into the lens, pulled faces, posed as muscle-men, jumped in front of the camera, or appeared behind other groups I was photographing, waving, grinning, putting two fingers up at the camera. They refused to take my fiction seriously and even the boys who initially went along with the idea of being pictured as 'learners', began to produce exaggerated parodies of what I wanted, holding the books too close to their faces or frowning with exaggerated concentration before collapsing into laughter. Why do these boys reject their roles in the story of the 'good' English classroom, while the girls willingly collaborate with it? . . .

There are no 'bad' girls in my photo-story, but what are the alternative stories that the boys, 'good' boys and 'bad' boys, are telling about themselves as they caper their resistance to my narrative? What other stories circulate around them, about boys, about English, about women teachers?[23]

That these boys should be thought by their teacher to 'caper their resistance to my narrative' is so radically different as a formulation of the 'problem' that it seems to me necessary to dwell on its implications for a moment. Just as it is possible to see how the teacher and the girls conspire in their readiness to 'play the game', so it is important to see the boys as conspiring to play another game, defined as *not* what the teacher and the girls are playing. Where the HMI see the choice of text and the teacher's tactics in presenting the text as cardinal, this teacher starts from the predictable tensions in any relationship between teacher and students. Each person in the classroom functions in terms of 'fictions', which articulate individual, as well as potentially shared or shareable, intentions; humour; a private and a public sense of self. Indeed, those fictions will form the substance of what goes on in English lessons. Some fictions will be shared, some will be idiosyncratic and some contested; but the notion that certain fictions are so clearly transcendent and, therefore, binding and uniting, that they will sweep all the other tiresomely alternative fictions out of the way and take their place, is something a teacher like Kate Pugh knows to be unhelpful. The 'fictions' of literature will have to find a place for themselves amongst all the other fictions. Much time and thought will, of course, be devoted to all those fictions, and much talk and writing will be performed in the interests of making sense of them. These activities will in their turn constitute the altered cultural possibilities made available to the class.

So, within a classroom which is hospitable to the tensions inherent in its own diverse cultural make-up, why should it be that the girls are, relatively speaking, willing at least to go along with their teacher's version of things: with the forms and outcomes she will encourage? Rather than blaming the boys for their disruptiveness and the teacher for either pandering to their brutish tastes or failing to persuade them 'to explore their feelings through written work and to consider the affective in literature',[24] we need to understand why English in any of its manifestations – but especially in the often broader and richer forms of itself to be found in what the HMI call 'disadvantaged' schools like Kate Pugh's – is negotiable with most of the girls, when it is not with a large number of boys, or is not except with a struggle.

One strand of the complex kind of explanation we might look for must relate to the future work and life prospects of these boys and girls. Kate Pugh points out that 'school failure amongst working-class boys is not . . . confined to counter cultural groups', as it is in Paul Willis's chronicle of his heroic 'school refusers' preparing themselves for unskilled manufacturing work in the seventies.[25] Very few, if any, of the children in Kate Pugh's school anticipate going on to university, so that even the relative success of the girls is limited by their sense of what is possible for them after school too. Good levels of literacy competence will be useful – indeed necessary – for almost all the jobs the girls might try for: as office clerks or secretaries, keyboard operators, shop assistants, receptionists, and so on. A few of them may aim higher, towards nursery nursing, hospital nursing, even teaching. The boys will have fewer options anyway, and though modest levels of literacy would in fact help them, they understand that the so-called 'rewards' for doing well at English are too insecure and unreliable to compensate for what may be the boredom, the loss of face and the considerable effort of working to achieve them.

It is probable, though, that most younger secondary-age children are not yet looking for any exact match between what they are learning at school and qualifications for future employment, though their family and community experience will exert an increasing influence on the sense they are making of these things. It does seem, however, that boys are more likely to think of their learning instrumentally, in terms of its immediate and future usefulness as knowledge, skills and qualifications. English is not an area of the school curriculum which delivers sure-fire examination results as a consequence of the effort put into it, nor does it offer itself as training of a straightforward kind for definable kinds of work. It may be that girls, can imagine futures for themselves in which reading and writing, even of a very different kind, will play a part, and they know that in the clerical and secretarial jobs they envisage, neatness, accuracy, conscientiousness will get them marks. But more than this, they know that most of life, perhaps the most important part, can't be measured in terms of linear progress towards a defined goal. When their mother placates an irate toddler; arranges for someone to pick a little brother up from school; works out when money for the school trip can be handed over; rings the housing office; work is being done, but no one is watching or directing it, it doesn't get measured, it doesn't get paid, it has no end-product. They don't conceptualise work and leisure, 'my time' to play and 'their time' for paid work, in the same way. They know that much work has to be self-directed, cooperative, on-going, a part of living.[26]

Within such an apportioning of time among multiple responsibilities, reading fits (as knitting does). It does not require whole days or even afternoons. Like everything else in so much of women's lives, it can be done in snatches: accommodated to the expectation of the unexpected, to the incessant demands of others on time and energy and silence.[27]

In just the same way, girls may perceive purposes in writing which go beyond the classroom. Carolyn Steedman wrote a book about 'The Tidy House', a story told and written by three eight-year-old working-class girls about the world they inhabited and the lives they anticipated for themselves as adult women. Steedman sets the writing of the story within a history of girls (mostly middle-class girls) writing diaries and stories and autobiographies, in which they explore their ambiguous futures as grown-up women, usually by way of a beady scrutiny of their actual experience of adult behaviour. These are futures simultaneously dressed in romance and circumscribed by the known lives of their own mothers. Steedman's presentation of the story of 'The Tidy House' offers us vital insights into girls' uses of literacy, as readers and as writers. They have learned to read and write in school, yet the story they construct together is entirely about the life they know outside school. As Steedman expresses it,

> what writing 'The Tidy House' provided Carla, Melissa and Lindie with was a powerful notion of change. The idea of change functioned in several ways, the simplest and most accessible being the children's understanding that as writers they could alter the words on the page, cross them out, start again. They were able to alter the sequence and effect of events witnessed in the real world by constructing a fiction. By writing, and particularly by making use of dialogue, they were able to analyse the way in which the words of adults altered events and to envision for themselves possible changes in circumstances. It is probable that children who are illiterate are quite unable to make these analyses or perform these transformations.[28]

The life the girls described was a mother's life, and a mother's life as it might appear to a daughter, who has double motives for imagining such a state for herself. In so doing the daughter recognises that as a child she has herself been simultaneously wanted, even the *raison d'être*, it might be said, of both house and motherhood – which in their turn measure out the mother's special realm of power – and that she is also a principal source of the mother's 'irritation and regret'. Writing, reproducing the speech that effects change, the speech women employ to direct and comment on the complexities of life in their own 'Tidy House', may be seen to have clear purposes. For girls know that as adults they will have to negotiate and then order the occupation of spaces and days for themselves and their children, and that it is through language that they will do this.

For boys to adjust to such regimes of adaptable time and altered purposes, articulated in a language of conversation rather than of monologic commentary, would be to do more than acknowledge the feminine. It would be to assume it and then to lose their right to a quite different destiny: one which exceeds 'The Tidy House' and attending to children and the organisation of time for others. The temptations of the domestic have to be resisted by boys if they are to stand a chance in the world outside. Little girls, in their play, are apt to burlesque, with manic and bustling energy, those endless tasks: washing, cooking, shopping, cleaning, smacking, rocking. Their longing for miniature ironing boards and dolls in prams may astonish their modern mothers. And their simultaneous desire for fairy dresses with wings and a make-up kit will scarcely redress the balance. Yet reading and writing may work as a way for them to make sense of those contradictions. Literacy provides them with stories of princesses and beggar maids, and of bad girls as well as good ones. These become something more, I think, than a comfort or an escape. Literacy becomes a mode of living femininity as more than just 'negative capability'. It offers scope for imagining multiplicity and change, and for resisting, as well as yielding to, the seductions of the domestic and the feminine.

How different, for instance, are the stories told by those men who loved English at school and grew up to become writers or teachers of English. I am thinking, for instance, of American critics like Wayne Booth or Frank Lentricchia or Richard Rodriguez, who have found it possible to write of their youth as an apprenticeship, however improbable, to a literature which was able to prefigure their future labours on its behalf.[29] For them the lesson learned, usually as a favourite student, was always of a career, of a life's work that might be forged out of what was learned at school, through reading and writing, through literature. Not for them the domestic narrative or the improbable romance, but the *Bildungsroman*, the life which is its own education, the epic struggle or perhaps even the tragic defeat. And how unsuited are the clichés of eulogy, of *Who's Who* entries, of the *Festschrift* or of obituary writing, after all, to the stories of most women's lives. How wholly inappropriate are those ritual tales of soaring, if often unfulfilled, promise, that bring a lump to the throat as, in bewilderment and uneasy soul-searching, we bow our heads at the funerals of the men we knew. And yes, of course, they are inappropriate to a majority of the human race: a state of affairs which does not in itself cancel out their gendered character.

English did not offer these men, as it seems to have offered girls, encouragement to settle for books as the repository of what will always be just beyond one's reach. Reading may indeed be there as emollient, escape. But its appeal also lies in the access it offers to lives created out of the vision of others, and assembled from the vagaries of narratives designed to give meaning to the lives of people who are quite different from us. I do not believe that most women find themselves in Anna Karenina or Emma Bovary. They may learn of the dangers and the disappointments there are in presuming on men's affection for women and on their hospitality. For girls, other people's narratives become grist to their mill; and English, that crown of the Humanities, offers them a profusion of stories they can use. Amongst them will be all those other stories – men's stories and the voices that recite them – which helpfully mark out forbidden territories and the small enclaves within them where women may lurk and spy out the land.

How reduced, and apparently unaware of literature as potentially explosive and unpredictable stuff, is the new pared-down 1994 Dearing version of the English curriculum, with its lists of good books, its antibiotic view of grammar and its multitude of occasions for instilling Standard English.[30] Each of us could as easily have come up with our longer or shorter list of the essential ingredients of English; and for teachers like Kate Pugh these ingredients will all, to

some degree, seem a hindrance and beside the point, because
they will ignore what she could have told anyone who asked.
Authors of curriculum proposals – however inter-galactic in
scope – are unlikely to have imagined what the nature of her
task may be in a school, where

> 70% of the pupils come from various immigrant groups,
> some from large, long-established local communities
> like the Cypriot community, others, for example
> Somalis and Kurds, from recently arrived refugee
> communities. What almost all the pupils have in
> common is relative poverty. Boys outnumber girls
> two to one in many classes in the school, but white
> working-class boys who would define themselves as
> English are now a minority.[31]

And her problem is not – as it has so often been represented
as being – that she, as a woman teacher, is simply out of
sympathy with working-class boys or the problems they
might have with school. Quite the reverse. Theirs are
recognisably the problems she remembers from her own
schooldays, where

> as we understood it, according to our teachers we came
> from homes with no books, could not speak properly
> and had parents who were too busy watching television
> to take much interest in our education. I can remember
> my anger at these assumptions, an anger that arose
> because my own working-class mother largely shared
> these prejudices. She was an avid reader and attender of
> W.E.A. courses, refused to have a television in the
> house and her insistence on 'correct English' had
> made me suffer throughout my primary school days
> for 'talking posh'.[32]

Girls are as susceptible as boys are to the limiting expectations
schools and teachers may have of working-class children.
Yet we still have to account for the relative willingness of girls

to use reading and writing both for the purposes of school and for purposes of their own.[33]

We have already seen how middle- and upper-class women have been imagined as readers and indeed depended on as teachers of children and as consumers of novels. As Gill Frith has pointed out, the expectation that some women would and should read has been a complex one, always subject to regulation and proscription as to how and what they read. Frith quotes an early example of such advice, from James Fordyce's *Sermons to Young Women*, first published in 1765, which prefigures in some ways the advice George Gissing offered his sisters.

> There is an influence, there is an empire which belongs to you, and which I wish you ever to possess: I mean that which has the heart for its object, and is secured by meekness and modesty, by soft attraction and virtuous love.
>
> But now I must add, that your power in this way will receive a large accession from the culture of your minds, in the more elegant and polished branches of knowledge. When I say so, I would by no means insinuate, that you are not capable of the judicious and the solid, in such proportion as is suited to your destination in life. This, I apprehend, does not require reasoning or accuracy, so much as observation and discernment. Your business chiefly is to read Men, in order to make yourselves agreeable and useful. It is not the argumentative but the sentimental talents, which give you that insight and those openings into the human heart that lead to your principal ends as Women. Nevertheless, in this study you may derive great assistance from books.[34]

The interesting question is how that injunction 'to read Men', offered here as the source and character of female power, should have become the touchstone for girls' successes in

English relative to boys'. Reading books and reading men acquire equivalent weight and purpose, besides being mutually dependant. And feeling and sympathy, as opposed to logic, become the qualities reading both kinds of thing produces and demands. Frith is clear about the connection between what she calls the female reader's necessary 'double vision' and her skills as a student of English:

> she both identifies with the heroine and is distanced from her, since she is positioned to draw distinctions and make predictions which are not available to the heroine.
>
> The particular qualities which are demanded of the reader by the mass-market romance have close affinities with those which James Fordyce hoped to inculcate in his youthful female reader. In both cases, there is an obvious link with women's familial role – with her place as the central point of connection, anticipating the needs and desires of others, suspending judgement, guiding and governing the emotions. But if, as I suggested earlier, we see the central constituent of feminine subjectivity not as 'lack' or 'passivity', but rather as *adaptability*, there is a further connection with the 'feminine' at work here: the reader's control over the narrative depends upon her 'feminine' capacity to alternate roles, shift subject-positions and identifications. At the same time, the empathetic and discriminating qualities described here are also, of course, those generally required of the 'good' reader. I am suggesting, then, that the idea that the 'normal' position of the reader is male is a very odd one. The required position of the reading subject, the reading *process*, conforms much more closely to the conventional prescriptions of femininity than to those of masculinity. It is hardly surprising that most students of English Literature are women.[35]

Frith's analogy is between women's having to learn to read men and their learning how to read texts. Is it possible to extrapolate from those students of English literature to, say, teenage girls in a working-class school who have become expert readers of both Mills and Boon romances and Jane Austen? There has been an important debate amongst teachers about the place of popular fiction in girls' reading in school. Indeed, the passionate positions taken up round this issue have come to represent a good deal of recent theoretical and critical discussion about the relation between readers and texts and, by extension, about English teachers' responsibilities for making explicit the public values accorded particular texts. No one has made the case better than Anne Turvey, I think, in her discussion of how some of her pupils in an East London girls' school (the school as it happens, to which many girls were proceeding by the nineteen twenties, after their time at Kensington Avenue School) came to understand the formal characteristics of the romance. Turvey contrasts many people's anxious disapproval of popular novels themselves, and, by implication, of their readers, with the girls' active 'exploitation' of their reading.

> The critic has not wanted to adopt an élitist position which condemns the reader as a passive consumer of mass culture, but at the same time has been reluctant to endorse the literature itself. Even when the readers of romance were shown to be anything but passive or mindless, they have remained, at least in relation to the romance, strangely inert, weighed down by the text. In the case of teenage girls, the readers emerge as vulnerable, impressionable, in need of the teacher's critical armour to fend off the dangers of these texts, dangers which can usually be reduced to various versions of 'Read the book; now live the life'.[36]

How can that anxious concern be justified in the light of this aside from fifteen-year-old Helen to her teacher during a discussion of *Pride and Prejudice*, 'I love this book: it's just like a Mills and Boon! I mean, the way we know what Elizabeth and Darcy *don't* know. That's in Mills and Boon. I love that!'[37] And should we sensibly worry about these two thirteen-year-old girls, who write an eight-chapter outline of their own romance, called 'Artist's Impression' (and it may be worth remembering that Jane Austen's first version of *Pride and Prejudice* was, in fact, called *First Impressions*), the first chapter of which goes like this?

> Anne Richards, journalist and part-time painter, is with her office associate, Steve White, at a galery in east New York, cool pale colours, dim lights, and low voices, where Anne is exhibiting a recent painting. A stranger approaches Anne, he's about 6ft 3″ with sandy hair, a muscular build and roguish good looks. He stands behind her and inspects the painting next to Anne's. He is wearing a smart pair of jeans with a short sleeved T-shirt just right for the temperature where as Anne is hot in the expensive, once-in-a-lifetime, wool suit bought with the money from a previous painting. As he comments on the painting she catches the scent of his colonge and turns to regard him. She is instantly struck by his strength and masculinity but as he looks down at her she quickly returns her attention to the painting. They move on together. As they reach Anne's painting the stranger finds himself looking at a young boy playing, on the beach, with a bucket and spade and is amazed at the similarity between the woman he is with and the child. Realishing the connection a boyish grin creaps into his features.
>
> 'I don't like it! The light is wrong and the whole scene is quite ridiculous.'
>
> Anne, appauled by the unsensitivity, begins to defend her painting but later leaves to join Steve for a celebratery dinner. Totaly ignoring her companions request for a date.[38]

This is intended as pastiche and may be read as parody: genres, as it happens, recommended by Professor Cox, and much used by teachers of writing for as long as anyone can remember. I wonder whether contemporary readers of Mary Anne Evans's story, 'Edward Neville', written when she was fifteen, would have predicted that its author would one day write *Romola*, as George Eliot, let alone, *Middlemarch*.

Edward Neville was the only son of (the) a favourite sister of Henry Marten who (died in giving him birth his father had been the staunch friend of his) had early in life married a staunch friend of her brother's Sir Hugh Neville whose political opinions and sentiments being the same as Martens had ripened a youthful intimacy into the strongest bonds of friendship: but not many months did Julia Neville enjoy the society of her beloved husband he fell in battle within a year after their marriage and his loss so shattered the constitution of his bereaved wife that not long after the brith of her son Edward she (fell) declined slowly into the grave: Edward was immediately taken into the family of his Uncle who having no children of His own, and possessing but little love for his wife, whom fortune alone had induced him to marry, lavished all the love his stern (comp) heart could hold upon his young newphew – [39]

Both pieces of writing show that their young authors are developing an ear for particular genres and styles. George Eliot had clearly read a good deal of Scott, and her biographer, George S. Haight, suggests also that she read and used a book called *An Historical Tour in Monmouthshire* by William Coxe, published in 1801, from which she borrowed actual words and phrases, many of which she then 'touched up'. It is the playing with style and the distance these young writers take on a particular genre which links them; and the pleasure they have in mimicry, in controlling their characters, but also in rewriting, updating, replenishing, satirising.

This is the substance of Anne Turvey's quarrel with the abstractions of curriculum prescription: with the privileging of the 'technologies' or conventions of written English over the pleasures, and the knowing and using of other texts, in the making of your own. The Nathalie she mentions is a black A-level student, whose interventions Turvey discusses elsewhere in her article.

> For a start, what these girls are up to when they read and write romances, is very much *not* part of that whole reductive framework of imperatives – 'shoulds', 'oughts', 'musts', 'will be taughts' – which underpins 'Cox', a deeply embedded network of literary value and hierarchies which wraps students and teachers and classrooms in a cocoon of assessable levels. It is not that Caroline and Rebecca's activities cannot be accounted for by such levels: the accuracy and authentic style of their writing are indeed impressive and I have no doubt I could find the right slot for it in the various Attainment Targets. But its significance for the writers and for any teacher is much more than that and is to be looked for partly in all those complex social relationships central to education. How are these two girls positioned in relation to their families, to each other, to their all-girls' school in East London, to the English classroom, and crucially, how does their writing relate to these questions, questions which ought to be central to this soi-disant 'national' curriculum? Caroline, a black girl who shares some of Nathalie's personal history, reads widely outside the romance genre; Rebecca, who is white, does not . . .
>
> Writing, in school and out, is involved in the ways gender is constructed. It seems likely that a teacher would want to explore with Caroline and Rebecca links between the autobiographical and the romance genres which are, on the surface, such different modes. Both

forms offer the writer opportunities for reflection and critique, as well as a sense of independence and control.[40]

It is not difficult to see why girls might prosper with teaching like that: teaching which took them seriously as readers and writers and which exposed the pitfalls inherent in the peddling of supposedly impermeable and superior forms and values as somehow transcendent ones. Such teaching is not the consequence of chance 'good practice', but part of what is by now a carefully theorised account of language and learning and teaching. In offering a challenge to the reduction of English teaching to no more than a set of methods and procedures, Tony Burgess argues that

> once language is seen as an aspect of people's personal and social practice, as being crucial to their experience in lived and living history, technologies of whatever kind recede. Teaching itself becomes handmaiden or critic to wider processes. The technologies are subordinate to what may be constructed in active, committed and shared classroom encounters and to ways in which these moments in people's lives may be described and theorised.[41]

The difference, as Burgess expresses it, is between an abstract and a historical or organic view of language. It is between an English 'projected not merely as a foreign language, but as actually no longer spoken, and surviving, like Latin and Greek, only in written and in school-mediated forms', on the one hand, and 'an advocacy for what children collectively and individually make [that] is not divided from a critical investigation of the cultural processes which they inhabit',[42] on the other. It is a massive shift, and one which cannot be said to have had much of a hearing in recent years in all the debate round English and the National Curriculum. An emphasis on language and on learning makes for discomfort amongst those who would rather itemise what a curriculum should contain than consider how children are to come to terms with the hermetic and excluding traditions embedded in school subjects. The shift entails starting from difference: from the languages and cultures children bring with them to school. For girls, it will mean an understanding of the conflicting fictions they are subjected to and amongst which they will make their way.

Yet there is always more to it than that. For if girls have taken to reading and writing, and have – at least recently – been encouraged to exploit literacy for their own ends, there remains the likelihood that easing the entry of girls and women into certain kinds of public language – off-the-cuff speech-making, for instance, or stand-up comedy – continues to be difficult. That is not because girls are unable to manage such forms, but because of social arrangements which make entry into such activities in the real world difficult, if not impossible, for them. Some might say that it is, after all, difficult, if not impossible, to ease anyone's entry into literary language too, and that most people who write can only do so if they are clear about the possible positions they may plausibly occupy in relation to an established industry of letters. Women writers and writers in English from India, Africa and the West Indies, for instance, have often testified to their struggle to achieve some sort of accommodation with the exclusions performed on them by the public language of English literature.[43]

The Irish poet, Tom Paulin, demonstrates one version of this in his essay, 'Writing beyond Writing: Emily Dickinson', through an exploration of how 'Dickinson's eruptive, intense vernacular challenges the way in which men use language as a means of achieving and consolidating power'. He goes on,

> only seven of Dickinson's poems were published during her lifetime; it is probable that her dislike of seeing them become printed texts was partly caused by a wish never to see them subordinated to male editorial control. As a

puritan she is hostile to the formal tyranny of print: it arrests the intense process of letter-writing and speech. Although Dickinson shares a vernacular aesthetic with Robert Frost – a consuming worship of speech-sounds – she appears to have viewed letter-writing as superior to speech because of the spoken word's debt to 'attitude and accent'. A letter 'always feels to me like immortality because it is the mind alone without corporeal friend'.[44]

That straining between the sounds and rhythms of speech and the subordinations and the soaring abstractions produced by its public, written presentation may be read as gendered. There are ways in which it also characterises the aggressive invasion of written English which many post-colonial writers feel bound to make, from the vantage point of their own spoken language and its disparaged local energies.

A similar duality could be said to organise Dorothy Richardson's vast novel, *Pilgrimage*. For women, the novel asserts, language is always either a battlefield or a negotiating table. At the least, Richardson's novel may be thought of as an attempt to drown out 'the man's hilarious expostulating narrative voice'[45] in favour of a last-ditch countering of the fat woman Richardson's heroine sees at a concert, who is 'two-thirds of the way through a life that had been a ceaseless stream of events set in a ceaseless stream of inadequate commentary without and within'.[46] Men may have hijacked writing and narrative, and they are always 'talking *about* people and things',[47] but women cannot afford simply to turn and run. For the history of men commandeering language is also the only history of language that women have. They cannot easily break free if that has been their history too; and to deny that history and invent another which is not theirs would be feckless and even banal.

Yet Dorothy Richardson's novel narrates the battle itself from within a felt failure or incapacity ever quite to deliver 'what is left out' by men in their novels or to offer in its place, 'current existence, the ultimate astonisher'. Miriam Henderson will move between resentful acceptance that 'if you can speak of a thing, it is past . . . Speaking makes it glow with a life that is not its own'[48] and those marvellous moments when she registers 'years falling into words, dropping like fruit'.[49] Richardson records her heroine's struggle for a language which might just begin to be adequate to an experience submerged beneath the postures of support or acquiescence women have learned to adopt in relation to men. An efficient secretary could be said to embody the language proficiency men have required of women. Dorothy Richardson demands more, and so do English teachers. From 'the convention that kept urbane women alert at the front gates of consciousness to guard the ease of men waiting to be set going on their topics'[50] – women as greyhound handlers – women must move on towards a language which will carry and exploit their ambivalence, their uncertainty and the peculiar brilliance of their contributions in the past and now to both literature and education.

8

Hirelings and Pedagogues

Imagine the teacher who, as both student and researcher, assembles her own intellectual history in the interests of a theoretical and reflective project about learning and teaching. That is not, by and large, something women teachers are much encouraged to do, though such things are beginning to happen. Such a teacher puts herself in touch with a line of narratives about female education, which runs more or less uninterruptedly from the middle of the eighteenth century to the present day and from, for example, Samuel Richardson's *Pamela* to Alice Walker's *The Color Purple*. In envisaging such a continuity, indeed such community, I need to admit to trip-wires and contradictions. For what, in some lights, may look like a common enterprise or even a single, but endlessly reworked, narrative, has also to be understood in relation to alternative and usually male accounts of what a young woman's moral, physical and mental development might be and the education that might be thought necessary to support it. We are also dealing here with diverse traditions of fiction, memoir and commentary, and with a number of attempts to define the meaning of those traditions for women.

Ellen Moers, the American critic, once identified as a central component of a possible women's literary tradition the use novelists have made of the pedagogic relation between an older and a younger woman, and the twin postures of teacher and taught, which she saw as characterising the development of the heroine herself in most nineteenth-century women's novels.[1] I suppose that Jane Austen's *Emma* might be thought of as exemplary. Moers argued this with bravura. And that heroine, who is, during the course of the novel, both student and pedagogue, stands for the rich possibilities that exist for women to grow and learn within the domestic setting, as an alternative to formal schooling, where teachers are paid to teach. The literary version of education in the family derives from the realities of bourgeois and aristocratic life up to at least the middle of the nineteenth century, and it is seen by Moers as the guaranteed model for all female development, and as one which has been used by novelists as separated in time and space as, say, Jane Austen and Willa Cather.

It is true that some such ideal of female education has sustained and fortified women – teachers amongst them – not least because it relied on notions of a specifically women's culture and reflected recognisable aspects of family life. It has also been adapted by writers of school stories as a way of interpreting the otherwise arcane rituals of school, and especially boarding school. But because it has been allowed to survive as an ideal beyond its historical time, it has also worked to undermine those women who, for whatever reason, have been paid to teach in schools or in family schoolrooms. Moers makes no bones about this. 'The educating heroine is a domestic figure, not a hireling; she teaches in the home, and it looks very like a palace.'[2] Such patrician imagining of what education has been, is, and ought to be for most girls relies on memories of some genuine grandee educationalists; and I will come to them. And it works to romanticise the mother as a girl's first, and best, teacher, even where the home is not a palace. But it also disparages in the process the efforts of those women who became schoolteachers, the 'hirelings' Moers drives out of her heroine tradition, and also the potential of those women and others as readers and writers within the literary tradition she is marking out.

Terry Lovell makes another kind of connection between teaching and writing, when she remarks that 'so many women novelists in the nineteenth century and earlier were the daughters of clergymen' and that for women of this class the only occupation outside marriage was as governess or writer, so that the business of both could seem interchangeable.[3] *Pamela* and *The Color Purple* share aspects of both sorts of lineage, though they also possess another one. For both novels are concerned with the destinies made possible for poor girls by the acquisition of literacy and, therefore, of education. And they could also be said to initiate and contribute to a line of narratives, which recount their own construction and their narrators' gathering mastery of literacy, for purposes which are revealed through the process of learning to use written language. Both novels are – and surely not incidentally – written within Protestant communities, which link literacy with the Church, and both are written as a series of letters by women who have little reason to expect that their missives will either reach their destination or get a reading, let alone an answer.

Yet there are, of course, a number of vital ambiguities in such assertions of continuity, for not only was *Pamela* written by a man, it was written within a history of men providing the 'theory' and the principles of good teaching and good child care, as aspects of a belief that child-rearing could be managed scientifically and rationally, preferably within the family and preferably by men. The edifying narrative, written by a woman, to which so much women's writing alludes, was quite likely to be written by a man. And though both novels deal with the education of a poor girl, they emphatically do so outside any formal educational setting, and firmly within the home. So that both novels fulfil in this sense Ellen Moers's conception of 'educating heroinism'.

Jane Roland Martin, an American philosopher of education, provides another historical perspective on this separation of formal from informal schooling. She starts from the writings of both Rousseau and Pestalozzi and the educational regimes they proposed for girls, in the persons, respectively, of Sophie and Gertrude.[4] In 'Excluding Women from the Educational Realm', Martin shows how much twentieth-century philosophy of education has continued to exclude the education of women from its own history and arguments; and, even more significantly, how it has defined teaching as being precisely *not* what children learn from their mothers.[5] What she characterises as the analytic philosophy of an educationalist like Richard Peters, with its focus on the necessary 'voluntariness' and 'intentionality' of educational procedures, casts doubt on what mothers teach their children as *teaching*.

So that, as she puts it, 'the definition of education used by analytic philosophers today excludes the teaching, the training, and the socialization of children for which women throughout history have had prime responsibility'.[6] This emphasis, she suggests, relies on the absolute separation of traditional intellectual disciplines from all the things which, for instance, Rousseau ordains that Sophie should know about and from Pestalozzi's insistence that education had much to learn from Gertrude's bringing up of her own child. That emphasis also excludes from its definition of education, transactions between adult and child which do not involve a level of intentionality in the teacher and elements of voluntariness and formal comprehension in the learner. This bias goes beyond even the marginalisation of mother and child interaction. It departs from the unequivocal 'fairness' of Socrates on these issues, and from his concern for the public good. And it remains resolutely deaf to the voices and the contributions of women teachers and thinkers themselves. Not only are we denied the particular character of Wollstonecraft's quarrel with Rousseau, for instance, as a valuable contribution to discussion of such issues; her argument, when it is alluded to, is distorted, and removed from the larger social purposes of her *Vindication of the Rights of Woman*. Socrates expresses his views about women's education and work within an attempt to envisage a just society:

If, then, we find that either the male sex or the female is specially qualified for any particular form of occupation, then that occupation, we shall say, ought to be assigned to one sex or the other. But if the only difference appears to be that the male begets and the female brings forth, we shall conclude that no difference between man and woman has yet been produced that is relevant to our purpose. We shall continue to think it proper for our Guardians and their wives to share in the same pursuits.[7]

Similarly, Wollstonecraft argues for women's education in the interests of a rationally organised world and the possibility of more productive lives for men as well as women. And she accuses Rousseau of sacrificing such possibilities to men's transient sexual desire for young women, with results as disadvantageous for men as for women.

But according to the tenor of reasoning by which women are kept from the tree of knowledge, the important years of youth, the usefulness of age, and the rational hopes of futurity, are all to be sacrificed to render women an object of desire for a *short* time. Besides, how could Rousseau expect them to be virtuous and constant when reason is neither allowed to be the foundation of their virtue, nor truth the object of their inquiries?[8]

The consequences of such a bias, Martin suggests, so far as what counts as education is concerned and the exclusion from view of women as teachers and learners, are extravagantly falsifying.

When the experience of women is neither reflected nor interpreted in the texts and anthologies of the history of educational philosophy, women are given no opportunity to understand and evaluate the range of ideals – from Plato's guardians to Sophie and Gertrude – that the great thinkers of the past have held for them. When Wollstonecraft and Montessori are ignored in

these texts, students of both sexes are denied contact
with the great female minds of the past; indeed, they are
denied the knowledge that women have ever thought
seriously and systematically about education.[9]

I shall suggest in this chapter that women's participation
in the education of children, as mothers and as teachers,
has been consistently manipulated and misrepresented, not
least through a deliberate blurring of those roles. In the final
chapter, I shall demonstrate what I think of as the scope
of new narratives produced by teachers. These have made it
possible for women teachers to acknowledge and then
counter the dominance of a male theoretical discourse and the
uncomfortable reinforcements to that discourse issuing from
a female and aristocratic commentary, which has incongru-
ously (and I would like to think, inadvertently) survived to
query the role as well as the competence of paid teachers.
These new narratives are able to challenge both of these
entrenched and hugely influential visions and to confront some
perhaps irreconcilable contradictions inherited from them.
Before that, however, I need to return to further examples of
disagreement amongst women themselves about their own
education and its purposes, and to the possibilities there have
been for women to participate in intellectual life.

Throughout the years when groups of women, with the
assistance of a few men, were campaigning to expand education for girls, at first into forms of secondary schooling which
would approximate to the best boys' schools, in terms of
breadth and depth of curriculum, and then towards entry to
colleges and universities, there were always some women
who sought or hoped for absolute equality with men and
rejected all patronising offers of handicap arrangements, at
least for middle-class girls. This produced conflict with certain
reformers: for example, those who, led by Henry Sidgwick,
were working to improve the quality of education at

Cambridge and to extend access to women at the same time. Emily Davis and her supporters in the 1860s were convinced that if women were ever to ask for different conditions of study or assessment from men, on whatever grounds, it would be interpreted publicly as a sop to women's inferior intellects and nothing to do with reform.[10]

There were by the 1870s more and more women who wanted an advanced education and a validation of that education, in order to work in the professions which had barred them entry: medicine, the law, the civil service, university teaching, and so on. They were not to be fobbed off any longer with acquiring accomplishments, with amateur status or grateful discipleship. Their single-mindedness worked to break down barriers and to foster talent, of course, but also to deter the fainter-hearted majority, who might still hope to combine traditionally feminine ways of living with something rather less than professional parity with men. Again, we have to find ways of understanding the tensions and the contradictions for many of the women in this history. How were they to reconcile their own immediate educational needs, interests and capacities with those standards developed within educational institutions as something like a function of their exclusion of women? It has always been difficult for women to combine their often lonely invasion of male bastions with a political analysis, let alone a political activism, on behalf of other women: whether those who still chose to remain outside such enclaves, or those who had difficulty storming them on the terms especially designed to keep them (and most men, after all) out. Joining entails accepting the rules for doing so, and 'handicap' in this context is likely to have several and opposite meanings, after all.

In *Daniel Deronda*, George Eliot's last great novel, published between 1874 and 1876, at a time when women had started at last to study for degrees at Cambridge (though not officially as members of the university), she explores this predicament. She does so, not in terms of education, but in terms of talent, paid work and marriage, and of the persistant reality that women could not expect to earn a living in any area where there was likely to be strong male competition and professional supervision. It is clear that George Eliot is delivering a forked and canny warning against female hubris. The maestro Klesmer's condescension towards Gwendolen's pleasant, unsophisticated musical talents, and her speedily doused ambition to earn her living by them in order to support her family, is set alongside the only possible solution he envisages to her problem, and indeed to the problem presented by even the better disciplined talents of the heiress, Catherine Arrowpoint. Gwendolen Harleth is advised to marry instead: which she does, unwisely and unhappily. So, as it happens, does Miss Arrowpoint. She marries her master, Herr Klesmer himself; for marriage to a master was always the most desired, if not the most often achieved, career for a clever girl.

Yet these are not offered as satisfactory solutions, though they are each in their way seen as unavoidable ones. And they are returned to later in the novel, when Deronda finally tracks down his absentee mother, who has been an internationally celebrated singer and actress, and is now in her old age prepared to admit to the 'unnaturalness' of her life. Yet, as she explains to her son, 'you can never imagine what it is to have a man's force of genius in you, and yet to suffer the slavery of being a girl'. Daniel has learned his lesson. Mirah, whom he eventually marries, is possessed of an amateur and domesticable talent, which she is ready to relinquish as soon as she is married to him.[11]

Such ambivalence, for which Eliot has sometimes been arraigned, most memorably by Doris Lessing, signals the importance of this question to the moral worlds inhabited by Eliot's heroines.[12] All her novels deal with the possible lives of clever women, of women who are in some sense like George Eliot herself. Maggie learns as a child that she must repress her own intelligence. Dorothea escapes from her withered scholar, Casaubon, whom she had hoped to sustain and urge on, into the arms of his young and sexually interesting cousin, Will Ladislaw, and to a potentially happy marriage, though it is one that is looked at askance by her friends.

Romola's translation from amanuensis to her blind, scholarly father to wife of the corrupt but also glamorously clever Tito, is overlaid by the condescension and exploitation meted out to her – differently – by both men. In the process, she gains an equivocal sense of the quality and the purposes of male scholarship, and of the passivity enjoined on her by her secretarial role. Against the narrowness and self-referential character of so much of the learning and the religious debate she encounters, she finally comes to adopt the saintly and pedagogic persona of the wise patrician woman, though

> she had no innate taste for tending the sick and clothing the ragged, like some women to whom the details of such work are welcome in themselves, simply as an occupation. Her early training had kept her aloof from such womanly labours; and if she had not brought to them the inspiration of her deepest feelings, they would have been irksome to her. But they had come to be the one unshaken resting-place of her mind, the one narrow pathway on which the light fell clear.[13]

Romola's training has made her what we might now call a research assistant. Her intellectual interests, her knowledge and her skills as an archivist make her a scholar's dogsbody rather than a scholar. Without her father and her husband, and wrenched from the duties she has performed for them, she is left with no occupation and no role. George Eliot also means us to understand that nothing can compensate a woman for the absence or loss of a love relation with a man. Romola's search for an alternative, whether through participation in men's intellectual work, or in the religious life, does not disguise this truth from her.

> There is no compensation for the woman who feels that
> the chief relation of her life has been no more than a
> mistake. She has lost her crown. The deepest secret of
> human blessedness has half whispered itself to her, and
> then for ever passed her by.[14]

Talent, professional ambition, a sense of worth: these were
released and realised for many women by education, though
never unproblematically, never without trouble. For professional fulfilment was usually undermined by the expectation
(and in many cases the ruling, as we have seen) that such
women would not marry or have children; that they would
earn less than men, retire earlier and on lower pensions (if
any); and bear with fewer opportunities for promotion or
responsibility, or for exercising influence or power.

Pamela has been lovingly recovered in recent years as the
embodiment of one kind of female ordeal and progress
through life, from teenage servant to wife of Mr B, mother
of 'seven fine children, five sons and two daughters', to final
intrepid pedagogue. It is a progress recorded and attended by
texts, and as Carolyn Steedman has put it, 'all we laugh at in
Pamela is contained within the narrative she gives us of
herself',[15] though we can never know whether Richardson,
let alone Pamela, knew just how funny some readers might
find it. Eventually, she will do more than produce her own
story in the letters she writes to her parents and friends, she
will consult and comment on texts herself: most famously,
John Locke's *Treatise on Education*.[16] This, placed in her
hands by her husband, she will summarise and submit to
some intelligent practical criticism, particularly on the subject
of how to bring up the sons of the upper classes, for whom
it was intended.

   The notion that this task might be performed by a woman
was not, as it happens, unheard of in the second half of the
eighteenth century. Madame de Genlis, who was born in

France in 1746, only four years after the publication of *Pamela*, is sometimes described as 'the first woman teacher' and even 'the first woman to have a writing desk'[17]: claims suggesting an aristocratic disdain for the activities of middle-class and working-class women in these areas, rather than attested fact, I should think. In fact, Ellen Moers makes Madame de Genlis the emblematic figure of her chapter, 'Educating Heroinism: Governess to Governor',

> In the Genlis world, adulthood succeeds to childhood, and childhood to the principal function of adulthood – the teaching of children – with an astonishing rapidity due not to fantasy but to fact: the very early marriages of aristocratic women in her day.[18]

Madame de Genlis became the mistress of the Duc de Chartres (later to acquire the ambiguous sobriquet, Philippe Egalité) not long after her marriage, and he appointed her governess (the position she occupied was, in fact, as *Gouverneur* rather than *Gouvernante*) of his two daughters and his two older sons. She ran a small school for the royal children and for her own, for which she was handsomely paid, and she became well known for her regime and her pedagogy – which were based partly on the principles of Rousseau, but also in opposition to some of them – and for the huge number of books, many of them novels, she wrote on education. She named the illegitimate daughter she had by the Duke, Pamela, which cannot have been a coincidence; and when, in her old age, she was asked whether teaching 'had been a passion' with her, she loftily replied that 'it has always bored me, but now that I am old it is the only way that I can do any good'.[19] It is a story which it is hard not to read as yet another offshoot of *Pamela*.

In Richardson's novel, Pamela's letters tell the story of her courage and ingenuity in successfully outwitting the seducer she secretly loves and wishes to marry, but as a virgin. Of course, Pamela has often been found foolish as well as a heroine, and devious as well as cunning: it is not merely that her victory could be read as Pyrrhic, but that it has been fixed beforehand, so that her good sense and literacy skills may be repaid and put to maximum use by both husband and creator. She will, as patient and exemplary Griselda, tolerate and survive her husband's adulterous skirmishes and live to regard herself as having spent a useful life: her children, as her 'editor' writes,

> being educated, in every respect, by the rules of their inimitable mother, laid down in that book which she mentions to have been written by her for the revisal and correction of her consort; the contents of which may be gathered from her remarks upon Mr Locke's *Treatise on Education*.[20]

In a novel that was often one of the few books owned by Flora Thompson's villagers in the 1880s, a poor village girl becomes first servant and then student of a benevolent upper-class woman. We follow Pamela from there into her life as mother and unpaid teacher of her own children and from there to unpaid teacher of generations of other women. Pamela has in the process written a novel and an educational textbook, as Madame de Genlis would later do. She has also provided sport for her future husband and sport for a literary tradition which mocks her artlessness and wonders at Richardson's designs on her. As in every sense a 'best-seller', she is often read as Richardson's *alter ego* (her class and gender standing in for Richardson's sensitivity about his own lower middle-class origins), or as the unmediated voice of virtuous English womanhood, permanently under siege.

That *Pamela* and, indeed, Pamela, are texts about texts has helped to draw contemporary readers back to a novel which has been at least as often mocked and parodied as it has been admired. Mr B's designs on Pamela are also Richardson's: for both are grappling with the understandings and the secrets her letters contain; with what she learns and knows; with the possibility that all this writing may go too far, take her beyond herself and out of their control. Both could also be said to be grappling with the bodices and stays that her body and her letters are so ineffectually contained by.

> 'But where are the papers? – I dare say you had them about you yesterday: for you say in those I have, that you will bury your writings in the garden, lest you should be *searched*, if you did not escape. This,' added he, 'gave me a glorious pretence to search you; and I have been vexing myself all night, that I did not strip you garment by garment, till I had found them.'[21]

Pamela's attractions for Mr B. are embodied in her resistance to his determined control over her, and her letters come to represent these attractions literally, as they might be possessed and enjoyed. They also contain coveted and contradictory information: her constant readiness to make a break for it *and* her improbably resilient love for the tiresome Mr B. They 'furnish out a surprising kind of novel':[22] one in which the new 'companionate marriage', as it has been called, is proposed, if under protest: a marriage, that is, in which the husband teaches and tests out the young woman who will become his wife, fashioning her to his own tastes and even making the best of poorish raw material. The excitement set up in this new young woman by glimpses of independence, promised as the fruits of her education, become a form of heightened sexual provocation for Mr B., who may in this be seen as a precursor of all those champions of the 'new woman' in the late nineteenth-century – Meredith, Gissing, Wells, for instance – who saw that they had everything to gain from the freely-given submission of intelligent, well-educated women.

The novel also makes it clear that this young woman's adventure, indeed her education, may go so far, but no farther. These are not adventures or education for their own sake, or for hers, but a carefully regulated preparation for marriage and motherhood and child-rearing. It is a training overseen, monitored, corrected and evaluated in the interests of burnishing a young woman's services to men; and *Pamela*'s charms lie in the novel's seamless ventriloquism, in its manner of disguising these male injunctions, in the breathless, tripping delivery invented to persuade us that this girl is speaking her mind for us. Most men of Richardson's class were less inclined to wrap their plans for women in such tropes and disguises.

John Dobson and Eliza Barker, who were cousins, got married on 30 June 1810. They wrote to each other frequently throughout the four years leading to their marriage. John's letters survive, presumably because Eliza kept them. Hers to him do not, though later ones written to her sister, Mary, do still exist. Clara Collet, John and Eliza's granddaughter, pruned and privately published John's letters to his future bride, calling them, with characteristic edge, *The Letters of John to Eliza. A Four Years' Correspondence Course in the Education of Women. 1806–1810.*[23]

Sometimes, in fact, John's letters read like love letters (of a rather anxious kind, it is true, for he clearly wondered at times whether his future bride was quite good enough for him) to the eighteen-year-old cousin whom he was preparing for marriage to him. He wrote as a hopeful young businessman of twenty-seven, trying to establish himself in shipping and overseas trade. His sermon to this young woman is a good deal more practical and down-to-earth than James Fordyce's. As he expressed it, with delightfully egotistical logic, 'It is only in the event that you can avail yourself of opportunities to cultivate your mind, that I can rationally hope to make you permanently happy.'[24] He was, after all, writing to a young teacher; for Eliza and her sister Mary, who was four years younger than she was, were assistant teachers at Miss Devall's school in Sloane Street, Chelsea. This did not encourage John to regard Eliza as in any way his equal, however, and he was not reticent in offering his advice on virtually every aspect of her life: on shoes and hats and dresses; on health and the benefits of walks and dancing; on grammar, style and usage; on travel; on how to negotiate a pay rise without looking greedy; and on the miracles of inoculation. He assumed that she would have a globe or atlas as well as a dictionary by her side at all times, and particularly while she read his letters. It was her duty to teach the children in her school, as he saw it, and his to teach her. His letters may be read, as his granddaughter suggests, as a textbook, and Eliza seems sometimes to have found them wearisome. They came accompanied by books and papers and magazines – the *Edinburgh Review* and the *Weekly Messenger*, for instance – and always there were detailed instructions about *how* to read and about the good that will come from doing so. He sent her Maria Edgeworth's stories.

Keep them by you dear Girl, and now and then *when your heart* is so disposed read *one* of them. I send the Popular Tales with them which are also as excellent as the others. I have added two small volumes of poetry by Bowles which you have already seen but which I wish you at your leisure to *enjoy* – do not however in attending to the agreeable, forget the useful – study the Scientific Dialogues with steady and unwearied attention untill you find yourself completely mistress of them. Never take them up when you are not perfectly disposed for them – and never suffer anything to pass until you understand it – *it does not signify how little you acquire at a time provided that be accurately acquired* – do not disturb yourself if you should find you have forgotten what you had once acquired – *it is for a time the case with everybody* – begin again – if you meet with anything you cannot clearly comprehend give me the page and subject and I will try to render it more clear to you.[25]

The pedagogic tone is unrelenting and unacknowledged. John was pleased to think of her becoming a teacher, and admitted that he would never have the patience to work with children himself, whereas 'it is extremely pleasant to me to think of you as interested about children'.[26] He wanted her to dress fashionably and to take an interest in her clothes, but he was certain that 'there is much more Economy in your qualifying yourself to direct the Education of your children should you be blessed with any than there would be in saving the expense of making your new stock of Cloathes'.[27] The connection between her current work and her future responsibilities as a mother was spelled out as he pictured her surrounded by the children she taught, and imagined her, in particular, passing on to them information from the books and newspapers he supplied her with.

> Indeed I do conceive that you might very much increase your powers of usefulness & the interest you would take in many of the articles . . . were you to read them to the children you are fond of. Surely the little Girl who took so much delight in hearing Miss B— talk about Astronomy would love to listen to her – and would you not delight to fill their little minds with truths and drive away those prejudices which you say sometimes disturb you.[28]

Irritated occasionally by her apparent complacency and unwillingness to tell him her innermost thoughts he sometimes criticised her, for 'ludicrous blunders' in her letters, for using 'get' rather than 'become'; and 'that' as an expletive – not in fact, an easy word to utter in a way that is incontrovertibly offensive. Quite early in the correspondence he wrote frankly of his misgivings.

> And to begin – I will confess to you that I am sensible you are deficient in many of those accomplishments which are universally considered of some importance to

a female. You do not sing, or play, or paint, or speak Italian, or write French with fluency – you possess no extraordinary taste in dress – converse very little – are neglectful of the trifling forms & ceremonies which are thought essential in society – and would not shine particularly in cutting up a goose for a large party at the head of your own *table*, nor in doing the general business of it. I am farther sensible that although you have read much, it has been in a desultory manner (without any plan) and that it has consequently *hitherto* been but of little advantage to you. I am aware that you are not a perfect beauty – that there are figures much more graceful than yours is. I know that your constitution is indifferent – that it is such as to incline you naturally to be indolent – and that I must expect you to be frequently unwell . . . I think I hear you almost breathless cry out Stop – and ask me how I ever could have told you 'you were exquisitely dear to me – that I was satisfied with you and that you had more than answered all my expectations?' – I said so, my dear Friend, because I felt it was the truth – and I believe it still.[29]

That final sentiment did not let him off, and this was not the last time that he offended her. It is clear that her letters to him contained eruptions and resentments and tales of other quite interesting admirers. He was upset by this, wrote that he hadn't slept, had even wept. Then he puzzled that though her letters were becoming livelier and he was able to assure her that 'you now possess my perfect approbation and esteem' she was still strangely silent, sullen, shy when they met. But he was also able to congratulate her on the news that at last 'you have qualified yourself to be my friend and my companion'.[30]

Eventually, he would buy a grand piano for her future use, after four years of nagging her to practise, and to practise playing 'good' music rather than bad, indeed 'scientific' music rather than the simple tunes she was used to, by which he appears to have meant the more complex counterpoint of Handel and Haydn. There are harangues on poetry, on taste, on science and mathematics and on reading about foreign affairs. These were the years of Napoleon's dominion over most of Europe, and John's business took him abroad, especially to Malta. Years later, his granddaughter Clara's pretty sparingly used editorial pencil was wielded mainly to amputate some longish tirades on electricity, magnetism and other modern marvels.

The cousins were brought up amongst Unitarians. Indeed, a shared great-grandfather was amongst the earliest of Unitarians in this country.[31] Yet God makes no appearance in John's letters at all, and their wedding, for which John made all the preparations, took place in Chelsea Church: down the road, as it happens, from the house where I have lived for thirty-six years. The couple seem to have been well suited, after all, and six of their children lived to adulthood. But John's business prospered only intermittently, and it seems that his children inherited little and even suffered a drop in their living standards. This may have contributed to the fact that three of them left England to make lives for themselves in New Zealand and Australia. Eliza's younger sister Mary lived to be ninety-three. She did not marry and was loved and emulated by her great-niece Clara, for her intellect and spirit; much preferred indeed to her duller and eventually domesticated sister, Eliza.

Pamela is not one of the novels John recommended to Eliza, though it is difficult to believe that she did not read it anyway. The peculiar wooing she received may well have provided her with an interpretive strategy for reading Richardson which was markedly different from mine or from any recent reading. For in the place of Dobson's unflagging transmission of his own views on matrimony and the duties of women,

Richardson imagined the woman herself and literally gave voice to her as she struggled to become the mother and teacher who would validate – through her enchanting (but also enchanted) submission – the limitations set on her own education, and the efficacy of a regime organised to produce men.

It is possible to trace back a tradition of male advice to women on the principles of modern child care, even within the family of John and Eliza. Fifty years earlier, in 1752 (only twelve years after *Pamela* was published, and still ten years before Rousseau's *Emile* burst upon the world) a great-uncle shared by John and Eliza, called Joseph Collet, wrote three long letters to his future sister-in-law, Sarah Lasswell, apparently in response to her request for his 'Opinion on that most Difficult Subject The Education of Children.'[32] Neither of them had children of their own when the letters were written, so one may presume that experience was not an essential qualification for an exercise of this kind. It seems likely that Joseph (like Pamela) would have read John Locke's *Some Thoughts Concerning Education*, and that his own thoughts were influenced by a need to adumbrate a quite different educational regime, which was not intended for Locke's 'young Gentleman', but for the sons of Dissenting middle-class families.[33] Indeed, the overall tone of the letters suggests that rationality, moderation and good sense are the essential qualities for child-rearing; that education is principally a family responsibility; but that the chief hazards faced by young children are likely to be at the hands of nurses and servants and mothers themselves. Childhood had not yet been marked out as a separate terrain, requiring a specially trained workforce. But whereas Locke is concerned with the figure of the Tutor, Joseph Collet regards the family and especially the father as a boy's principal educators.

The letters move through the years of the child's growing up (and the child is, of course, a boy), so that the first letter takes him to five or six and the establishment of good habits, through kindly persuasion and truthfulness. There will be early formal teaching of the alphabet, numbers, world geography, the reading of moral stories and fables, and a persistent focus on children's developing habits of care, accuracy and attention. Punishment is to be avoided, by and large. It is clear that this is an upbringing designed for children growing up in the Dissenting middle class of the mid-eighteenth century: anti-aristocratic, anti-classical, liberal, and in favour of French and Dutch (the mercantile languages of the period, though an earlier generation of the family put Portuguese before French) rather than Latin and Greek. Latin and Greek are fine for children, Joseph insists, 'if you design them for Law, Physick or Divinity', but certainly not otherwise.

> I could wish our School learning for young Gentlemen from 10 or 12 years of age to their prenticeships was Carry'd on in a Different manner than it is at present, of what use can be their reading Ovid and many other Heathen authors but to Learn their Superstitions, and what Service can all their nonsense of their Gods and Godesses amours, dissensions, Battles &c. be of but only to fill Children's Tender minds with foolish Ideas, Ridiculous fancys, Idle Superstitions and above all (as they are growing to an age so susceptible of and Inclinable to amorous desires) Their Lewd and Wanton Storys must Infallibly tend to the blowing up the Sparks of Lust and Impurity which it is one great design of Education to damp and extinguish; How much better would it be if some books of Christian morality were read in the place of those heathen authors.

However, this education will not be pious, but will serve as a practical preparation for modern life and for business. Children will, for instance, be encouraged to show kindness and generosity to the poor, but must learn early on to distinguish the industrious poor from beggars, to whom they should not give money. The concentration is firmly on boys' education, for it is through boys and then through men as fathers that family order and happiness are to be achieved,

> How Happy is the Father of an Orderly and Well Govern'd Family. He acts as a King in his own house and sees his Laws Chearfully and punctually obey'd, as they are not the effects of meer Arbitrary will and absolute Power but wise, usefull and necessary to the Hapiness of every one of his Children, To Him therefore they readily come to decide any little differences amongst themselves and willingly abide by his determinations because they see his whole concern is to do exact justice to everyone of them and to promote the peace, Harmony and universal Hapiness of them all.

Leisure needs supervision as well, in Joseph's view.

> I could also wish we had better Sports, and Diversions for them than we have at present, especially when they have a whole day for a Holiday or an afternoon. It is to long for the young folks to be entirely left to themselves, to play at Cricket or worse Games, I should rather like their taking a walk into the feilds and forming themselves into knots or little Companys engage in Conversation on some moral subjects.

By the age of ten or eleven – and the third letter confirms this – the overall purpose of education is set towards the future, when the young 'must soon quit their fathers House and go into the wide World, the young men to their prenticeship and the young ladys to be mistresses of familys Themselves'. And these families are the model of order and sense, with the father presiding as inspiration for, and regulator of, a regime of relative permissiveness. The historian, Rosalind Mitchison, once put a helpful gloss on the notion that by the middle of the eighteenth century there had been a rise in both individualism and permissiveness.

Individualism may mean permissiveness. In the reaction
to both formalism and puritanism it often did. But it
could also mean the expression of the personality of the
father at the expense of everyone else . . . The private
person with whom Locke's political thought was
concerned was an adult male landowner. No one else
counted as an individual, certainly not a servant, an
employee, a woman. Some of the finest sentiments
about liberty of the individual and the rights of man can
be culled from the papers of the Scottish judge, Lord
Grange. 'It cannot be agreeable to the Use for which
God design'd Creatures . . . to be Slaves subjected
to the absolute Arbitrary Power and Pleasure of one
or more', he wrote. Yet when his wife became tiresome
to him she was, at his instigation, kidnapped by
Highlanders and carried off to St. Kilda. We should not
accuse Lord Grange of hypocrisy, merely of a narrow
idea of which of God's 'Creatures' did have rights. If
daughters were allowed to express a choice in marriage
partners in the eighteenth century, or wives to regard
themselves as companions, this was so long, and only
so long, as it pleased the head of the family.[34]

Joseph Collet, as a man of his time, did not altogether ignore
the education of girls. A final image reverberates for me with
many of the themes of this book.

Where there are several young Ladies in a family it is a
very Good Method to let the Eldest read for an Hour
whilst the rest work and then the Second take it for
another hour and the eldest sit down to work, and so
on till each has read Her hour, Thus they'll Improve in
reading and working at once, and have food for the
mind as well as Employment for the hands, and when
your son is at home and can be spared from other
Studys or bussiness, Let him read to them (as of an
Evening) whilst all the Ladies work, The books to be

Chosen are such as will both divert and Instruct as Telemachus and the Travels of Cyrus, Love makes a Man, the Provoked Husband, and Cato are the best Romances and plays I know of, but I should be very Carefull of these sort of books, Good History, as Prideauxs Connection of ye old and New Testamts; Echards Eclesiastical History, Rollins Roman and Antient History, Rapins History of England &c. are what I should prefer, as giving us a real account of things and not filling the mind with foolish Romantick Ideas, without any foundation in truth, but of all books for young Ladies I prefer the Spectators Tatlers and Guardians, as soon as ever they are Capable of understanding them.[35]

Carefully circumscribed and marked out here are the circumstances and purposes of a woman's education, the uses to which it might be put, its domestication within the family, and a sense of reading as accompaniment to useful activity, rather than as an end in itself. There is the separation of the male and female economies of space and time: the time spent or wasted by women compared with the time used profitably by men. Even the care of young children, if it is to be taken seriously, is best performed by men.

It is not surprising to learn that the Infant School Society, set up in the first quarter of the nineteenth century to remedy what were seen as the dangers and the deprivations suffered by working-class children in cities, should have insisted that these children be taught by men from their earliest years. As Karen Clarke has pointed out, 'almost all the authors of the books on infant schools were men who were themselves masters of infant schools'.[36] She quotes the rationale that was offered for this by a certain David Stow, in 1839.

After the family order of father and mother, there ought to be a man at the head of every juvenile and infant training school, and when practicable, his wife or sister ought to be an assistant. This proposal to carry the family system into school is not to supersede parental training at home, but to assist and strengthen it.[37]

I have been diverted – in more ways than one – by these men's educational bulletins from the mid-eighteenth century and the early nineteenth century away from the stories women have told about their own lives and learning; and it is to these I shall return in the next chapter. I think it is a necessary diversion, however, since the continuities I have gestured towards from *Pamela* to *The Color Purple* or the novels of Toni Morrison are at least partly defined by the equivocations they contain and by the transvestism that is apparent in those novels and in many others. And then the defining of childhood as a separate terrain, with its own needs and character, brought with it demands for schooling, as a process apart from the family. Gradually, and reluctantly it might be said, such demands came to be made on behalf of all children. And though at first the belief prevailed that men were the best teachers for even the youngest children, this gave way, finally, to an equally grudging acknowledgement that women, first as mothers, then as teachers, would be required willy-nilly to take responsibility for a good deal of child-rearing in schools as well as in the home. That history has left its traces in the ambiguities women teachers express about their role in schools even today: their uneasiness as educational theorists; their backing into pastoral positions in schools; and their frequent reluctance to name and stand by their authority, knowledge and expertise as teachers. Just as Ellen Moers could trace a tradition in which a girl's education was firmly contained within the boundaries of domesticity, so there is a contrary tradition, which has defined education as specialised precisely in opposition to the maternal relation.

Current views on childhood tend to focus on the breakdown of families and the inability of schools to compensate for that breakdown. It is a scenario which finds double fault, as it were, with women's presence, while regretting men's absence, in families and classrooms. And even though it has often been pointed out that family breakdown in the past, caused most often by poverty and the early death of parents, was scarcely less frequent or damaging than it is today, the sense of crisis in our conception of what childhood is has returned us to the inadequacies of women, whether as mothers on their own or as teachers of children who are badly in need of fathers and father figures.

The total collapse of family order in *The Color Purple*, produced by demoralisation in the context of the extreme racism and poverty undermining black family and community life in the American South between the wars, is the starting point for a novel of redemption. Alice Walker's novel rewrites the class inequalities of *Pamela* for the second half of the twentieth century, in terms of the wholesale depredations of racism and poverty. Celie's first letter, written when she is fourteen, is addressed to God and asks for 'a sign letting me know what is happening to me'.[38] God does not reply to her letters. Yet by the end of the novel Celie has developed a written language, capable of expressing her new knowledge and confidence, which is speculative, critical, humorous and, ultimately, creative and optimistic. Her sister Nettie becomes a missionary in Africa and writes letters to Celie, which are intercepted by Celie's husband and never delivered. Since neither God nor boys, as we shall see, much 'like girls' stories' literacy does not, cannot (any more than religion can) liberate Pamela or Celie or the narrators of hundreds of other novels from the particular social and cultural deprivations of their time and place. But literacy is equivalent to education in such women's narratives, and it does expose the character of those deprivations and even provide ways of demonstrating some of the underlying causes of inequality and oppression. It also recovers for Celie her family and some control over her own life, while releasing her creativity (she makes trousers by the dozen and in every conceivable shape and colour) and her capacity for sexual pleasure, with a woman.

In the next chapter I shall be considering the stories teachers may come to tell about their work and their lives. As teachers, they are in a position to become expert listeners to children, and expert readers of their narratives. The ambiguities of teachers' own position may encourage an interest in and a responsiveness to other kinds of narrative which are incomplete, or unresolved, or peripheral, or even submerged. There is no doubt that in recent years the stories of black women writers have come to mean a great deal to some of these teachers, partly because such stories are implicated in the problems their students have in developing fictions of their own within the coercions of those promoted by the dominant culture. But teachers have also to recognise that they are themselves implicated, and less benignly than that, in these fictions. For schools and teachers are part of the stories of damage and deafness that Toni Morrison tells, and not a beneficent part. For instance, she starts her first novel *The Bluest Eye* – about young Afro-American girls growing up in a Midwestern ghetto of the 1940s – from the mindless triumphalism of a child's first Reader encountered in school.

> Here is the house. It is green and white. It has a red door. It is very pretty. Here is the family. Mother, Father, Dick, and Jane live in the green-and-white house. They are very happy.[39]

And so on. As Morrison marvellously hustles the Reader's blithely neat and empty sentences towards what must be their pernicious nonsense for any poor black child growing up in an urban ghetto, we experience the language as dangerously snarled and tangled. It is as if schooling and learning to read spell out with idiotic finality the chasm between the 'normality' of a white childhood and the 'pathology' of a black one. And later, in *Beloved*, that chasm is still more graphically exposed, when Paul D learns about Sethe's infanticide from a newspaper clipping he can't actually read,

> Paul D slid the clipping out from under Stamp's palm. The print meant nothing to him so he didn't even glance at it. He simply looked at the face, shaking his head no. No. At the mouth, you see. And no at whatever it was those black scratches said, and no to whatever it was Stamp Paid wanted him to know. Because there was no way in hell a black face could appear in a newspaper if the story was about something anybody wanted to hear. A whip of fear broke through the heart chambers as soon as you saw a Negro's face in a paper, since the face was not there because the person had a healthy baby, or outran a street mob. Nor was it there because the person had been killed, or maimed or caught or burned or jailed or whipped or evicted or stomped or raped or cheated, since that could hardly qualify as news in a newspaper. It would have to be something out of the ordinary – something whitepeople would find interesting, truly different, worth a few minutes of teeth sucking if not gasps. And it must have been hard to find news about Negroes worth the breath catch of a white citizen of Cincinnati.[40]

I find it hard to think of any writing which conveys more exactly than this the solid reality of a world in which literacy and its uses may come to hold and stand in for such extremes of ambiguity and tension.

9

Stories of Hope and Disappointment

Stammerers and stutterers have been known to repair to writing as to a haven, avoiding not so much the drawbacks of speech as of conversation. There are women who have made that sort of a move, and for most of their lives. One eighty-year-old woman explained to her daughter,

> I think personal writing and letter writing is more a woman's occupation. I think men find it difficult to listen, and often women themselves can't imagine that anyone will listen to them, so they write their thoughts down instead . . . I was the only girl with four brothers and I think I had a need to express myself and to be heard. It's the same now in the church. The influence of the men is so ingrained and so unconscious and it's hard. Even the men's voices are louder so they prevail in meetings. If two people start to speak and one is a man, the man's voice will be the one that is heard unless you have a very sensitive chairman.[1]

The business of writing, whether in a classroom or outside it, certainly includes its own hiccups, but it can be performed within some sort of insulation, even uninterruptedly, and there is no question that girls have seen the point of it more readily than boys, and that women continue to do it, usually for their own purposes, long after most men have given it up.

Yet the appropriation of writing by girls and by women
for their own purposes must be set within the realities of
writing in society. These include the specialising of most
genres and the reifying of the formal conventions that have
been historically developed round most kinds of written text.
The institutions for standardising and evaluating writing
– publishing and reviewing, for instance, and even examining,
whether in schools or universities – are mostly under male
control. Writing by women has passed the various gate-
keepers so long as it conformed to such standards. It is, as
Terry Lovell has put it, 'woman-to-woman writing which
is excluded'.[2] Yet, as I have begun to argue, there is a long
history of private or domestic writing performed by women.
Indeed, one of the themes which is apt to erupt within
current disagreements about the teaching of literacy in school
is that this private or domestic kind of writing is allowed to
prevail as a model, at least in the early years of schooling, at
the expense of more practical, instrumental uses of writing,
which are thought to be required by the modern industrial
world.[3]

In making claims – as many feminist teachers have done
– for autobiography as a necessary form for women and as a
challenge to conventional kinds of academic writing, it is
important to start from the problems of doing so. For the
published autobiography is still more likely to be male than
female, and is still likely to derive from a life valued in terms
of its public achievements according to one of a number of
relatively conventional trajectories through life. Many men's
autobiographies have generic titles like 'A Life', 'Childhood',
'Boyhood and Youth', 'Confessions', 'Diaries', even 'Our
Age', which deliberately allude to the shared, recognisable
character of the life that has been written and the shape
which the story of that life can be expected to take. Women
are not always able to find themselves within such at least
rhetorically asserted versions of common experience, or if
they do it will be in one of several split or dependant roles,

such as loyal or disloyal wives and daughters, perhaps, or even as good- or bad-sport *grandes horizontales*. Mothers may figure too, of course: usually as guarantee of lineage or sensibility, or both. Women are rarely there as participants, workers, friends or equals, though it is possible to think of some women who have watched the particular male world they know from the pavilion, as it were, and recorded its antics from a position of cheering, or anyway cheerfully clear-eyed acceptance of the peripheral (or scoring) role they occupied in it all. My metaphor is not a random one: a brief devotion to cricket at school – or perhaps to the cricketers – landed me in the pavilion, scoring for the boys' team.

In this last chapter I shall consider a number of connected themes which have been touched on in earlier parts of the book. First, there are the voices and the testimonies of teachers, which offer collectively, I hope, the possibility of a rewritten history of education in this country and a revitalised argument about that history. Then there is the recent use of, even the reliance on, forms of autobiographical writing by women teachers and students. This may be pursued in the interests of a certain kind of pedagogy, but it may also be a way of writing their own submerged histories and knowledge into public educational debate in order to become visible players rather than tiresomely irrepressible adjuncts or irritants to that debate.

Initiating autobiographical writing in the classroom, and reading it, entails thinking in new ways about language and the social relations it mediates. For if, as Volosinov, the Russian philosopher of language, expressed it, 'meaning belongs to a word in its position between speakers',[4] writing cannot be generated or made sense of solely as a kind of monologue conducted within a private, unread vacuum. Its communicative potential is intrinsic rather than arbitrary, and must be registered in the language, if only as suppressed or stifled. By that I mean that the process and the character of the writing must be judged in terms of the manoeuvres required of its writers if they have reason to believe they have no readers or only particular kinds of readers, for that is often the fate of women's writing. Another theme, collected from the last chapter and vital to this one, is the voice of the amateur male pedagogue, the spectral father, whose instructions to women about teaching and mothering, indeed about how to be a satisfactory woman (who acknowledges and even welcomes her natural limitations), for centuries constituted the lines of women's education. That voice presented women with many of the genres they now employ and subvert in the stories they tell about themselves as teachers and mothers. Lastly, there is the possibly interchangeable character of writing and pedagogy, in which diaries and letters may be read as part of a female self-education and pedagogic style. From such beginnings have emerged new analyses, new pedagogies and even some of the new literary forms which characterise contemporary women's writing.

Celia Burgess Macey, a teacher and educationalist, and the daughter of that eighty-year-old woman who told her why she had always written, and mostly for herself, is one of a group of teachers whose studies I shall consider in this chapter. Her particular focus is on the writing of girls in the primary school (most of them bilingual) and she starts by setting her own learning of writing and reading within the family history which lead her, if indirectly, to teaching. She grew up in a Nonconformist family in the Midlands, where, as her mother suggests, writing was a gendered activity, learned within a tradition where young women were educated and trained for work, but expected to give it up as soon as the first child was born. So the specific tradition Burgess Macey inherited was of intelligent, well-educated women who read widely and wrote for their own purposes rather than for public scrutiny, and where the notion of being paid to work (or write) after childbirth was unacceptable. Her father kept a journal too, noting down 'the sighting of the first swallow and bee, the date of the first cuckoo call and coltsfoot and crocus flower'[5] and her grandfather was a Unitarian minister, who wrote books. So it was not that writing or even diary writing were experienced as necessarily female in themselves, but that they came to be associated with the private realm: with feeling and with the unspoken.

Burgess Macey's professional concern with young children learning to become literate is shot through, therefore, with what may be thought a female experience of literacy and particularly of writing. For instance, she says of herself, 'All my important relationships with men and women have gone through the diarying process. It is as if I trust my feelings better if they have been written down.'[6] The audience for her writing, she tells us, 'is partly myself, but I often have an idea that someone, sometime, will read the diaries'.

That context for her own writing has a particular origin, which will not necessarily be shared by young working-class girls learning to write in the primary school, or indeed, by bilingual girls growing up in families where writing is differently used. The acquisition of a context for *their* writing may start by being centred in school and school values, in their wanting to communicate with their teachers and do well. However, the differences from boys that Burgess Macey found in young girls' writing suggested to her that 'in their preference for stories and personal and autobiographical writing, girls are learning to manipulate the forms of language best suited to reflect on female experience as it is communicated to them in cultural terms'.[7]

A tradition of private and domestic writing hinges on the question of who is likely to read it. Writing for daughters and granddaughters will seem a disingenuously modest ambition to many professional women today. And an insistence on the therapeutic, or even the hermeneutic, value of the activity, will hardly meet the needs of politically active and sophisticated teachers, who have seen their best practice and its by now well-elaborated rationales overridden and treated with contempt in recent years. Yet women who write as women are rarely read by men, even by those men who may be thought to be their political allies, and to some extent that must influence the way women write. If, as one six-year-old girl said to Celia Burgess Macey, 'boys don't like girls' stories, they never want to read them',[8] what are girls to do? I imagine that most women write *as if* men were going to read what they write. Indeed, it might be said that there are forms of feminist polemic which are especially intended for men: the most plangent and enraged, perhaps, or the most deferential. And there can be no doubt that much auto-biographical and fictional writing by women is *meant* for men, just as much as for women. Yet most women also know that they are, in fact, writing for women, and that determines to a considerable extent what and how they write.

Forms of confessional and argumentative writing have developed, with their own styles and jargons and reference points, which many women read almost as if they were distributed amongst them through some system of *samizdat*. An obstacle to the establishment (or, indeed, the invention) of female literary traditions – a continuous if erratic preoccupation during the last twenty-five years – has been a disinclination to consider the question of who reads texts produced by women; for where women's writing is read by men as well as women it surely joins some sort of mainstream tradition. It is the sanctifying of forms of writing which travel only between women, but underground, as it were, inspiring recognition and even a response in kind, that may all too easily work to maintain women's absence from effective public discussion. This may have been one of the effects of having had something of a feminist press and feminist publishing outlets during the last twenty years: a sense that women have had their say, and that that exonerates men from reading what they write. I too believe that 'boys don't like girls' stories', but I also think it vital that they get written and that a simultaneous battle be waged to find ways of inserting these stories into the protected enclaves of male debate. This seems to me an intensely difficult dilemma and a central one for feminism, especially in education.

More than twenty years ago, when I was teaching English in the large London comprehensive school I have already written about, a friend, flipping idly through a pile of my corrected exercise books, came upon my scribbled question, 'Where is your autobiography?' This, I am sorry to say, was addressed to a small eleven-year-old boy, who had been in the school less than a month. It was a moment in the early seventies, when I might well have been under the influence of the emerging work on writing development being carried out by James Britton, Nancy Martin and others at the London Institute of Education, where I now work.[9] Actually, I hadn't heard of Britton or Martin at that point and I had no connections yet with the Institute of Education. Looking back, I see the use I made of autobiography and especially of diary writing in English lessons as inspired in part by the 'Child Art' movements of the thirties and forties,[10] which had affected my own schooling, and, much more generally, by the emancipatory politics of the sixties, which had propelled me into teaching in an inner-city school in the first place, and which had provided me – I was a mother as well as a 'mature' and untrained teacher – with views about teaching English which smacked a little, I now think, of the Salvation Army.

That moment collects a number of entangled issues for me: first, autobiography as pedagogy, and a whole set and sequence of arguments for it. And that reminds me as well of all that may seem continuous, while being utterly changed, since what look from here like the golden days of the seventies. Why was I so insistent that all my eleven-year-olds wrote me the story of their lives? Maggie Humm, who has written about the use she and her colleagues make of autobiographical writing with first-year undergraduate students, many of them 'mature', claims that 'writing an autobiography can give students that sense of a narrated identity'[11] which enables them to move more confidently towards the translation from 'subjective readings into the critical analysis of texts' that the subject English requires of them. However, as she also points out, 'educational paradigms absorb radical intentions',[12] and this preparatory manoeuvre all too easily transforms itself into a competition for grades. There was always the danger, my class of eleven-year-olds may well have felt, that their teacher would give them low marks for their own lives.

Educational autobiography – or autobiography as pedagogy – has a complex history, with mostly literary and linguistic beginnings, I suppose. These were later reinforced by political as well as psychotherapeutic designs on such writing, some of which have been transported wholesale into feminist teaching. This is the reason for my doubts about one or two of the uses that have been made of it. Yet I also want to suggest that women teachers are beginning to develop a new kind of analysis of their work, which I believe to be invaluable. It is one which challenges conventions of academic writing and – perhaps even more importantly – undermines the mostly spurious claims of detachment and objectivity inscribed in a good deal of educational research.

When teachers come to do master's (or doctoral) studies in the department where I work – and almost all of them are women working in primary or secondary schools, or in further or higher education – they have to produce, amongst other things, a 25,000-word dissertation in the area of language and literacy and literature teaching. Most of them are very experienced teachers, and most of them will have had a fairly conventional four years or so of academic and professional training. Few of them, however, will have had much experience as what might be called public writers or as researchers. More than that, they may have encountered what is often unhelpfully termed 'theory' as dogma rather than debate or a history of ideas, presented with apparently impermeable authority, in the unreadable prose of 'written-up' research, and usually by men.

Some of us suggest that they start from what we have come to call 'the autobiography of the question'; *their* question, that is. This means beginning with the story of their own interest in the question they are asking and planning to research into. From that initial story, they may move towards mapping their developing sense of the question's interest for them on to the history of more public kinds of attention to it. This becomes a way of historicising the questions they are addressing and of setting their lives and educational history within contexts more capacious than their own. It is also a way of formalising a particular kind of self-consciousness; and that in its turn may reveal the absence of women, or of girls, or of gender, in the history and the debate within which they are seeking to find a place for themselves.

This way of approaching academic writing does not meet with the approval of all my colleagues, by any means. I have heard it anathematised as an incitement to self-indulgent introspection; as a recipe for *ad hominem* argument; as a pedagogic strategy that takes its in-built assumptions all too literally; and as likely to produce bad history and bad research. Too often, I think, I defend the approach because it works, or rather because it seems to produce more confident writing and thinking than other approaches I know of, and a more swashbuckling sense of equality with the looming gurus who will, at some point, need to be consulted and invoked. Yet I am clear that that won't do, and that my reasons for working like that need to be exposed to the light of day and also separated from the quite different rationales for autobiography and personal writing with which they actually have rather little in common, although they are often confused.

Apart from anything else, many people would regard this as a somewhat exiguous notion of autobiography, focused as it is upon an educational question and upon aspects of the student's own schooling and work, which – in a possibly self-fulfilling way – must be demonstrably relevant to the initial question. The strategy is organisational, perhaps, rather than therapeutic or hermeneutic. Then, it may even be that this writing is 'personal' in only a formal or tactical sense. That is, the narrative 'I' is foregrounded at least in part as a challenge to the efficacy of principles of detachment, disinterestedness, impartiality, and so on, as if declaring who you are and where you come from might offer some unassailable guarantee that only the most modest moves will be made towards theoretical transcendence or gross generalisability. A story full of children, classrooms, moments, admissions, will eschew – one can seem to be implying – abstractions that are deaf to questions of 'Who?', 'When?', 'Where?'. I begin to see the whole procedure as no more than an altered style: a highlighting of the conventions of academic writing by denial or negation, but ultimately just as formulaic and constraining as any other. Perhaps this is another trick, a merely rhetorical invitation to students to put their own lives and development into the argument, and to set their knowledge and experience as teachers alongside the authorities we all study and quote. Are we, in fact, deluding a group of mature professional women, who are already exploited and overlooked, into believing that all this will finally get them a hearing?

I have to read my own uncertainty about a successful pedagogic manoeuvre within that question and as part of more miasmic confusions round the position of women as teachers and what a feminist practice might be for them. Feminist educational writing is full of the occupational scepticism of its practitioners, who characteristically worry and wonder even about what the Canadian academic, Deanne Bogdan, has beautifully described as her dream class or 'Singing School' of 1988. I recognise all too well the questions she asks when the creative harmony of that one class turns out to be mysteriously unrepeatable.

Was it that the more democratic collaborative setting had allowed me to comfortably shed my role as 'expert'?

> Was it the carefully sequenced readings and exercises?
> Was it that the students enjoyed reader-response journal
> writing, for most of them a 'first' in graduate education
> – or were we all just nice people? And how accurate, in
> any case, is the absence of factional strife or the presence
> of a mutually reinforcing class dynamic as a barometer
> of productive learning?[13]

How accurate indeed? And how often do most university
teachers – and I am thinking of some of the most admired
and remembered of them all – measure the success of their
teaching in terms of students' learning anyway? Susan Sellers,
translating what she'd learned in Paris from Hélène Cixous,
the feminist writer and teacher, to a different group of
women she was teaching in Amsterdam, recalls how hard her
students found a practice which had been designed especially
to engage them all.

> As was the case with the attempt to abandon traditional
> student/teacher hierarchies, the attempt to adopt the
> non-judgemental practice of Hélène Cixous' seminar
> created problems. Many of the women found our refusal
> to sit in judgement on their work one of the most difficult
> aspects of the whole course.[14]

In some ways, Bogdan and Sellers are writing about the
predictably unpredictable character of teaching and the problems students may have with unfamiliar modes of teaching
and assessment, particularly perhaps where these have been
conceptualised and offered as democratic and 'empowering'.
These writers are not after all formulating pedagogic or curriculum theory in a vacuum, but describing their own work
and its pitfalls, and arguing from that. They are also telling us
how difficult it is for a teacher (and especially perhaps a
woman teacher) to be the one who initiates procedures
designed to expose and rupture precisely those social relations
which buttress her own always ambiguous position of power.

Is a woman teacher ever unequivocally in a position to 'empower' anyone? And what, as Bogdan asks, do we do with resistance or even mutiny? Predict it, accommodate it, ignore it, or work with its disturbances?

We met Michael Apple's analysis of the increased 'proletarianization' and 'intellectual deskilling' of teachers in Britain and North America in Chapter 4, and what he sees as the particular vulnerability of women to those processes. We also saw that though he was prepared to concede that women teachers had contributed to movements which set out to resist the centralised undermining of teaching, he was readier still to notice their susceptibility to conservative forces. Similarly, Apple acknowledges that women teachers have often been radicalised by their understanding of the ways in which the patriarchal education establishment exploits and regulates its female teaching force in the interests of controlling curriculum change. However, his analysis also presents women teachers as coerced into implementing reactionary, as well as progressive, innovations, in a process which deludes them into misinterpreting the more and more time-consuming paperwork they are expected to do, 'as a symbol of their increased *professionalism*'.[15] All this acknowledges women teachers only as joiners or refusers, more or less deluded, more or less in need of special pleading. There needs rather to be a sense of how women have used such scope for creativity as teaching afforded them, within and against the constraints imposed on their labour as intellectual workers.

It has been partly in an attempt to break out of this tangle of contradictions that feminist teachers in all areas of education are looking, in their teaching and their writing, for patterns and voices which might allow for less reductive accounts of what goes on in education and of the scope for change. They look for change from a position which assumes the centrality of class, race and gender differences and inequalities. Similarly, they start from the importance of the relations between teacher and taught; between the culture of children's families and the culture of the school; between curriculum and assessment; and between subject knowledge and 'real-life' versions of that knowledge. Characteristically, such looked-for change is outside the current managerial obsession with alternative administrative structures, record-keeping, reduced provision, quality assurance and accounting in all educational establishments. Those moves make the business of initiating genuine educational change more difficult, as in some cases they are meant to. However, the achievement of the changes feminist teachers are urging will depend in the end on their learning to insert the impossibilities and the incongruities of their teaching narratives into the academic discourses which have so far proved deaf to them. And the hybridisation of those discourses will be a significant by-product of that process.

One characteristic area of impossibility for women teachers lies in the approach taken in most schools to their responsibility for pastoral care. In principle, most schools present this as an important area of their provision. In practice, it will be performed by women to an overwhelming extent, will be thought to require nothing more than a little common sense, rather than intelligence or experience or training, and it will sit low within the school's range of preoccupations, though it will offer some purchase as a determining lever in the career possibilities of its staff.

Jo Cross made a study of her own formation as a teacher and set that against her qualifications for making sense of the autobiography written by her student Riffat, from Pakistan, which narrates a series of episodes from her life and the gathering sense of disappointment and powerlessness she took from them. In many respects, Jo Cross, as Riffat's English teacher and Head of Year in a large North London comprehensive school, inhabits a narrative with quite opposite features and outcomes from the one Riffat is embarked on. Yet there are chimings and overlaps. Here is Jo, characterising one day of her work at school.

By looking at my diary I can see my involvement on that one day with three different mothers: the white, Irish, working-class mother of the habitual truant, the Afro-Caribbean mother of the boy who was to run away; and the Asian mother of Umesh who was seen to have serious behaviour problems which had already caused his incarceration in an adolescent mental ward. Each of these mothers . . . could be judged as having failed in their sensitivity as their children were all involved in behaviour that was other than 'normal'. My positioning in their relationships with their children was as an advisor and judge of their failure, a role invested in me by the authoritative position of the school in the culture. But I was not a mother, I was younger than them, and did not share their life experiences nor their cultures. How was I qualified to advise and judge these women? A further contradiction was inherent between my own working-class upbringing and my social elevation to the middle-class professionally which put me in the position of judging by an example of child care I had not even experienced. What were the messages taken by the children at the centre of these triads, each of them the single male in the group – that the women in their lives felt a responsibility for their deviation from the 'norm'? What were they learning about the ways their cultures were perceived by the authorities of society – the Social Services and the Psychological Services were involved in all three situations but with the mothers and myself as central actors all the time?

. . . It is perhaps significant that two of these boys had widowed mothers and were seen as becoming traumatised due to their lack of a father figure and all three were deemed as having unstable and unsupportive homes.[16]

This seems to me to offer an analysis of a central dilemma faced daily by schools, while also addressing the impossibly conflicting demands made on the woman teacher caught within it. This teacher is simultaneously bound by 'professional' codes and 'mothering' ones. Whatever her experience or proclivities, she risks criticism if she cannot perform her pastoral duties adequately. And doing so brings her into equivocal contact with government agencies and other professionalisms. Yet young male teachers, as Jo Cross points out elsewhere, may safely reveal that they are incompetent, callous and perfunctory form tutors or pastoral agents without in any way spoiling their chances of rapid promotion. More than that, the conscientious Head of House also runs the risk of being thought to spend too much time on non-academic questions, of missing important staff meetings on their account, of being 'soft' on intractable children and parents and of getting the problems of individuals out of proportion.[17] Jo Cross concludes,

A further contradiction of the pastoral role is inherent in the positioning of teacher to parent. If we recognise the meritocratic fantasy that all children could be successful (i.e. middle-class) if their development was properly handled by a 'sensitive mother', does not this same fantasy indicate that if the child is seen as a problem at school then in some way a mother has failed and must be judged as such? In fact, the fault would have to be placed at the feet of the biological mother or the mother role of the school, one or other of which may be deemed not sensitive enough. So this places school and home in conflict and, because Heads of Year are more often women, and mothers more often deal with school than fathers, then it places two women in conflict and puts one (the teacher) in a judgemental role in relation to the other.[18]

I quote Jo Cross at this length for a number of reasons. First, her offering of this example from her own experience incorporates and develops its own theory and analysis in ways which are hard to find in educational writing anywhere: the circumscribed powers of the woman teacher occupying a pastoral position in the school, which will often be read by the mother/parent as equivalent to the school's hegemony and therefore out of sympathy with her own ordeal. Second, this example is only one of several Jo Cross considers, which connect her work as a teacher with her working-class girlhood: as one of three daughters who were encouraged to believe in the possibility of, as she puts it, 'having it all', by parents who had themselves missed out on grammar school because their parents could not afford to keep them at school for long enough. Education becomes worth any sacrifice, an unequivocal good, which as a teacher she must uphold against all contrary pressure. Her own ambivalence especially has to be suppressed in the conduct of her professional duties. And third, her own story is offered in careful counterpoint to the story of a Pakistani student's autobiography: the two reverberating together to illustrate 'the silence, the inability to talk about that feeling which typifies the experience of many a working-class achiever – especially, I would suggest, girls whose socialisation process is towards moderation and passivity'.[19]

Riffat's story of neglect, an arranged marriage and an education truncated and made futile by the deafness she encounters, is a quite different story from Jo's. Yet, as I have said, the two narratives chime at many points. The arranged marriage is dangerously protean in its meanings: at once the predictable reward for virtuous young womanhood, the promise of future security and the end of an unhappy childhood, it is also an experience of restraint and coercion which cancels out her free will and, therefore, her capacity for virtue and growth. There is the raw discrepancy between the woman writing her own text and her existence as a body destined to a life of sexual compliance: an impermissible conjunction. Think of Samuel Richardson's Clarissa, and the spectre of her willing herself to an anorexic death as the only way of denying her body to Lovelace, whilst penning her marvellous letters on the coffin she plans so resolutely to inhabit.

It is possible that I and others who encourage students to begin from 'the autobiography of the question' assume too easily that the approach is likely to be more popular with women students than with men. I have met with greater initial resistance from some men, who appear to believe that as graduates they are (and should be) unintimidated by the impersonal academic style. Some of them seriously doubt the respectability of research or writing which can seem to be declaring its own limitations through the brazen use of the first person. Women students have their ways, particularly if they are also teachers, and this resistance in their fellow students is usually overcome. But when men are prepared to be autobiographical they are likely, as Maggie Humm has put it, to make 'their lives into patterns of self-chosen events set in a rational pursuit of well-defined education goals'.[20] This, Humm suggests, is quite unlike the ways in which women write about their lives, besides being more acceptable to teachers in higher education. But then, as we have seen, men may have found voices not so unlike their own in a long history of pedagogic writing, where women will not have done. It is also sometimes the case that until teachers actually begin to construct the story of their question, as Jo Cross has done, they are quite likely to believe too that they have been offered a beginner's guide to research, which must, therefore, be a second-rate one.

If some of us persist – and we do – with the idea of 'the autobiography of the question' it is certainly not because students find it an easy way into research and writing. Nor is it because the construction of a story out of their own experience and thought is able in some miraculous way to provide them with a missing self or identity (for that has sometimes been a feminist ambition). Nor is it possible to view this manoeuvre as either a short cut to some tidy truth, or a guarantee of truth at all. Rather, the purpose is to confront and foreground the intolerable difficulty of embarking on any kind of serious investigation of education which engages with the dilemmas of teaching at any level beyond what 'works'. For there is no easy way of knowing for certain what is productive, expedient, necessary in teaching; and any commitment to a pedagogy which presents itself as certain ought to arouse our instant suspicions. There is not very much educational research, after all, which escapes the pattern of gathering in data to illustrate the proposition you started from.

Lest I be thought to be saying that a teacher's remembering her own history in education, as student and teacher, is likely to provide some sort of sure-fire recompense for the absence of her voice in most academic discussion of education, let me swiftly offer yet another proviso. I am haunted by the warning from the novelist, Dorothy Richardson, that memory itself is not to be trusted: not just because it is faulty and unreliable, but because its modes of operation have been schooled to turn the past into history, providing what is recalled with a usually spurious and partial significance, of a sort absolutely not equivalent to what a novelist is out to capture. Carolyn Steedman, a historian rather than a novelist, casts another kind of doubt on the possibility that autobiography either is or delivers history. In a lecture she gave about her own autobiographical book, *Landscape for a Good Woman*, she admitted that in using fragments of her own remembered experiences and extrapolating from them to a longer and broader history of working-class women, she was flouting the practices of at least some historians.[21]

These both seem to me quite proper kinds of scepticism about memory. The dredging-up of possible continuities in our experience, the search for relevant connections, the reliance on the sequences proposed by the conventions of autobiographical narrative, as if these manoeuvres were inevitably committed to discovering an integrity of the self or of experience: these are not in themselves the stuff of research or fiction or history. But nor are they to be thought of as therapy or some sort of consolatory second-best mode of reflecting on the world, suitable for those with undeveloped expository skills, or women.

Feminists in education have contributed a number of vital insights and strategies for teaching and learning: usually, as Julia Kristeva ordained, through negation.[22] They have shown, for instance, that while most teaching is done by women, most theorising about schools and classrooms and teaching and learning has been done by men; and that this has removed more than girls and women from the picture: it has encouraged the simplification and the etiolation of some key issues.

Certain feminist writers have pointed to the anomalies produced by this: to the wilful separation of theory from practice and of research from teaching.[23] They have argued that while most cultures are primarily concerned with the regulation of female sexuality, women have usually occupied ambiguous roles in relation to the transmission and evaluation of the culture's forms and practices.[24] Such writers have also shown what happens to a profession which refuses to acknowledge its own class, gender, colonial and/or race history. For example, the character and durability of Bell's monitorial system of teaching and of training teachers in the late eighteenth and early nineteenth century – which was and perhaps still is hugely influential in this country – look rather different when its origins as an experiment for teaching the illegitimate and mixed-race offspring of military personnel in Madras are considered. Similarly, issues of classroom 'management and control' look a good deal more complex when an analysis like Valerie Walkerdine's is brought to bear on the ambiguous figure of the woman teacher, as we saw in Chapter 5. We have to start from an acknowledgement of difference and difficulty if we are ever to describe the complex and changing relations women have with the theoretical discourses which mark out their professional activities.

Much writing on literacy in North America and Britain during the seventies and eighties relied on an abstracted and ungendered person, usually known as 'the child'. The child was attended by parents and teachers, none of whom was identified. The dangers of that were not simply that working-class children's and girls' lives were made invisible, but that they were also subsumed (usually to their detriment) within normative accounts of 'mainstream' children's 'natural' as well as educational development. What was lost in those studies was not just difference, but history and conflict. And schooling, teaching, the education of children got written up in just those academic languages of psychology or sociology or linguistics which have cast the woman teacher as the more or less efficient implementer of the curriculum philosophies of the time, as promulgated by other people. It is not over-emphatic to claim, I think, that during my time as a teacher in school – the late sixties and the seventies – most classroom research cast the woman teacher as at fault in some way or other: either as insensitive to questions of social class, or as foolishly optimistic and wholly unable (or unwilling) to organise or control the classroom when it was occupied by working-class children, particularly boys.

Both Dorothy Richardson and Carolyn Steedman had more to say, as it happens, than simply to disparage memory and autobiography. Memory and its erratic behaviour organises Richardson's remarkable novel, *Pilgrimage*, and she was as wary of human experience stripped of language as of language emptied of the world it articulates. Similarly, for all her misgivings about treating autobiography as if it were history, Carolyn Steedman can also declare that 'it is for the potentialities of that community offered by historical consciousness, I suppose, that I want what I have written to be called history, and not autobiography'.[25]

Too many of the arguments for the writing of autobiography have concentrated on its benefits for individuals rather than on its potential for the discovery and definition of new kinds of community. I want to suggest that the power of autobiographical writing, as an aspect of teachers' reflection and scholarship and research and theorising, is in its potential for rethinking teaching and schooling from a critical and feminist vantage point. This is by no means a matter of minting new categories of experience, but of rereading and remaking for ourselves those traditions of narration which have measured out women's learning and teaching in the past, traditions which have had to absorb the material and mental deprivations lived by women who were denied education and intellectual sustenance.

June Levison, another London teacher, wrote the story of her own childhood in working-class, Jewish Manchester in the fifties, as an at first effortless ascent from home to school, her mother's impeccable preparation for her daughters' schooling propelling them towards the smooth certainties of success. June wonderfully and wryly remembers herself as the charming little princess, good and clever, and poised for perfection as 'we girls learned the obligations that we were born to'.[26] And then, as she remembers, how surreptitiously goodness could tip over into coquettishness, how oddly elation was combined with fear, even in school, where all was sunshine and triumph. Always, as she writes, 'I knew I was destined to succeed.' But at what?

Grammar school brings 'the first flutter of self-doubt'.[27]

She is put in the B stream and there are richer, blonder, prettier girls. Then,

> When my gaze fell upon the new fourth year English teacher, however, it was a falling in love with a future vision of myself – fiercely academic yet thoroughly approachable, teacherly but sensual. She allowed us glimpses into her life which cast her family as solid, ordinary, working-class Mancunians and herself as surprisingly exotic. In the slides she showed us of her Indian trek, her normally tightly bound hair was flowing down her back, and she looked carefree and joyful in the embrace of her dark-skinned, Indian boyfriend.[28]

Curiously, success in literature and writing coincided with a withdrawal from speech.

> As my written voice became more and more eloquent, I became less vocal in the classroom and when I left that school I entered a long period of silence in the public domain.[29]

Levison's recurrent image is of inflation followed by deflation, of being elaborately set up for disappointment, of hope and aspiration containing their own drop, their own built-in gravity. Even the wonderful teacher recedes as torch and inspiration, though Levison herself becomes just such a teacher. She ties up the disappointments at last in an exasperated bow, 'My work will never be valued by my mother and others as much as that of my relatives who are Doctors or Lawyers.'[30] She quotes the wise question put by that wise teacher of teachers, Josie Levine:

> When teaching is so complex a set of practices, when it is so important to the development of individuals and of society, when it is culturally and economically of such importance, how is it that it can be so negatively positioned?[31]

Yet June Levison's story of becoming a teacher – indeed becoming the wonderful teacher she remembers, if only momentarily, wanting to be – works in some way to dispel the sour taste of memory she discovers in an otherwise comically golden childhood. The process has entailed contextualising and then theorising the constant and unnerving conjunction of pleasure and pain she felt as a daughter and a schoolgirl and now feels as a woman, a teacher, a mother, an intellectual. It has been a process of recovering a voice that went silent, muffled and unstrung by the breathless promise and disappointment of being a girl, and a clever girl, and learning to use that voice by trying it out all over again in the public domain: 'the autobiography is a means of legitimising the writer's claim to enter a particular debate – it advises the reader who it is discussing these ideas and declares her interest in it.'[32]

The writing connects her with her own past and with a shared female experience. That in its turn helps her to read her students and their writing. More than that, it links her, and teachers like her, with the informing ideas which matter to them, not as anxious, doting Marthas, but as thinkers. Bakhtin's theory of language as utterance learned and practised in conversations is internalised to become part of her own way of thinking about herself and the language she uses.

> I have also discovered some things about the process of writing itself which may help me to understand what it really means when I ask students to write in the classroom. Firstly I have discovered the immense pleasure and power involved in gaining confidence as a writer, and autobiographical writing is a useful place to start for someone who believes she lacks the imagination to invent stories for herself. I have also discovered the astonishing truth that autobiographical writing actually releases memory and insight – most of what I have written was

recalled during the writing. I have discovered that to write is to lie, by which I mean that aesthetic considerations often supercede the quest for absolute truth and although I have tried to produce some sort of historical record I am aware that at times I have distorted or invented in the interest of 'literary' effect. It is impossible to tell it as it really is and most glaringly, the mother of these pages is not my mother. Perhaps the most crucial discovery, and this applies to the dissertation as a whole, is that I cannot write without hearing others' voices – the voices which make up my entire reading history. I have a very real sense that these are not my words and my reading of Bakhtin . . . tells me that in a sense they are not.[33]

Women who teach have to learn how to speak (and write) out of the history of the accommodations they have made to male theories of culture and education. To do that we need to expose and then to eliminate the obfuscations of much academic writing, but also to insist that all writers on education begin with a declaration of their starting point, their strengths or weaknesses as commentators. We are learning to work consciously within and against the voices of authority. No research paradigm available to teachers that I know of allows them room to consider how teaching matches and conflicts with other aspects of their lives: how contradictory conceptions of femininity may impede, confuse, distort; but how they may also – once they are confronted and understood – enhance and even illuminate what they do as teachers.

'Only in the last third of the twentieth century have women broken through to a realization of the narratives that have been controlling their lives',[34] writes Carolyn Heilbrun, in her *Writing a Woman's Life*. She also writes of women's coming of age, as portending 'all the freedoms men have always known and women never – mostly the freedom from fulfilling the needs of others and from being a female impersonator'.[35] And that 'coming of age' is meant literally: women's new-found time and scope as their lives open out after youth into these new narratives, rather than ending abruptly with marriage, as the old narratives required. It is a precarious optimism, perhaps, coming from a writer and a teacher, but one which is due, given women's gains and what these owe to literacy and to education.

What is probably the most important effect of education on people's lives is currently forgotten in the rush towards 'standards' and standardisation, towards the frozen lineaments of a curriculum rather than an imaginative engagement with the lives and language of learners and teachers. Education has always revealed new possibilities. No one could know in the early nineteenth century, when Eliza married John, what women's lives might be. Even the expansion of education for middle-class girls relied on sublime acts of faith and vision, and achievements there fired those who believed in the transforming possibilities of education for all. A history of girls' and women's education shows women learning all the time about what they could want and what they could accomplish. Needless to say, this has been felt as a threatening business, for its potential may well be boundless. Government orders, by contrast, have usually been minimalist, bogged down by notions of entitlement to a provision which can be anticipated because it is always tied to the past and can, therefore, be calculated in advance. It is education's capacity to confront the unknown and to accommodate it that so terrifies a government obsessed with its budgets, and prepared to attack education and denigrate teachers in order to meet them.

Women teachers have often been utopian in their ambitions for their students, and as a parent one might count this an advantage rather than the consequence of some foolhardy innocence, as it is sometimes allowed to seem. Many of the finest women teachers are nowadays driven out of the classroom by the poor prospects, by public condescension towards them, and – most recently – by the ceaseless flow of ill-considered and swiftly countermandered claims on their time, energies and expertise, imposed from outside. Many trained, talented and enthusiastic young teachers will not get jobs in school this year or next because of cuts and the increase in the size of classes. Most women went into teaching in the first place because it was work which interested them. Most of them knew it was demanding work and that teaching is not thought much of in this country. Their interest in teaching was complex in origin and unlikely to be understood by analogy with women's experience of domestic relations and arrangements. The interest was often in the subjects they were to teach as they had encountered them in their own studies, but it was also in the philosophical, psychological and historical issues raised by all kinds of educational engagement. And if in addition teachers have, as young people, chosen to work within an impoverished state system, that has often been because they had good reason to believe in children's intelligence and in their capacity to benefit from good teaching.

We need to become a society in which everybody has access to decent forms of educational provision throughout their lives. We also need to have a far more flexible and diversified sense of what such provision might need to be. Progress towards that point is hopelessly hobbled by successive government moves to reduce what is on offer and to make judgements about quality on the back of auditing procedures rather than knowledge.

An acknowledgement of the anomalies lived by women teachers would be a beginning. It would do something to explain the history of public pessimism and discouragement in relation to schooling. It might also alert women in other professions to the dangers there are in denying their own difference and the implications of that difference. Reading the autobiographical writing of women teachers reminds one of the impossibilities of teaching, and there have always been voices which have warned of those impossibilities, particularly for women. In the end, though, women themselves are implicated in the successes and the failures of education, and they are committed to making it work. To recognise that is to recognise some important truths about women and work and culture as well as education.

Notes

Introduction

1 Ivan Reid and Erica Stratta (eds), *Sex Differences in Britain*, 2nd edn, Gower, 1989.

2 I am all too aware of the stern warnings against such writing and the illusory 'self' it may seem to invoke and rely on. Most of these warnings come from Australia, where teaching children the ostensibly more useful genres of writing – reports and so on – is promoted by some with considerable fanaticism and faith in a range of post-structuralist dogma. I allude to my own misgivings about autobiographical writing in Chapter 9. I am sure we should be sceptical and encourage children to be sceptical about the 'truths' supplied by memory and shaped by the social determinations of the autobiographical form. However, it is not clear that we can live without learning about the ways that exist to represent what we think we know about ourselves; so that too much scepticism in this area should simply not detain us, in my view. Some of the arguments for giving up autobiographical writing in favour of more 'useful' genres are to be found in F. Christie, *Teaching English Literacy. A Project of National Significance on the Preservice Preparation of Teachers for Teaching English Literacy*, vol. 2, *Papers*, Canberra: DEET, 1991; and P. Gilbert and S. Taylor, *Fashioning the Feminine: Girls, Popular Culture and Schooling*, Allen & Unwin, 1991.

3 Jane Miller, 'Tell him, Miss', *The New Review*, 2, no. 16 (1975).

4 The *Black Papers* were started in 1969 by Professor Brian Cox and Rhodes Boyson, the Tory MP. In their words,

'The original *Black Paper* . . . was the first serious attempt in Britain to provide a critique of the move to progressive education.' The papers appeared irregularly, and the issue to which my article was a response, *Black Paper, 1975: The Fight for Education*, emerged after a five-year gap. Its contributors included Kingsley Amis, G.H. Bantock, H.J. Eysenck, Max Beloff and Iris Murdoch. John Carey, 'Down with Dons', *The New Review*, 1, no. 10 (1975).

5 Jane Miller, 'Tell him, Miss', p. 30.

1 *Culture and Paradox*

1 In *Freud's Women*, Weidenfeld & Nicolson, 1992, Lisa Appignanesi and John Forrester argue for the attractions of psychoanalysis for women as practitioners as well as patients, and go on to show how some women made a career and a life for themselves as psychoanalysts. It is interesting to consider how the progressive professionalism of the work accompanied this move: not simply in order to keep women out, but in order to assert the respectability of psychoanalysis as a science and a branch of medicine, it became necessary to downplay its 'femininity' as a practice and as a mode of analysis.

2 Frances Rafferty and Neil Munro, 'Lonely Men seek Gender Balance', *The Times Educational Supplement*, 10 June 1994.

3 David Budge, 'A World made for Women?', *Times Educational Supplement*, 24 June 1994.

4 Leading article in the *Independent*, 18 December 1993.

5 CSE stands for Certificate of Secondary Education. This was an examination system introduced in 1965 and phased out nearly twenty-five years later to make way for the GCSE examinations. The CSE was introduced at a time when only 20 per cent of the school population was expected to manage O levels, and was originally intended for 40 per cent of the remaining school population. The administration of the examination and its setting and marking were, if not directly, far more accessible to teacher involvement than the university- run system was. A 'Mode' referred to the form of examination and to the form and the extent of teacher involvement. A Mode 3 was a school-initiated course and assessment scheme, overseen by the central examinations board, which was likely to include more continuous assessment, less in the way of timed examinations, and was in

general popular with teachers, because it could be tailored to the pupils involved. It was enormously successful in many 'difficult' London schools because it elicited such high levels of attendance and entry to the examination. For instance, my school went from having a 40–50 per cent involvement in fifth-year English examinations to between 80–90 per cent by the mid-seventies.

6 I borrow this summary of the qualities of the eligible candidate for teacher training from Sue Smedley's 'Versions and Visions: Women Primary School Teachers, their Initial Education and their Work', thesis submitted for MA in Language and Literature in Education, University of London Institute of Education, 1992, p. 59.

7 Carolyn Steedman, 'Prisonhouses', in her *Past Tenses: Essays on Writing, Autobiography and History*, Rivers Oram Press, 1992, p. 60.

8 See Anna Davin's 'Imperialism and Motherhood', *History Workshop Journal*, 5, (Spring 1978), pp. 9–65.

9 Dorothy Thompson makes this point about Queen Victoria much more intricately than I am doing, in her *Queen Victoria: Gender and Power*, Virago, 1990.

10 Louis Althusser, 'Ideology and Ideological State Apparatuses (Notes towards an Investigation)', in his *Lenin and Philosophy and Other Essays*, Monthly Review Press, 1971, p. 157.

11 From Simone de Beauvoir's *The Prime of Life*, trans. Peter Green, Penguin, 1965, p. 94.

12 The heroine of Muriel Spark's novel about a teacher, *The Prime of Miss Jean Brodie* (1961), Macmillan, 1969.

13 I am thinking particularly of her characterisation of the woman teacher in the book she wrote with Helen Lucey, *Democracy in the Kitchen: Regulating Mothers and Socialising Daughters* (Virago, 1989), but also of her more 'academic' research pieces, for instance, 'From Context to Text: A Psychosemiotic Approach to Abstract Thought', in Michael Beveridge (ed.), *Children Thinking through Language* (Arnold, 1982), in which a subtle analysis of children's problems with classroom discourse and its difference from everyday practices is produced out of the mandatory errors and confusions of the teacher.

14 Madeleine R. Grumet, *Bitter Milk: Women and Teaching*, University of Massachusetts Press, 1988, p. 25. It should also be said that Grumet's purpose is in part to persuade

women teachers to reclaim the benefits of the feminine and the maternal in their pedagogy.

15 From *College of St. Matthias: Annals*, 1977, p. 36.

16 Quoted in ibid., p. 15, from the College Council Report on their plans to reserve eight vacancies for such students for a one-year course.

17 I am thinking here of a solid piece of research undertaken by Professor R.K. Kelsall of Sheffield University into the vexed question of 'wastage' amongst women teachers, who left teaching, temporarily or permanently, when they had children. This became a theme of post-war employment policy, and was never accompanied by any attempt to offer nursery facilities or other support for the teachers in question. The report on the survey is called *Women and Teaching: Report on an Independent Nuffield Survey Following-up a Large National Sample of Women who Entered Teaching in England and Wales at Various Dates Pre-War and Post-War*, HMSO, 1963.

18 Carolyn Steedman, *Policing the Victorian Community: The Formation of English Provincial Police Forces, 1856–80*, Routledge & Kegan Paul, 1984, p. 160–63.

19 Anita S. Barley, 'Reading Black Literature in School', thesis submitted for MA in Language and Literature in Education, University of London Institute of Education, 1994, pp. 7–9.

20 ibid., pp. 10–11.

21 Peter Conrad, review of Harold Bloom's *The Western Canon: The Books and School of the Ages*, *Observer*, 22 January 1995.

22 Edward W. Said, *Culture and Imperialism*, Chatto & Windus, 1993, p. 385.

23 Gauri Viswanathan, *The Masks of Conquest*, Columbia University Press, 1989, p. 4.

2 *The Feminisation of Schooling in Two Countries*

1 Jessie Chambers, *D.H. Lawrence: A Personal Record* (1935), Cambridge University Press, 1980, p. 28.

2 See note 24 on Queen's Scholarships. These became King's Scholarships in 1901, and were abolished after 1906. See H.C. Dent, *The Training of Teachers in England and Wales 1800–1975*, Hodder & Stoughton, 1977, p. 53.

3 Jessie Chambers, *D.H. Lawrence*, p. 45.

4 There is a useful treatment of these years of Lawrence's life, his friendships with young women who became teachers, and a more general discussion of what teaching meant to men and women of Lawrence's background and generation in John Worthen, *D.H. Lawrence: The Early Years 1885–1912*, Cambridge University Press, 1991.

5 There are other sources of information about Nottingham University College. Perhaps unfairly, I wanted to hear the peculiar disparagements I remember so well from my youth and from my own time as a student in the fifties. I have relied, therefore, on A.C. Wood's *A History of the University College Nottingham 1881–1948*, Blackwell, 1953.

6 Ibid., p. 29.

7 Ibid., p. 31.

8 D.H. Lawrence, *The Rainbow* (1915), Penguin, 1950, p. 440.

9 Jessie Chambers, *D.H. Lawrence*, p. 161.

10 A.C. Wood, *A History of the University College of Nottingham*, p. 142.

11 Andy Green, *Education and State Formation: The Rise of Education Systems in England, France and the USA*, Macmillan, 1990, p. 7.

12 I have made use here of Andy Green's useful book, though it is not at all helpful about women teachers or, indeed, about the education of girls.

13 June Purvis, *A History of Women's Education in England*, The Open University Press, 1991, p. 11. See also June Purvis, *Hard Lessons: The Lives and Education of Working-Class Women in Nineteenth-Century England*, Polity Press, 1989. Both books are wide-ranging and detailed, though they have surprisingly little in them about women teachers.

14 A powerful account of the disastrous hold of so-called 'Home Economics' on the curriculum for girls is to be found in Dena Attar's excellent *Wasting Girls' Time: The History and Politics of Home Economics*, Virago, 1990.

15 See chapter 1 of Geoffrey Partington, *Women Teachers in the 20th Century in England and Wales*, NFER Publishing Co., 1976.

16 It was common for girls of thirteen or fourteen to become student teachers in schools and to attend local centres or even colleges for part of the week. In many cases they continued to teach without a formal certificate of qualification to do so

from the college. This would have made them ineligible for the salary supplements available to certificated teachers.

17 I have been enormously helped in this comparison of the American position with the English by Geraldine J. Clifford, '"Lady Teachers" and Politics in the United States, 1850–1930', in Martin Lawn and Gerald Grace (eds), *Teachers: The Culture and Politics of Work*, Falmer Press, 1987. Also by Madeleine Grumet, *Bitter Milk: Women and Teaching*, University of Massachusetts Press, 1988.

18 Geraldine J. Clifford, '"Lady Teachers" and Politics'.

19 In L.M. Montgomery's *Anne of Windy Willows* (1936), Puffin Classics, 1992.

20 In Laura Ingalls Wilder's *On the Banks of Plum Creek* (1953), Puffin Books, 1973 p. 101.

21 This episode is in Wilder's *These Happy Golden Years* (1943), Puffin Books, 1970.

22 ibid., p. 177.

23 The monitorial system of training seems to have had twin origins: in the system of teaching introduced by the Revd Dr Andrew Bell (an Anglican priest) in Madras in India and by Joseph Lancaster (a Quaker) in this country. Both were operating in the very first years of the nineteenth century. H.C. Dent, in his *The Training of Teachers*, puts it like this, 'Use pupils as teachers, they both said. Then, you will need only one adult, a "Superintendent", for any school, however large. The Superintendent will teach selected scholars, and these, under his observant eye, will teach the rest. So easy! And so cheap! For, of course, the teacher-scholars, the "Monitors", would not be paid. Again, the idea was not new; but what *was* new was the systematic and detailed fashion in which it was worked out, especially by Lancaster, whose "British" scheme was a masterpiece of intricate planning. Organisation, administration, curriculum, methodology, examination, discipline, welfare: each was broken down into small units, to be mastered by the Monitors, and by them passed on to the other pupils' (p. 3).

24 From 1852, certain pupil-teachers, who had completed a satisfactory apprenticeship in school, could receive a certificate which entitled him or her to sit a public examination, held annually, for the award of the Queen's Scholarships. These qualified their holders for places in recognised training colleges, with annual maintenance grants of £25 for men and £20 for women. The scheme was ended in 1863 and then

restored in the mid-1870s, when the demand for teachers increased dramatically in response to the 1870 Education Act. See H.C. Dent, *The Training of Teachers*, p. 20.

25 Frances Widdowson, *Going up into the Next Class: Women and Elementary Teacher Training, 1840–1914*, Hutchinson, 1983, p. 47.

26 M. Vivian Hughes, 'Pioneer Days in a Woman's Teacher Training College' in L.J. Lewis (ed.), *Days of Learning: An Anthology of Passages from Autobiography for Student Teachers*, Oxford University Press, 1961.

27 Frances Widdowson, *Going up into the Next Class*, p. 12.

28 See Chapter 3 for details about Kensington Avenue School, East Ham during the first twenty-nine years of this century.

29 See Chapter 2 of Madeleine Grumet, *Bitter Milk*; and Michael W. Apple, *Teachers and Texts: A Political Economy of Class and Gender Relations in Education*, Routledge, 1989, pp. 58ff.

30 I have no solid evidence for this, of course, but I do possess a 'Confessions Album', given to Clara Collet on her sixteenth birthday in 1876, in which her friends confess – amongst other things – to their favourite literary heroines. Jo runs Romola a close second, with Jeanie Deans as third. Amongst those who filled in their confessions were Jenny and Eleanor Marx, two of Karl Marx's three daughters, and friends of the Collet girls.

31 Quoted in Andy Green, *Education and State Formation*, p. 204.

32 Clara E. Collet, 'Secondary Education – Girls', in Charles Booth (ed.), *Labour and Life of the People*, vol. 2 *London Continued*, Williams and Norgate, 1891, p. 578.

33 See H.C. Dent, *The Training of Teachers*, p. 67.

34 See Annie E. Ridley, *Frances Mary Buss and her Work for Education*, Longmans, Green, 1895, p. 283.

35 From C. Bird's *Born Female*, Pocket Books, 1968, quoted in Geraldine J. Clifford, '"Lady Teachers" and Politics', p. 12.

36 Quoted in Geraldine J. Clifford, '"Lady Teachers" and Politics', p. 14, from L.P. Ayres, 'What Educators Think About the Need for Employing Men Teachers in Our Public Schools', *Journal of Education Psychology*, 2 (1911), pp. 89–93. Clifford also notes that 'the "woman peril" was frequently commented on in the years before World War I'.

37 In Alison Prentice and Marjorie R. Theobald (eds), *Women who Taught*, University of Toronto Press, 1991, p. 6.

38 Alison Oram has written well about the history of a whole range of inequalities between male and female teachers and, in '"Sex Antagonism" in the Teaching Profession: Equal Pay and the Marriage Bar, 1910–39', in Madeleine Arnot and Gaby Weiner (eds), *Gender and the Politics of Schooling*, Hutchinson, 1987, about the marriage bar particularly. See also Alison Oram, 'Inequalities in the Teaching Profession: The Effect on Teachers and Pupils, 1910–1939', in Felicity Hunt (ed.), *Lessons for Life: The Schooling of Girls and Women, 1850–1950*, Blackwell, 1987.

39 Gillian Sutherland, *Elementary Education in the Nineteenth Century*, The Historical Association, 1971, pp. 21, 22.

40 Indeed, I called the pamphlet I wrote on this subject in 1992, *More has meant Women: The Feminisation of Schooling*, Institute of Education and The Tufnell Press. I was adapting the phrase coined by Kingsley Amis, 'More will mean worse', which was his warning response to the new universities being built in the late sixties.

41 Ursula Howard, Paper delivered at 'The Future of English' conference at Ruskin College, Oxford, 15, 16 June 1991.

42 See June Purvis, *Hard Lessons*.

43 Margaret Bryant, *The Unexpected Revolution: A Study in the History of the Education of Women and Girls in the Nineteenth Century*, University of London Institute of Education, 1979.

44 There are useful accounts of such pockets of alternative provision in, for instance, Ann Thompson and Helen Wilcox (eds), *Teaching Women: Feminism and English Studies*, Manchester University Press, 1989; and in many of the pieces in the last two sections of Lynda Stone (ed.), *The Education Feminism Reader*, Routledge, 1994.

45 Clara E. Collet, *Educated Working Women*, (dedicated to Frances Mary Bun) P.S. King, 1902, p. 6.

46 Ivy Pinchbeck, *Women Workers and the Industrial Revolution 1750–1850* (1930), Virago, 1981; see tables starting on p. 317.

47 Margaret Bryant, *The Unexpected Revolution*, p. 107.

48 Clara E. Collet, *Educated Working Women*, p. 56.

49 Letter from Professor Robin Alexander of the University of Leeds School of Education to the Editor of the *Guardian*, 9 August 1991. The report was eventually published in

1992: R. Alexander, J. Rose and C. Woodhead, *Curriculum Organisation and Classroom Practice in Primary Schools*, HMSO, 1992.

50 Geoffrey Partington, *Women Teachers*, gives a helpful account of this struggle. So do Alison Oram, '"Sex Antagonism" in the Teaching Profession'; and Margaret Littlewood, 'The "Wise Married Woman" and the Teaching Unions', in Hilary de Lyon and Frances Widdowson Migniuolo (eds), *Women Teachers: Issues and Experiences*, Open University Press, 1989. Hilda Kean, *Challenging the State? The Socialist and Feminist Educational Experience 1900–1930*, Falmer Press, 1990, and her *Deeds not Words*, Pluto, 1990, treat the earlier period of women's involvement with the teaching unions.

51 Alison Oram, 'Inequalities in the Teaching Profession', p. 102. NAS (The National Association of Schoolmasters), was formed in 1922 as a breakaway union from the NUT (The National Union of Teachers, which was a mixed-sex union) to defend male interests. It has now become a part of the NAS/UWT (The National Association of Schoolmasters and the Union of Women Teachers). NUWT (The National Union of Women Teachers), broke away from the NUT in 1919 and disbanded in 1961, when women teachers won equal pay. It is now also amalgamated with the NAS to form NAS/UWT.

52 Alison Oram, 'Inequalities in the Teaching Profession', p. 103.

53 Mary Evans, *Life at a Girls' Grammar School in the 1950s*, The Women's Press, 1991.

54 ibid., p. 117.

55 Doris Lessing, *Under My Skin: Volume One of my Autobiography, to 1949*, HarperCollins, 1994, p. 149.

56 ibid., p. 87.

57 ibid., p. 73.

58 ibid., p. 133.

59 ibid., p. 112.

3 Children's Teachers

1 I have just learned that Miss Cocker married Mr Messingham almost fifty years ago.

2 My copy of *Ameliaranne Keeps School*, the one I read as a child, has no author and no publisher or other sign of its provenance.

3 In the first volume of Simone de Beauvoir's autobiography, *Memoirs of a Dutiful Daughter*, trans. James Kirkup, Penguin, 1963, p. 45.

4 Ruth Adam, *I'm Not Complaining* (1938), Virago, 1983.

5 ibid., p. 343.

6 ibid., p. 346.

7 ibid., p. 26.

8 ibid., p. 14.

9 ibid., p. 58.

10 ibid., p. 100.

11 Sue Smedley, 'Versions and Visions: Women Primary School Teachers, their Initial Education and their Work', thesis submitted for MA in Language and Literature in Education, University of London Institute of Education, 1992, p. 37.

12 Flora Thompson, *Still Glides the Stream* (1948), Oxford University Press, 1979, p. 10.

13 Flora Thompson, *Lark Rise to Candleford* (1945) Penguin, 1973 p. 155. The trilogy was originally published in three parts. The first part, *Lark Rise*, was published in 1939.

14 ibid., p. 156.

15 ibid., p. 207.

16 ibid., p. 328.

17 ibid., p. 182.

18 ibid., p. 189.

19 Michael W. Apple, *Teachers and Texts: A Political Economy of Class and Gender Relations in Education*, Routledge, 1986, p. 21.

20 ibid., p. 64.

21 Kathryn Hughes, *The Victorian Governess*, The Hambledon Press, 1993, p. 200. Mary Poovey's chapter 'The Anathematized Race: The Governess and *Jane Eyre*' in her book *Uneven Developments: The Ideological Work of Gender in Mid-Victorian England*, Virago, 1989, covers similar ground and charts the changes in female employment up to the 1850s, and their effect on public discussion of the governess and her 'plight'.

22 Kathryn Hughes, *The Victorian Governess* p. 148. In Charlotte Brontë's *Shirley* (1849) as in Mrs Henry Wood's *East Lynne* (1861) a disgraced wife returns to become the governess of her own children. It seems likely that such slippage between the two roles arose out of the kind of anxiety Hughes indicates.

23 Quoted in Frances Widdowson, *Going Up into the Next Class: Women and Elementary Teacher Training, 1840–1914*, Hutchinson, 1983, p. 30.

24 Flora Thompson, *Lark Rise to Candleford*, p. 185.

25 ibid., p. 186.

26 ibid., p. 188.

27 ibid.

28 ibid., p. 192.

29 ibid., p. 196.

30 For a marvellously illuminating analysis of how teachers fare within the representations of popular culture, and particularly in terms of Barbie Doll images, see Sandra Weber and Claudia Mitchell, *'That's Funny, You Don't Look Like a Teacher'*, Falmer Press, 1995. The study considers the contradictory character of children's perceptions of their teachers in a contemporary setting.

31 'Vatican II' is the name given to the series of liberalising moves initiated by Pope John XXIII in 1962, which introduced reforming change to the Catholic Church.

32 Mary Loudon, *Unveiled: Nuns Talking*, Chatto & Windus, 1992, p. 2.

33 ibid., p. 144.

34 Antonia White, *Frost in May* (1933), Virago, 1978, p. 118.

35 ibid., p. 132.

36 Jackie Bennett and Rosemary Forgan (eds), *There's Something about a Convent Girl*, Virago, 1991, p. 92.

37 ibid., p. 62. Michael Mason asks why there has been such a long tradition amongst feminists of condemning many aspects of sexual emancipation in favour of austerity. He answers his own question by suggesting that many of us would see the virtue in taking 'a leaf from the nineteenth-century anti-sensualist book' in relation to paedophilia, and that similarly, many women – including nuns and some feminists from Mary Wollstonecraft onwards – were surely right to warn young women that their own sexual fulfilment would be hard to come by without some kind of endorsement of the social and sexual exploitation of women. Michael Mason, *The Making of Victorian Sexual Attitudes*, Oxford University Press, 1994, pp. 215ff.

38 René Weis, the author of *Criminal Justice: The True Story of Edith Thompson*, Hamish Hamilton, 1988, very kindly lent me his copy of this log-book. It is very nearly 500 pages long, written entirely in long-hand, and runs from 16 August

1901, when the Kensington Avenue Schools first opened, to 24 July 1929.

39 ibid., p. 151.

40 Charles Booth, *The New Survey of London Life and Labour*, vol. 1 *Forty Years of Change*, P.S. King and Son Ltd., 1930, p. 245.

4 *Teaching as Work*

1 I am thinking particularly of Madeleine Grumet's very intelligent *Bitter Milk: Women and Teaching*, which does seem to me to rely on an ultimately unreliable double vision of the maternal relation as both central to productive pedagogy and what is most specifically repressed and ruled out by conventional schooling.

2 Sandra Acker, 'Women and Teaching: A Semi-Detached Sociology of a Semi-Profession', in Stephen Walker and Len Barton (eds), *Gender, Class and Education*, Falmer Press, 1983; see also p. 12. Acker's work in this field has been immensely helpful to me; in particular, the collection of essays she edited and introduced: Sandra Acker (ed.), *Teachers, Gender and Careers*, Falmer Press, 1989.

3 Northrop Frye, *On Education*, Fitzhenry & Whiteside, 1988, p. 11. I am particularly grateful to Professor Deanne Bogdan, both for introducing me to the work of Northrop Frye, as a writer on education and on the reading of literature, and for her arguments with him in the book she edited with Stanley B. Straw, *Beyond Communication: Reading, Comprehension and Criticism*, Boynton/Cook, Heinemann, 1990; and in her *Re-Educating the Imagination: Toward a Poetics, Politics, and Pedagogy of Literary Engagement*, Boynton/Cook, Heinemann, 1992.

4 I owe this insight to Carolyn Steedman's '"The Mother Made Conscious": The Historical Development of a Primary School Pedagogy', in her *Past Tenses: Essays on Writing*, p. 179. See also Irene M. Lilley, *Friedrich Froebel: A Selection from his Writings*, Cambridge University Press, 1967, particularly pp. 84–5: 'A mother does this naturally and spontaneously without any instruction or prompting, but this is not enough. It is also necessary that she should influence the child's growing awareness and consciously promote the continuity of his development, and that she should do this by establishing a positive and living relationship with him. So it is our concern

to arouse intelligent parental love and show the modes in which childhood expresses itself.'

5 In, for instance, Cathy Urwin, 'Constructing Motherhood: The Persuasion of Normal Development', in Carolyn Steedman, Cathy Urwin and Valerie Walkerdine (eds), *Language, Gender and Childhood*, Routledge & Kegan Paul, 1985.

6 Geraldine J. Clifford, '"Daughters into Teachers": Educational and Demographic Influences on the Transformation of Teaching into Women's Work in America', in Alison Prentice and Marjorie R. Theobald (eds), *Women who Taught*, University of Toronto Press, 1991, p. 124.

7 Clara E. Collet, 'The Age Limit for Women', in her *Educated Working Women*, P.S. King, 1902, p. 91.

8 ibid.

9 Sabrina Broadbent, 'Sex, Lies and the Media: A Gendered Account of State Intervention in Schools and the Subject of English in the 1980s, thesis submitted for MA in Language and Literature in Education at the University of London Institute of Education, 1991, pp. 44–5.

10 ibid.

11 Carolyn Steedman, 'Prisonhouses', in her *Past Tenses*, p. 56.

12 An extremely interesting history of changes in the forms of schooling, and their relation to issues of classroom control, curriculum and pedagogy, is David Hamilton's, *Towards a Theory of Schooling*, Falmer Press, 1989. Predictably, however, it does not consider the position of women teachers in relation to these often crucial changes, some of which women must have provoked or inspired, if not initiated.

13 Sandra Acker, 'Rethinking Teachers' Careers', in Sandra Acker (ed.), *Teachers, Gender and Careers*, p. 10.

14 Gerald Grace, *Teachers, Ideology and Control: A Study in Urban Education*, Routledge & Kegan Paul, 1978.

15 Michael W. Apple, 'Work, Gender, and Teaching', *Teachers College Record*, 84, no. 3 (1983), p. 620.

16 This exists only as a typescript, which is in my possession.

17 The letter, which is in my possession, reads 'My dear Clara, I congratulate you heartily on your success in the Examination – you are our first graduate. With love & good wishes Believe me, Affectly yours, Frances M. Buss.'

18 See Geoffrey Partington, *Women Teachers in the 20th*

Century in England and Wales, NFER Publishing Co., 1976, p. 6; and Annie E. Ridley, *Frances Mary Buss and her Work for Education*, Longmans, Green, 1895, p. 177.

19 H.C. Dent, *The Training of Teachers in England and Wales 1800–1975*, Hodder & Stoughton, 1977, p. 15.

20 ibid., p. 25.

21 This division has had the most pernicious effects, I believe: first, by separating knowledge and skills that are to be taught to children from knowledge about teaching and learning, creating artificial barriers in the process between teachers' knowledge and children's knowledge, when we need to be sharing the implications of both kinds of knowledge with children; then, by rationalising a reduction in all those aspects of teachers' education and training, which cannot be justified as immediately relevant or as having obvious practical outcomes.

22 ILEA stands for the Inner London Education Authority, which was responsible for all levels of public education except for university education in the capital between 1964 and 1990, when it was abolished as part of the destruction of the GLC, the Greater London Council. London County Council (LCC) ran the London Schools until the creation of the ILEA in 1964.

23 See chapter 1, note 5.

24 ROSLA, Raising of the School Leaving Age, from fifteen to sixteen, in 1972.

25 In the 1970s London teachers had most to fear from the *Evening Standard*. On several occasions journalists from that paper waylaid pupils at my school as they were leaving to go home. Now, I can think of no paper of any kind that is not capable of attacking teachers. And few if any of them ask teachers for their views.

26 *Liber Amoris* was William Hazlitt's painful and much criticised account of his love for Sarah Walker, published in 1823.

27 I am thinking of writers like Neil Postman and Herbert Kohl in America and Nick Otty in this country.

28 Margaret Littlewood, 'The "Wise Married Woman" and the Teaching Unions', in Hilary de Lyon and Frances Widdowson Migniuolo (eds), *Women Teachers: Issues and Experiences*, Open University Press, 1989, p. 182.

29 Clara E. Collet, 'The Economic Position of Educated Working Women', in her *Educated Working Women*, P.S. King, 1902, p. 3.

30 John Newsom, *The Education of Girls*, Faber & Faber, 1948, p. 20.

31 Gerald Grace, *Teachers, Ideology and Control*, p. 15.

32 ibid.

33 Hilda Kean, *Challenging the State? The Socialist and Feminist Educational Experience 1900–1930*, Falmer Press, 1990, p. 129.

34 In the excellent anthology he edited with Martin Lawn: Martin Lawn and Gerald Grace (eds), *Teachers: The Culture and Politics of Work*, Falmer Press, 1987.

35 For instance, Alison Prentice and Marjorie R. Theobald (eds), *Women who Taught.*

36 I am thinking of several of the teachers I taught on a Masters course at McGill University in Montreal during the summer of 1993.

37 Antonio Gramsci (1891–1937), founder, and leader for some years, of the Italian Communist Party, and also the writer who initiated the most significant rereading of Marx within a study of twentieth-century capitalism and the political and cultural relations that have sustained it.

38 See Antonio Gramsci, *Selections from Prison Notebooks*, ed. and trans. Quintin Hoare and Geoffrey Nowell Smith, Lawrence & Wishart, 1986, p. 8.

5 Boys and Girls

1 Raymond Williams, *Politics and Letters: Interviews with New Left Review*, Verso, 1979, p. 28.

2 WEA, Workers' Educational Association. Raymond Williams, *Politics and Letters*, p. 78.

3 Raymond Williams, *Politics and Letters*, p. 27.

4 LEA: Local Education Authority.

5 I think of Valerie Walkerdine's powerful memoir of her childhood, in which she describes her sense of being fobbed off with the second-rate, and her determination to achieve more than was ever expected of her. She succeeded triumphantly, of course. Valerie Walkerdine, 'Dreams from an Ordinary Childhood', first published in Liz Heron (ed.), *Truth, Dare or Promise: Girls Growing up in the Fifties*, Virago, 1985.

6 Carol Dyhouse, *Girls Growing up in Late Victorian and Edwardian England*, Routledge & Kegan Paul, 1981, p. 10.

7 George Eliot, *The Mill on the Floss* (1860), Penguin, 1983, p. 220.

8 For instance, Caroline Gipps and Patricia Murphy, *A Fair Test: Assessment, Achievement and Equity*, Open University Press, 1994.

9 Section Two, the *Independent*, 18 October 1994. The article was written by Judith Judd.

10 These words come from Iris Murdoch's firm assertion of 'the importance of acknowledging that there *are* sheep and goats, and acting accordingly' in her 'Socialism and Selection', in Brian Cox and Rhodes Boyson (eds), *Black Paper, 1975: The Fight for Education*, J.M. Dent, 1975, p. 8.

11 Brian Jackson and Dennis Marsden, *Education and the Working Class*, Penguin, 1962, p. 179.

12 Paul Willis, *Learning to Labour: How Working-Class Kids get Working-Class Jobs*, Saxon House, 1977, p. 52.

13 Michael T. Hamerston, 'On Becoming a Plumber', thesis submitted for MA in Language and Literature in Education, University of London Institute of Education, 1981.

14 ibid., p. 103.

15 ibid., pp. 100–102.

16 Terry Lovell, *Consuming Fiction*, Verso, 1987, p. 141.

17 Valerie Walkerdine, 'Sex, Power and Pedagogy', in her *Schoolgirl Fictions*, Verso, 1990, p. 13.

18 ibid., p. 4.

19 The *Independent*, 6 September 1994.

20 D.H. Lawrence, *The Rainbow* (1915), Penguin, 1950, p. 372.

21 ibid., p. 388.

22 ibid., p. 410.

23 ibid., p. 406.

24 Catherine Pugh, 'Boys and English: A Consideration of Some Issues Raised by the 1993 OFSTED Report', thesis submitted for the MA in Language and Literature in Education, University of London Institute of Education, 1994, p. 15.

25 ibid., p. 17.

26 Rosalind Coward, 'Whipping Boys', *Guardian*, 3 September 1994.

27 P. and H. Silver, *The Education of the Poor: The History of a National School 1824–1974*, Routledge & Kegan Paul, 1974, p. 49.

28 ibid., p. 56.

29 ibid., p. 103.

30 ibid., p. 153.

31 ibid., p. 70.

32 ibid., p. 158.

33 J-J. Rousseau, *Emile* (1762), trans. Barbara Foxley, Everyman's Library, 1911, p. 331.

34 Andrew Bell, in *Education Guardian*, 6 August 1991.

35 These figures are taken from Alan Smithers and Pamela Robinson, *Post-18 Education: Growth, Change and Prospect*, Executive Briefing, The Council for Industry and Higher Education, February 1995.

36 Harriet Martineau, *Autobiography: Volume I* (1877), Virago, 1983, p. 100.

37 See, for instance, Myron Weiner, *The Child and the State in India*, Princeton University Press, 1991, pp. 175–9.

38 Ken Jones, *Right Turn. The Conservative Revolution in Education*, Hutchinson Radius, 1989, p. 1.

6 Literacy

1 Caroline Gipps and Patricia I. Murphy survey recent research on the question of sex differences in specific abilities in their *A Fair Test? Assessment, Achievement and Equity*, Open University Press, 1994, Chapter 2, pp. 28ff. They are, by and large, sceptical of the grosser claims, particularly those which generalise from age-specific samples to overall differences. They quote particularly in this context the research of A.W.H. Buffery and J.A. Gray, 'Sex Differences in the Development of Spatial and Linguistic skills' in C. Ounsted and D.C. Taylor (eds), *Gender Differences: Their Ontogeny and Significance*, Churchill, 1972; T. Moore, 'Language and Intelligence: A Longitudinal Study of the First Eight Years. Part 1: Patterns of Development in Boys and Girls', *Human Development*, 10 (1967), pp. 88–106; and E.E. Maccoby and C.N. Jacklin, *The Psychology of Sex Differences*, Stanford University Press, 1974.

2 Reprinted from the *Guardian*, 19 July 1936, in *Guardian*, 19 July 1994.

3 Shirley Brice Heath, *Ways with Words*, Cambridge University Press, 1983.

4 Judith Solsken, *Literacy, Gender and Work in Families and in School*, Ablex Publishing Company, 1993, p. 31.

5 ibid., p. 43.

6 ibid., p. 166.

7 ibid., p. 217.

8 Flora Thompson, *Lark Rise to Candleford*, p. 182.

9 ibid., p. 180.

10 ibid., pp. 109–12.

11 ibid., p. 331.

12 ibid., p. 381.

13 I am thinking of Shirley Brice Heath's marvellous study of the literacy practices of three communities in North Carolina during the 1970s and of Brian Street's very interesting work, which, in focusing on those literacy practices which function outside and independently of school, is perhaps too inclined to leave schooled literacies untheorised within his useful opposition of an ideological model of literacy to what he calls an 'autonomous' model. However, he also very helpfully suggests the ways in which a pedagogic approach to literacy infects literacy behaviour outside school. His own work and work he has anthologised are to be found in Brian V. Street, *Literacy in Theory and Practice*, Cambridge University Press, 1986; J.C. and B.V. Street, 'The Schooling of Literacy' in D. Barton and R. Ivanic (eds), *Writing in the Community*, Sage Publications, 1991; and Brian V. Street (ed.), *Cross-Cultural Approaches to Literacy*, Cambridge University Press, 1993.

14 René Weis, *Criminal Justice. The True Story of Edith Thompson*, Hamish Hamilton, 1988.

15 'The Newbolt Report' was, in fact, *The Teaching of English in England. Being the Report of the Departmental Committee Appointed by the President of the Board of Education to Inquire into the Position of English in the Educational System of England*, HMSO, 1921, whose chairman was Sir Henry Newbolt, and which reported in 1921. Amongst the recommendations relating to elementary schools are the injunctions to teach children to speak Standard English and to aim, not 'at the suppression of dialect, but at making the children bi-lingual'. The last of the recommendations in this section is 'that if literature is to be enjoyed by the children it must be entrusted to teachers with a love of it'.

16 René Weis, *Criminal Justice*, p. 9.

17 ibid., p. 6.

18 ibid., p. 7.

19 ibid., p. 9.

20 ibid., p. 261.

21 ibid.

22 ibid., p. 293. Margaret Fry was the wife of Roger Fry, the painter and art critic.

23 ibid., p. 235.
24 ibid., p. 43.
25 ibid., p. 140.
26 In Raymond Williams, *The Long Revolution*, Penguin, 1965, pp. 67–76.
27 ibid., p. 278.
28 Q.D. Leavis, *Fiction and the Reading Public* (1932), Chatto & Windus, 1978, p. 7.
29 OFSTED (Office for Standards in Education), *Boys and English 1988–1991*, (report from the office of Her Majesty's Chief Inspector of Schools), pamphlet distributed by the Department of Education and Science, 1993.

7 A Civilising Influence

1 Brian Doyle, *English and Englishness*, Routledge, 1989, p. 2.
2 ibid., p. 3.
3 ibid., p. 4.
4 See, for example, Ken Jones, 'The "Cox Report": Working for Hegemony' in Ken Jones (ed.), *English and the National Curriculum: Cox's Revolution?*, Kogan Page, 1992, p. 19.
5 'There has been an English Tripos in Cambridge since 1917, and an independent Tripos and Faculty since 1926,' see Raymond Williams, 'Cambridge English and Beyond', in *London Review of Books*, 5, no. 12, 1983. The first examinations in the new Oxford degree, *Literis Anglicis*, were taken in 1896. See John Dixon, *A Schooling in 'English': Critical Episodes in the Struggle to Shape Literary and Cultural Studies*, Open University Press, 1991, p. 62. The first Professor of English and Rhetoric was appointed at University College London in 1829. In 1857, Professor Masson was congratulated on the numbers of students taking English classes, and the university regulations were changed to allow for an Honours degree in English. The first students were awarded an Honours degree in English in 1862. Women were first admitted in 1872.
6 I wrote a version of this section on George Gissing as an article called 'Gissing may Damage your Health', *London Review of Books*, 13, no. 5, 7 March 1991. This was, in fact, a review of George Gissing, *The Collected Letters of George Gissing*, vol. 1, *1863–1880*, ed. Paul F. Mattheisen, Arthur C. Young and Pierre Coustillas, Ohio University Press, 1990.
7 This is included in Gissing, *The Collected Letters*.

8 From Raymond Williams, *The English Novel from Dickens to Lawrence*, Chatto & Windus, 1974, quoted in Chris Baldick, 'Raymond Williams and English Studies', *Changing English*, 2, no. 1 (1994), p. 19.

9 John Buchan, *Memory Hold-the-Door: The Autobiography of John Buchan*, J.M. Dent, 1984, p. 30.

10 Gissing, *The Collected Letters*, pp. 232–3: George Perkins Marsh, *Lectures on the English Language*, published in New York in 1860 and in London in 1862.

11 Richard Morris, *Historical Outlines of English Accidence*, 1872; and Ernest Adams, *Elements of the English Language*, 1866. Gissing, *The Collected Letters* pp. 83–4.

12 Gissing, *The Collected Letters*, p. 279.

13 John Dixon, *A Schooling in 'English'*.

14 John Dixon, *Growth Through English – set in the Perspective of the Seventies*, Oxford University Press, 1975.

15 James Britton, *Language and Learning*, 1970; new revised edn, Penguin, 1992; the Bullock Report is the Department of Education and Science's (DES's), *A Language for Life*, HMSO, 1975; Douglas Barnes, James Britton and Harold Rosen and the London Association for the Teaching of English (LATE), *Language, the Learner and the School*, Penguin, 1969; revised edn. Penguin, 1975. Peter Medway, *Finding a Language: Autonomy and Learning in School*, Writers and Readers/Chameleon, 1980.

16 All of these were important themes of the work on language and learning done by James Britton and his colleagues in the English Department of the University of London Institute of Education during the late sixties and early seventies.

17 I was impressed recently to read an anthology of conversations among women scholars of literacy and English, most of whom were in their fifties or much older. Their maturity and sense represented exactly what might have been included in all those earlier versions of progressive English teaching, but was not. I am thinking of people like Margaret Meek Spencer, Janet Emig, Louise Rosenblatt, Yetta Goodman and Margaret Gill. See Mary H. Maguire (ed.), *Dialogue in a Major Key: Women Scholars Speak*, NCTE (National Council of Teachers of English), 1995.

18 I am grateful to Leon Gore for these figures. He reported on the findings of his research in a pamphlet called 'Can Exams Be Fair? Race and Gender Differences in Brent student attainment in GCSE English', distributed by Brent LEA, 1991.

19 OFSTED (Office for Standards in Education), *Boys and English 1988–1991* (report from the Office of Her Majesty's Chief Inspector of Schools), pamphlet distributed by the Department of Education and Science, 1993, p. 1.

20 ibid., p. 9.

21 ibid., p. 10.

22 ibid., p. 23.

23 Catherine Pugh, 'Boys and English: A Consideration of Some Issues raised by the 1993 OFSTED Report', thesis submitted for MA in Language and Literature in Education at the University of London Institute of Education, 1994, p. 5.

24 ibid., p. 23.

25 ibid., p. 16. Paul Willis, *Learning to Labour: How Working-Class Kids get Working-Class Jobs*, Saxon House, 1977.

26 Catherine Pugh, 'Boys and English', p. 30.

27 A recent BBC/Mori poll, reported in the *Independent*, 22 October 1994, unearthed differences between the reading habits of men and women. Women are much more likely to read in bed than men and to read a book right through. They are also, apparently, more likely to read the end of a book before deciding whether to persevere.

28 Carolyn Steedman, *The Tidy House: Little Girls Writing*, Virago, 1982, p. 109.

29 I am thinking here of a lecture given by Wayne Booth in 1984, at the 17th conference of 'Language in Inner-city Schools', at the University of London Institute of Education, to mark the retirement of Harold Rosen. In this, he wonderfully described his early reading of Joyce's *Ulysses*, and how he read a passage in which 'Stephen Dedalus is walking on the shore, puzzling about his sensations' in a spirit of emulation of the philosophical and the learned and the witty man that Joyce creates in Stephen and must therefore – if only by implication – have been himself. I remember being struck by how difficult any such identification would have been for a young woman. 'Narrative as the Mold of Character', in University of London Institute of Education, *A Telling Exchange*, University of London Institute of Education, 1984; Frank Lentricchia, 'My Kinsman, T.S. Eliot', *Raritan*, 11, no. 4 (1992), p. 1; Richard Rodriguez, *Hunger of memory. The Education of Richard Rodriguez: An Autobiography*, David R. Godine, 1982.

30 Sir Ron Dearing was given the task by the government of simplifying the National Curriculum. The reduced version of

the English curriculum I refer to here is SCAA (Schools
Curriculum and Assessment Authority), *English in the
National Curriculum: Draft Proposals*, May 1994.

Even John Locke, in his *Some Thoughts Concerning
Education*, published in the 1690s, is more sceptical about
the usefulness of teaching grammar than recent secretaries
of state for education have been. See John Locke, *Some
Thoughts Concerning Education* (1693), in *The Educational
Writings of John Locke*, ed. James L. Axtell, Cambridge
University Press, 1968, p. 277, where he makes a good case
for and against the teaching of grammar.

31 Catherine Pugh, 'Boys and English', p. 15.
32 ibid., p. 18.
33 I have been enormously helped by the work of Gill Plummer,
   whose research has focused on the history of working-class
   girls who used their education as a way into middle-class
   work and lives. She has shown me how powerfully class has
   structured these women's lives, and how complex their sense
   of the educational process has been.
34 Gill Frith, 'Transforming Features: Double Vision and the
   Female Reader', in *New Formations*, no. 15, Winter (1991),
   p. 72; James Fordyce, *Sermons to Young Women*, 3rd edn, 2 vols,
   Millar, Cadell, Dodsley & Payne, 1766, vol. 1, pp. 272–3.
35 Gill Frith, 'Transforming Features', p. 72.
36 Anne Turvey, 'Interrupting the Lecture: "Cox" seen from a
   Classroom', in Ken Jones (ed.), *English and the National
   Curriculum: Cox's Revolution?*, Kogan Page, 1992, p. 52.
37 ibid., p. 53.
38 ibid., p. 54.
39 George Eliot, 'Edward Neville', written 16 March 1834 and
   included in Gordon S. Haight, *George Eliot: A Biography*,
   Oxford University Press, 1968, pp. 554–60. The words in
   brackets were crossed out in George Eliot's manuscript.
40 Anne Turvey, 'Interrupting the Lecture', p. 58.
41 Tony Burgess, 'The Question of English', in Margaret Meek
   and Jane Miller (eds), *Changing English: Essays for Harold
   Rosen*, University of London Institute of Education and
   Heinemann Educational Books, 1984, p. 3.
42 ibid., p. 4.
43 I have written about this in a chapter called 'A Tongue,
   for sighing' in Janet Maybin and Neil Mercer (eds)
   Using English: From Conversation to Canon, Routledge,
   1996.

44 Tom Paulin, 'Writing beyond Writing: Emily Dickinson', in his *Minotaur. Poetry and the Nation State*, Faber and Faber, 1992, pp. 99 and 103.

45 Dorothy Richardson, *Pilgrimage*, vol. 1. Virago, 1979, p. 215.

46 ibid., vol. 4, p. 305.

47 ibid., vol. 2, p. 373.

48 ibid., vol. 2, p. 317.

49 ibid., vol. 3, p. 288.

50 ibid., vol. 4, p. 158.

8 Hirelings and Pedagogues

1 Ellen Moers, *Literary Women*, Women's Press, 1978, particularly chapter 10, 'Educating Heroinism: Governess to Governor'.

2 ibid., p. 214.

3 Terry Lovell, *Consuming Fiction*, Verso, 1987, p. 42.

4 J-J. Rousseau (1712–78), wrote *Emile* in 1762, in which he established principles for a new scheme of education. J.H. Pestalozzi (1746–1827), the Swiss educationalist, whose *Leonard and Gertrude* (1781) and *How Gertrude Teaches her Children* (1801) expounded his educational theory.

5 Jane Roland Martin, 'Excluding Women from the Educational Realm' (1982), in Lynda Stone (ed.), *The Education Feminism Reader*, Routledge, 1994.

6 ibid., p. 111.

7 Plato, *The Republic of Plato*, trans. and ed. Francis Cornford, Oxford University Press, 1948, p. 148.

8 Mary Wollstonecraft, *Vindication of the Rights of Woman* (1792), Penguin, 1985, p. 189.

9 Jane Roland Martin, 'Excluding Women', p. 115.

10 Rita McWilliams-Tullberg, 'Women and Degrees at Cambridge University, 1862–1897', in Martha Vicinus (ed.), *A Widening Sphere: Changing Roles of Victorian Women*, Methuen, 1980.

11 George Eliot, *Daniel Deronda* (1874/6), Penguin, 1957, p. 694.

12 Doris Lessing in her 1971 Preface to *The Golden Notebook*, Granada, 1973, p. 11, writes, 'George Eliot is good as far as she goes. But I think the penalty she paid for being a Victorian woman was that she had to be shown to be a good woman even when she wasn't according to the hypocrisies

of the time – there is a great deal she does not understand because she is moral'.

13 George Eliot, *Romola* (1862/3), Oxford University Press, 1994, p. 366.

14 ibid., p. 471.

15 Carolyn Steedman, Introduction to her *Past Tenses: Essays on Writing, Autobiography and history*, Rivers Oram Press, 1992, p. 5.

16 John Locke, *Some Thoughts Concerning Education* (1693), in *The Educational Writings of John Locke*, ed. James L. Axtell, Cambridge University Press, 1968.

17 Violet Wyndham, *Madame de Genlis*, André Deutsch, 1958, p. 82.

18 Ellen Moers, *Literary Women*, p. 221.

19 Violet Wyndham, *Madame de Genlis*, p. 249.

20 Samuel Richardson, *Pamela*, Everyman's Library, 1962, vol. 2, p. 472.

21 ibid., vol. 1, p. 211.

22 ibid., p. 218.

23 Clara E. Collet transcribed and edited *The Letters of John to Eliza. A Four Years' Correspondence Course in the Education of Women. 1806–1810*, privately published and available in the British Library.

24 ibid., p. 22.

25 Clara E. Collet, *Letters of John to Eliza*, p. 19.

Maria Edgeworth, *The Popular Tales*. They were published in 1804. William Bowles was a poet much admired by Coleridge in his youth. He is remembered mainly for his *Fourteen Sonnets*, which were published in 1789.

Scientific Dialogues. Intended for the Instruction and Entertainment of Young People: in which the first principles of Natural and Experimental Philosophy are fully explained. These were written by the Revd. Jeremiah Joyce (1763–1816), and a second edition of seven volumes, published between 1803 and 1809, is probably the one John is referring to here. Joyce was, incidentally, secretary to the Unitarian Society for many years and tutor to the sons of Lord Stanhope, to whom the books are dedicated. The volumes were published by J. Johnson, at No. 72, St. Paul's Churchyard, St John's Square, Clerkenwell. The volumes were each devoted to one or a pair of topics: mechanics, astronomy, hydrostatics, pneumatics, optics and magnetism, electricity and galvanism. The final volume contained questions and exercises for examining pupils. Each volume had a few pages of engravings, mostly of diagrams, at the end, and on the title-page a quotation from Edgeworth's *Practical Education* (almost certainly written with his daughter, Maria): 'Conversation, with the habit of explaining the meaning of words, and the structure of common domestic implements to children is the sure and effectual method of preparing the mind for the acquirement of science.' The books are indeed written in dialogue form. The earlier volumes take the form of a conversation between Charles, Emma and their father. Emma and her father are dropped from the later volumes in favour of James and a tutor. A new enlarged edition was published in 1855. I am grateful to Eric Korn for his help in tracking down these books to the Wellcome Library.

26 ibid., p. 108.

27 ibid., p. 216.

28 ibid., p. 72.

29 ibid., p. 15.

30 ibid., p. 174.

31 Samuel Collet, known in the family as the Patriarch, partly to distinguish him from younger namesakes, was born in 1682 and died in 1773. He would not have called himself a Unitarian, rather a 'primitive' Christian, anxious to get to the fundamentals, the roots of Christianity, and to do away with what he regarded as the excrescences of current practices and beliefs. In letters to his brother Joseph on the subject he is, however, particularly exercised by the confusions incurred by Trinitarian beliefs, so that it is not illegitimate, I think, to see him as a very early Unitarian. These letters were published privately by Clara Collet in a booklet called *William Whiston's Disciples. In correspondence with each other 1723–1768.*

32 What must be the original manuscript draft of these letters, written in a handmade notebook and dated 1752, are in my possession, as is the version of them that Clara Collet had typed in 1932. She appeared to have no misgivings about her attribution of these letters to Joseph Collet, nor to the question of their recipient, Sarah Lasswell, his future sister-in-law. Mary Barker (Eliza's sister) also endorsed this provenance (though she inserted a question mark after Joseph Collet) in a pencilled note on the front page of the manuscript, written in 1878, in her extreme old age, and ending with the words, 'very much the principles on which *we* were trained'.

33 Clara sent my father a copy of her transcribed version of these letters a month before I was born.

34 Rosalind Mitchison, 'The Numbers Game', *The New Review*, 4, no. 47 (1978); a review of Peter Laslett's *Family Life and Illicit Love in Earlier Generations*, Cambridge University Press, 1977, and Laurence Stone's *The Family, Sex and Marriage in England 1500–1800*, Weidenfeld and Nicolson, 1977.

35 All three were literary periodicals, started in the early eighteenth century. Richard Steele was involved in all three.

36 Karen Clarke, 'Public and Private Children: Infant Education in the 1820s and 1830s', in Carolyn Steedman, Cathy Urwin and Valerie Walkerdine (eds), *Language, Gender and Childhood*, Routledge & Kegan Paul, p. 81.

37 Clarke is quoting from David Stow, *Supplement to Moral Training and the Training System*, Glasgow, 1839, p. 26.

38 Alice Walker, *The Color Purple*, The Women's Press, 1983, p. 1.

39 Toni Morrison, *The Bluest Eye*, Triad Granada, 1981, Prologue.

40 Toni Morrison, *Beloved*, Chatto & Windus, 1987, pp. 155–6.

9 Stories of Disappointment

1 Celia Burgess Macey, 'The Development of Girls' Writing in the Primary School: The Influence of Gender and Genre', thesis submitted for MA in Language and Literature in Education at the University of London Institute of Education, 1992, p. 21.

2 Terry Lovell, *Consuming Fiction*, Verso, 1987, p. 160.

3 See Introduction, note 2, p. 279, for references to this debate.

4 V.N. Volosinov, *Marxism and the Philosophy of Language*, Harvard University Press, 1973, p. 102.

5 Celia Burgess Macey, 'The Development of Girls' Writing in the Primary School', p. 21.

6 ibid., p. 24.

7 ibid., p. 124.

8 ibid., p. 8.

9 This work on writing produced several books, foremost amongst them: James Britton *et al.*, *The Development of Writing Abilities, 11–18*, Macmillan, 1975; Nancy Martin *et al.*, *Writing and Learning across the Curriculum, 11–16*, Ward Lock for Schools Council, 1976; and Carol Burgess *et al.*, *Understanding Children Writing*, Penguin, 1973.

10 These ideas were above all about art; the value of children's painting and drawing as art. Wilhelm Viola, for instance, in *Child Art*, University of London Press, 1942, traces the movement back to Germany and Austria in the early thirties, but also reminds us that there was a famous exhibition held at County Hall in London in 1938, where hundreds of pictures by London schoolchildren were seen by literally thousands of visitors. He also writes of private exhibitions in London where paintings by children were bought for five or ten guineas apiece.

11 Maggie Humm, 'Subjects in English: Autobiography, Women and Education', in Ann Thompson and Helen Wilcox (eds), *Teaching Women: Feminism and English studies*, Manchester University Press, 1989, p. 39.

12 ibid., p. 40.

13 Deanne Bogdan, 'When Is a Singing School (Not) a Chorus? The Emancipatory Agenda in Feminist Pedagogy and Literature Education' (1993), in Lynda Stone (ed.), *The Education Feminism Reader*, Routledge, 1994, p. 350.

14 Susan Sellers, 'Biting the Teacher's Apple: Opening Doors for Women in Higher Education' in Ann Thompson and Helen Wilcox (eds), *Teaching Women: Feminism and English Studies*, Manchester University Press, 1989, p. 28.

15 Michael W. Apple, *Teachers and Texts: A Political Economy of Class and Gender Relations in Education*, Routledge, 1986, p. 45.

16 Jo Cross, 'Reading Riffat: Gender, Culture and School – How do These Influence the Writing and Reading of Autobiography in the Classroom?', thesis submitted for MA in Language and Literature in Education at the University of London Institute of Education, 1990, pp. 25ff.

17 Moya O'Donnell also wrote about the mismatch between the school's offer of pastoral care and its actual priorities, and the effect of that mismatch on women's careers as teachers, in 'Mothers as Teachers and Teachers as Mothers: How this Patterning Affects the Status of Women whether Inside the Institution of Teaching or Out of it', thesis submitted for MA in Language and Literature in Education, University of London Institute of Education, 1988.

18 Jo Cross, 'Reading Riffat', p. 29.

19 ibid., p. 38.

20 Maggie Humm, 'Subjects in English', p. 40.

21 Carolyn Steedman, 'History and Autobiography: Different

Pasts', in her *Past Tenses*, Rivers Oram Press, 1992, p. 41.

22 For instance, in Julia Kristeva, 'Oscillation between Power and Denial', in Elaine Marks and Isabelle de Courtivron (eds), *New French Feminisms*, Schocken Books, 1981, p. 166, where she writes, 'If women have a role to play in this on-going process, it is only in assuming a *negative* function: reject everything finite, definite, structured, loaded with meaning, in the existing state of society.'

23 Perhaps one of the most useful synoptic accounts of what I have sometimes called the 'impossibility' of women's relation to education is Madeleine Arnot's 'Male Hegemony, Social Class, and Women's Education' (1982), reprinted in Lynda Stone (ed.), *The Education Feminism Reader*, Routledge, 1994, pp. 84–104.

24 See, for instance, Shirley Ardener (ed.), *Defining Females: The Nature of Women in Society*, Croom Helm, 1978.

25 Carolyn Steedman, 'History and Autobiography', p. 50.

26 June Levison, 'Autobiographical Writing: Gender, Culture and Classrooms', thesis submitted for MA in Language and Literature in Education for the University of London Institute of Education, 1994, p. 14.

27 ibid., p. 20.

28 ibid., p. 22.

29 ibid., p. 21.

30 ibid., p. 40.

31 From Josie Levine, 'Pedagogy: The Case of the Missing Concept', in Keith Kimberley, Margaret Meek and Jane Miller (eds), *New Readings: Contributions to an Understanding of Literacy*, A & C Black, 1992, p. 197.

32 June Levison, 'Autobiographical Writing', p. 30.

33 ibid., pp. 25–6. Levison is referring here to Mikhail Bakhtin's 'The Problem of Speech Genres', in his *Speech Genres and Other Late Essays*, trans. Vern W. McGee, ed. Caryl Emerson and Michael Holquist, University of Texas Press, 1986.

34 Carolyn G. Heilbrun, *Writing a Woman's Life*, Ballantine Books, 1988, p. 60.

35 ibid., p. 130.

Bibliography

Acker, Sandra, 'Women and Teaching: A Semi-Detached Sociology of a Semi-Profession', in Stephen Walker and Len Barton (eds), *Gender, Class and Education*, Falmer Press, 1983

Acker, Sandra, (ed.), *Teachers, Gender and Careers*, Falmer Press, 1989

Adam, Ruth, *I'm Not Complaining* (1938), Virago, 1983

Alexander, R., J. Rose and C. Woodhead, *Curriculum Organisation and Classroom Practice in Primary Schools*, HMSO, 1992

Althusser, Louis, 'Ideology and Ideological State Apparatuses, (Notes towards an Investigation)', in his *Lenin and Philosophy and Other Essays*, Monthly Review Press, 1971

Appignanesi, Lisa, and John Forrester, *Freud's Women*, Weidenfeld & Nicolson, 1992

Apple, Michael W., *Cultural and Economic Reproduction in Education*, Routledge & Kegan Paul, 1982

Apple, Michael W., 'Work, Gender and Teaching', *Teachers College Record*, 84, no. 3 (1983)

Apple, Michael W., 'Teaching and "Women's Work": A Comparative Historical and Ideological Analysis', *Teachers College Record*, 86. no. 3 (1985)

Apple, Michael W., *Teachers and Texts: A Political Economy of Class and Gender Relations in Education*, Routledge, 1986

Ardener, Shirley (ed.), *Defining Females: The Nature of Women in Society*, Croom Helm, 1978

Arnot, Madeleine, 'Male Hegemony, Social Class, and Women's Education' (1982), in Lynda Stone (ed.), *The Education Feminism Reader*, Routledge, 1994

Arnot, Madeleine, and Gaby Weiner (eds), *Gender and the Politics of Schooling*, Hutchinson, 1987

Attar, Dena, *Wasting Girls' Time: The History and Politics of Home Economics*, Virago, 1990

Avery, Gillian, *The Best Type of Girl: A History of the Girls' Independent Schools*, André Deutsch, 1991

Ayres, L.P. 'What Educators Think About the Need for Employing Men Teachers in Our Public Schools', *Journal of Education Psychology*, 2 (1911)

Bakhtin, M.M., *Speech Genres and Other Late Essays*, trans. Vern W. McGee, ed. Caryl Emerson and Michael Holquist, University of Texas Press, 1986

Baldick, Chris, 'Raymond Williams and English Studies', *Changing English*, 2 no. 1 (1994)

Ball, S.J., and I.F. Goodson (eds), *Teachers' Lives and Careers*, Falmer Press, 1985

Barley, Anita S., 'Reading Black Literature in School', thesis submitted for MA in Language and Literature in Education, University of London Institute of Education, 1994

Barnes, Douglas, James Britton and Harold Rosen, and the London Association for the Teaching of English (LATE), *Language, the Learner and the School*, Penguin, 1969; revised edn, Penguin 1975

Barton, D., and R. Ivanic (eds), *Writing in the Community*, Sage Publications, 1991

de Beauvoir, Simone, *The Prime of Life*, trans. Peter Green, Penguin, 1965

de Beauvoir, Simone, *Memoirs of a Dutiful Daughter*, trans. James Kirkup, Penguin, 1963

Bennett, Jackie, and Rosemary Forgan (eds), *There's Something about a Convent Girl*, Virago, 1991

Benstock, Shari, *The Private Self*, Routledge & Kegan Paul, 1988.

Bird, C., *Born Female*, Pocket Books, 1968

Bogdan, Deanne, *Re-Educating the Imagination: Towards a Poetics, Politics, and Pedagogy of Literary Engagement*, Boynton/Cook, Heinemann, 1992

Bogdan, Deanne, 'When Is a Singing School (Not) a Chorus? The Emancipatory Agenda in Feminist Pedagogy and Literature Education' (1993), in Lynda Stone (ed.), *The Education Feminism Reader*, Routledge, 1994

Bogdan, Deanne, and Stanley B. Straw (eds), *Beyond Communication: Reading Comprehension and Criticism*, Boynton/Cook, Heinemann, 1990

Booth, Charles, (ed.), *Labour and Life of the People*, vol. 2 *London Continued*, Williams & Norgate, 1891

Booth, Charles, *The New Survey of London Life and Labour*, vol. 1, *Forty Years of Change*, P.S. King and Son Ltd, 1930

Booth, Wayne, 'Narrative as the Mold of Character' (lecture delivered at the seventeenth conference of 'Language in Inner-City Schools'), in the University of London Institute of Education, *A Telling Exchange*, University of London Institute of Education, 1984

Borer, Mary Cathcart, *Willingly to School: A History of Women's Education*, Lutterworth Press, 1976

Bowie, Janetta, *A Clydeside School in the Thirties*, Constable, 1975

Britton, James, *Language and Learning*, 1970; new revised edn, Penguin, 1992

Britton, James, *et al.*, *The Development of Writing Abilities, 11–18*, Macmillan, 1975

Broadbent, Sabrina, 'Sex Lies and the Media: A Gendered Account of State Intervention in Schools and the Subject of English in the 1980s', thesis submitted for MA in Language and Literature in Education at the University of London Institute of Education, 1991

Bryant, Margaret, *The Unexpected Revolution: A Study in the History of the Education of Women and Girls in the Nineteenth Century*, University of London Institute of Education, 1979

Buchan, John, *Memory Hold-the-Door: The Autobiography of John Buchan*, J.M. Dent, 1984

Budge, David, 'A World Made for Women?', *Times Educational Supplement*, 24 June 1994

Buffery, A.W.H., and J.A. Gray, 'Sex Differences in the Development of Spatial and Linguistic Skills', in C. Ounsted and D.C. Taylor (eds), *Gender Differences: Their Ontogeny and Significance*, Churchill, 1972

Burgess, Carol, *et al.*, *Understanding Children Writing*, Penguin, 1973

Burgess, Tony, 'The Question of English', in Margaret Meek and Jane Miller (eds), *Changing English: Essays for Harold Rosen*, University of London Institute of Education and Heinemann Educational Books, 1984

Burgess Macey, Celia, 'The Development of Girls' Writing in the Primary School: The Influence of Gender and Genre', thesis submitted for MA in Language and Literature in Education at the University of London Institute of Education, 1992

Cadogan, Mary, and Patricia Craig, *You're a brick, Angela! A New Look at Girls' Fiction from 1839–1975*, Gollancz, 1976

Calley, M. and I. Portuges, *Gendered Subjects: The Dynamics of Feminist Teaching*, Routledge & Kegan Paul, 1985

Canadian Teachers' Federation, *Progress Revisited: The Quality of (Work) Life of Women Teachers*, with Foreword by Heather-jane Robertson, 1993

Carey, John, 'Down with Dons', *The New Review*, 1, no. 10 (1975)

Carson, Ann, 'The Glass Essay', *Raritan*, 13, no. 3 (1994)

Chamberlain, Mary, (ed.), *Writing Lives*, Virago, 1988

Chambers, Jessie, *D.H. Lawrence: A Personal Record*, (1935), Cambridge University Press, 1980

Chodorow, Nancy, *The Reproduction of Mothering: Psychoanalysis and the Sociology of Gender*, University of California Press, 1978

Christie, F., *Teaching English Literacy: A Project of National Significance on the Preservice Preparation of Teachers for Teaching English Literacy*, vol. 2, *Papers*, Canberra, DEET, 1991

Clarke, Karen, 'Public and Private Children: Infant Education in the 1820s and 1830s', in Carolyn Steedman, Cathy Urwin and Valerie Walkerdine (eds) *Language, Gender and Childhood*, Routledge & Kegan Paul, 1985

Clifford, Geraldine J., '"Lady Teachers" and Politics in the United States, 1850–1930', in Martin Lawn and Gerald Grace (eds), *Teachers: The Culture and Politics of Work*, Falmer Press, 1987

Clifford, Geraldine J., ' "Daughters into Teachers": Educational and Demographic Influences on the Transformation of Teaching into Women's Work in America', in Alison Prentice and Marjorie R. Theobald (eds), *Women who Taught*, University of Toronto Press, 1991

College of St. Matthias: Annals, 1977

Collet, Clara E., 'Secondary Education – Girls', in Charles Booth (ed.), *Labour and Life of the People*, vol. 2, *London Continued*, Williams & Norgate, 1891

Collet, Clara E., *Educated Working Women*, P.S. King, 1902

Collet, Clara E., (ed.), *The Letters of John to Eliza. A Four Years' Correspondence Course in the Education of Women. 1806–1810*, privately published

Conrad, Peter, review of *The Western Canon: The Books and School of the Ages*, by Harold Bloom, *Observer*, 22 January 1995

Coward, Rosalind, 'Whipping Boys', *Guardian*, 3 September 1994

Cox, Brian, and Rhodes Boyson (eds), *Black Paper, 1975: The Fight for Education*, J.M. Dent, 1975

Cross, Jo, 'Reading Riffat: Gender, Culture and School – How Do These Influence the Writing and Reading of Autobiography in the Classoom?', thesis submitted for MA in Language and Literature in Education at the University of London Institute of Education, 1990

Davin, Anna, 'Imperialism and Motherhood', *History Workshop Journal*, 5 (1978)

Deem, Rosemary, *Women and Schooling*, Routledge & Kegan Paul, 1978

Dent, H.C., *The Training of Teachers in England and Wales 1800–1975*, Hodder & Stoughton, 1977

Department of Education and Science (DES), *A Language for Life*, [The Bullock Report], HMSO, 1975

Dixon, John, *Growth Through English, Set in the Perspective of the Seventies*, Oxford University Press, 1975

Dixon, John, *A Schooling in 'English': Critical Episodes in the Struggle to Shape Literary and Cultural Studies*, Open University Press, 1991

Doyle, Brian, *English and Englishness*, Routledge & Kegan Paul, 1989

Dyhouse, Carol, *Girls Growing up in Late Victorian and Edwardian England*, Routledge & Kegan Paul, 1981

Eliot, George, 'Edward Neville' (1834), included in Gordon S. Haight, *George Eliot: A Biography*, Oxford University Press, 1968

Eliot, George, *The Mill on the Floss* (1860), Penguin, 1983

Eliot, George, *Romola* (1862/3), Oxford University Press, 1994

Eliot, George, *Daniel Deronda* (1874/6), Penguin, 1967

Evans, Mary, *Life at a Girls' Grammar School in the 1950s*, Women's Press, 1991

Evetts, Julia, *Women in Primary Teaching: Career Contexts and Strategies*, Urwin Hyman, 1990

Floud, J.E., A.H. Halsey and F.M. Martin, *Social Class and Educational Opportunity*, Heinemann, 1956

Fordyce, James, *Sermons to Young Women*, 3rd edn, 2 vols, Millar, Cadell, Dodsley & Payne, 1766

Frith, Gill, 'Transforming Features: Double Vision and the Female Reader', *New Formations*, no. 15, Winter (1991).

Frye, Northrop, *On Education*, Fitzhenry & Whiteside, 1988

Galton, M., B. Simon and P. Croll, *Inside the Primary Classroom*, Routledge & Kegan Paul, 1980

Gilbert, P., and S. Taylor, *Fashioning the Feminine: Girls, Popular Culture and Schooling*, Allen & Unwin, 1991

Gipps, Caroline, and Patricia I. Murphy, *A Fair Test: Assessment, Achievement and Equity*, Open University Press, 1994

Girls and Mathematics Unit, *Counting Girls Out*, Virago, 1989

Gissing, George, *The Collected Letters of George Glissing*, vol. 1, *1863–1880*, ed. Paul F. Mattheisen, Arthur C. Young and Pierre Coustillas, Ohio University Press, 1990

Gore, Leon, 'Can Exams Be Fair? Race and Gender Differences in Brent Student Attainment in GCSE English', distributed by Brent LEA, 1991

Grace, Gerald, *Teachers, Ideology and Control: A Study in Urban Education*, Routledge & Kegan Paul, 1978

Gramsci, Antonio, *Selections from Prison Notebooks*, ed. and trans. Quintin Hoare and Geoffrey Nowell Smith, Lawrence & Wishart, 1986

Green, Andy, *Education and State Formation: The Rise of Education Systems in England, France and the USA*, Macmillan, 1990

Grumet, Madeleine R., *Bitter Milk: Women and Teaching*, University of Massachusetts Press, 1988

Hamerston, Michael T., 'On Becoming a Plumber', thesis submitted for MA in Language and Literature in Education, University of London Institute of Education, 1981

Hamilton, David, *Towards a Theory of Schooling*, Falmer Press, 1989

Heath, Shirley Brice, *Ways with Words*, Cambridge University Press, 1983

Heilbrun, Carolyn, *Writing a Woman's Life*, Ballantine Books, 1988

Heron, Liz (ed.), *Truth, Dare or Promise: Girls Growing up in the Fifties*, Virago, 1985

Howard, Ursula, paper delivered at 'The Future of English' conference held at Ruskin College, 15, 16 June 1991

Hughes, Kathryn, *The Victorian Governess*, The Hambledon Press, 1993

Hughes, M. Vivian, 'Pioneer Days in a Woman's Teacher Training College', in L.J. Lewis (ed.), *Days of Learning: An Anthology of Passages for Student Teachers*, Oxford University Press, 1961

Humm, Maggie, 'Subjects in English: Autobiography, Women and Education', in Ann Thompson and Helen Wilcox (eds), *Teaching Women: Feminism and English Studies*, Manchester University Press, 1989

Hunt, Felicity (ed.), *Lessons for Life: The Schooling of Girls and Women, 1850–1950*, Blackwell, 1987

Jackson, Brian, and Dennis Marsden, *Education and the Working Class*, Penguin, 1962

Jones, Ken, *Right Turn: The Conservative Revolution in Education*, Hutchinson Radius, 1989

Jones, Ken, 'The "Cox Report": Working for Hegemony', in Ken Jones (ed.), *English and the National Curriculum: Cox's Revolution?* Kogan Page, 1992

Kean, Hilda, *Challenging the State? The Socialist and Feminist Educational Experience 1900–1930*, Falmer Press, 1990

Kean, Hilda, *Deeds not Words*, Pluto, 1990

Kelsall, R.K., *Women and Teaching: Report on an Independent Nuffield Survey Following-up a Large National Sample of Women who Entered Teaching in England and Wales at Various Dates Pre-war and Post-War*, HMSO, 1963

Kristeva, Julia, 'Oscillation between Power and Denial', in Elaine Marks and Isabelle de Courtivron (eds), *New French Feminisms*, Schocken Books, 1981

LATE (London Association for the Teaching of English), *English Exams at 16*, ILEA English Centre, 1980

Lawn, Martin, and Gerald Grace (eds), *Teachers: The Culture and Politics of Work*, Falmer Press, 1987

Lawrence, D.H., *The Rainbow* (1915), Penguin, 1950

Lawrence, D.H., *Women in Love* (1920), Heinemann, 1945

Leavis, Q.D., *Fiction and the Reading Public* (1932), Chatto & Windus, 1978

Lessing, Doris, Preface to *The Golden Notebook*, Granada, 1973

Lessing, Doris, *Under My Skin: Volume One of my Autobiography, to 1949*, HarperCollins, 1994

Lettricchia, Frank, 'My Kinsman, T.S. Eliot', *Raritan*, 11, no. 4 (1992)

Levine, Josie, 'Pedagogy: The Case of the Missing Concept', in Keith Kimberley, Margaret Meek and Jane Miller (eds), *New Readings: Contributions to an Understanding of Literacy*, A. & C. Black, 1992

Levison, June, 'Autobiographical Writing: Gender, Culture and Classrooms', thesis submitted for MA in Language and

Literature in Education at the University of London Institute of Education, 1994

Lewis, L.J. (ed.), *Days of Learning: An Anthology of Passages from Autobiography for Student Teachers*, Oxford University Press, 1961

Lilley, Irene M., *Friedrich Froebel: A Selection from his Writings*, Cambridge University Press, 1967

Littlewood, Margaret, 'The "Wise Married Woman" and the Teaching Unions', in Hilary de Lyon and Frances Widdowson Migniuolo (eds), *Women Teachers: Issues and Experiences*, Open University Press, 1989

Llewellyn-Smith, H., 'Education', in Charles Booth, *The New Survey of London Life and Labour*, vol. 1, *Forty Years of Change*, P.S. King and Son Ltd, 1930

Locke, John, *Some Thoughts concerning Education* (1693) *The Educational Writings of John Locke*, ed. James L. Axtell, Cambridge University Press, 1968

Loudon, Mary, *Unveiled: Nuns Talking*, Chatto and Windus, 1992

Lovell, Terry, *Consuming Fiction*, Verso, 1987

de Lyon, Hilary, and Frances Widdowson Migniuolo (eds), *Women Teachers: Issues and Experiences*, Open University Press, 1989

Maccoby, E.E., and C.N. Jacklin, *The Psychology of Sex Differences*, Stanford University Press, 1974

McRobbie, Angela, and Mica Nava (eds), *Gender and Generation*, Macmillan, 1984

McWilliams-Tullberg, Rita, 'Women and Degrees at Cambridge University, 1862–1897', in Martha Vicinus (ed.), *A Widening Sphere: Changing Roles of Victorian Women*, Methuen, 1980

Maguire, Mary H. (ed.), *Dialogue in a Major Key: Women Scholars Speak*, NCTE, 1995

Marks, Elaine, and Isabelle de Courtivron (eds), *New French Feminisms*, Schocken Books, 1981

Martin, Jane Roland, 'Excluding Women from the Educational Realm' (1982), in Lynda Stone (ed.), *The Education Feminism Reader*, Routledge, 1994

Martin, Nancy, *et al.*, *Writing and Learning across the Curriculum, 11–16*, Ward Lock for Schools Council, 1976

Martineau, Harriet, *Autobiography: Volume I* (1877) Virago, 1983

Mason, Michael, *The Making of Victorian Sexual Attitudes*, Oxford University Press, 1994

Maybin, Janet and Neil Mercer (eds), *Using English: From Conversation to Canon*, Routledge, 1996

Medway, Peter, *Finding a Language: Autonomy and Learning in School*, Writers and Readers/Chameleon, 1980

Miller, Jane, 'Tell him, Miss', *The New Review*, 2, no. 16 (1975)

Miller, Jane, *Seductions: Studies in Reading and Culture*, Virago, 1990

Miller, Jane, 'Gissing may Damage your Health', *London Review of Books*, 13, no. 5 (1991)

Miller, Jane, *More has meant Women: The Feminisation of Schooling*, Institute of Education and the Tufnell Press, 1992

Miller, Jane, 'A tongue, for sighing', in Janet Maybin and Neil Mercer (eds), *Using English: From Conversation to Canon*, Routledge, 1996

Mitchison, Rosalind, 'The Numbers Game', *The New Review*, 4, no. 47 (1978)

Moers, Ellen, *Literary Women*, Women's Press, 1978

Montgomery, L.M. *Anne of Windy Willows* (1936), Puffin Books, 1992

Moore, T., 'Language and Intelligence: A Longitudinal Study of the First Eight Years. Part 1: Patterns of Development in Boys and Girls', *Human Development*, 10 (1967)

Morrison, Toni, *The Bluest Eye*, Triad Granada, 1981

Morrison, Toni, *Beloved*, Chatto & Windus, 1987

Morrison, Toni (ed.), *Race-ing, Justice, En-gendering Power*, Chatto & Windus, 1993

Murdoch, Iris, 'Socialism and Selection', in Brian Cox and Rhodes Boyson (eds), *Black Paper, 1975: The Fight for Education*, J.M. Dent, 1975

Nava, Mica, 'The Urban, the Domestic and Education for Girls', in Gerald Grace (ed.), *Education and the City: Theory, History and Contemporary Practice*, Routledge & Kegan Paul, 1984

Newsom, John, *The Education of Girls*, Faber & Faber, 1948

O'Donnell, Moya, 'Mothers as Teachers, and Teachers as Mothers: How this Patterning Affects the Status of Women whether Inside the Institution of Teaching or Out of It', thesis submitted for MA in Language and Literature in Education at the University of London Institute of Education, 1988

OFSTED (Office for Standards in Education), *Boys and English 1988–1991* (report from the Office of Her Majesty's Chief Inspector of Schools), pamphlet distributed by the Department of Education and Science, 1993

O'Keefe, Dennis J., *The Wayward Elite: A Critique of British Teacher-Education*, Adam Smith Institute, 1990

Okely, Judith, 'Privileged, Schooled and Finished: Boarding Education for Girls' in Shirley Ardener (ed.), *Defining Females: The Nature of Women in Society*, Croom Helm, 1978

Olivia [Dorothy Strachey], *Olivia*, Virago, 1987

Ong, Walter J., *Orality and Literacy: The Technologizing of the Word*, Methuen, 1982

Oram, Alison, 'Inequalities in the Teaching Profession: The Effect on Teachers and Pupils, 1910–39', in Felicity Hunt (ed.), *Lessons for Life: The Schooling of Girls and Women 1850–1950*, Blackwell, 1987

Oram, Alison, '"Sex Antagonism" in the Teaching Profession: Equal Pay and the Marriage Bar, 1910–39', in Madeleine Arnot and Gaby Weiner (eds), *Gender and the Politics of Schooling*, Hutchinson, 1987

Oram, Alison, 'A Master Should Not Serve under a Mistress: Women and Men Teachers 1900–1970', in Sandra Acker (ed.), *Teachers, Gender and Careers*, Falmer Press, 1989

Ounsted, C., and D.C. Taylor (eds), *Gender Differences: Their Ontogeny and Significance*, Churchill, 1972

Parker, Julia, *Women and Welfare*, Macmillan, 1988

Partington, Geoffrey, *Women Teachers in the 20th Century in England and Wales*, NFER Publishing Co., 1976

Pattison, Robert, *On Literacy*, Oxford University Press, 1982

Paulin, Tom, 'Writing beyond Writing: Emily Dickinson', in *Minotaur: Poetry and the Nation State*, Faber & Faber, 1992

Percival, Alicia C., *The English Miss To-day and Yesterday*, George G. Harrap, 1939

Phillips, M., and W.S. Tomkinson, *English Women in Life and Letters*, Oxford University Press, 1927

Pinchbeck, Ivy, *Women Workers and the Industrial Revolution 1750–1850* (1930), Virago, 1981

Plato, *The Republic of Plato*, trans. and ed. Francis Cornford, Oxford University Press, 1948

Poovey, Mary, *Uneven Developments: The Ideological Work of Gender in Mid-Victorian England*, Virago, 1989

Prentice, Alison, and Marjorie R. Theobald (eds), *Women who Taught*, Universiy of Toronto Press, 1991

Pugh, Catherine, 'Boys and English: A Consideration of Some Issues Raised by the 1993 OFSTED Report', thesis submitted for MA in Language and Literature in Education at the University of London Institute of Education, 1994

Purvis, June, *Hard Lessons: The Lives and Education of Working-Class Women in Nineteenth-Century England*, Polity Press, 1989

Purvis, June, *A History of Women's Education in England*, Open University Press, 1991

Rafferty, Frances, and Neil Munro, 'Lonely Men Seek Gender Balance', *Times Educational Supplement*, 10 June 1994

Reid, Ivan, and Erica Stratta (eds), *Sex Differences in Britain*, 2nd edn, Gower, 1989

Richardson, Dorothy, *Pilgrimage*, 4 vols, Virago, 1979

Richardson, Samuel, *Pamela*, 2 vols, Everyman Library, 1966

Ridley, Annie E., *Frances Mary Buss and her Work for Education*, Longmans, Green, 1895

Rockhill, Kathleen, 'Gender, Language and the Politics of Literacy' in Brian V. Street (ed.), *Cross-Cultural Approaches to Literacy*, Cambridge University Press, 1993

Rodriguez, Richard, *Hunger of Memory. The Education of Richard Rodriguez. An Autobiography*, David R. Godine, 1982

Rousseau, J-J., *Emile* (1762), trans. Barbara Foxley, Everyman's Library, 1911

Said, Edward W., *Culture and Imperialism*, Chatto and Windus, 1993

SCAA (Schools Curriculum and Assessment Authority), *English in the National Curriculum: Draft Proposals*, May 1994

Schmuck, Patricia A. (ed.), *Women Educators: Employees of Schools in Western Countries*, State University of New York Press, 1987

Sellers, Susan, 'Biting the Teacher's Apple: Opening Doors for Women in Higher Education' in Ann Thompson and Helen Wilcox (eds), *Teaching Women: Feminism and English Studies*, Manchester University Press, 1989

Silver, P. and H., *The Education of the Poor: The History of a National School 1824–1974*, Routledge & Kegan Paul, 1974

Simon, Kate, *Bronx Primitive: Portraits in a Childhood*, Harper Colophon, 1982

Simons, Michael, and Mike Raleigh, 'Where We've Been: A Brief History of English Teaching', *The English Magazine*, no. 8, Autumn (1981)

Smedley, Sue, 'Versions and Visions: Women Primary School Teachers, their Initial Education and Their Work', thesis submitted for MA in Language and Literature in Education, University of London Institute of Education, 1992

Smithers, Alan, and Pamela Robinson, *Post-18 Education:*

Growth, Change, Prospect, Executive Briefing, The Council for Industry and Higher Education, February 1995

Solsken, Judith, *Literacy, Gender and Work in Families and in School*, Ablex Publishing Company, 1993

Spark, Muriel, *The Prime of Miss Jean Brodie* (1961), Macmillan, 1969

Squires, Geraldine, *Diary of a School-Marm*, Arthur H. Stockwell, 1984

Steedman, Carolyn, *The Tidy House: Little Girls Writing*, Virago, 1982

Steedman, Carolyn, *Policing the Victorian Community: The Formation of English Provincial Police Forces, 1856–80*, Routledge & Kegan Paul, 1984

Steedman, Carolyn, *Childhood, Culture and Class in Britain: Margaret Macmillan, 1860–1931*, Virago, 1990

Steedman, Carolyn, *Past Tenses: Essays on Writing, Autobiography and History*, Rivers Oram Press, 1992

Steedman, Carolyn, Cathy Urwin and Valerie Walkerdine (eds), *Language, Gender and Childhood*, Routledge & Kegan Paul, 1985

Stone, Lynda (ed.), *The Education Feminism Reader*, Routledge, 1994

Stow, David, *Supplement to Moral Training and the Training System*, Glasgow, 1839

Street, Brian V., *Literacy in Theory and Practice*, Cambridge University Press, 1986

Street, Brian V. (ed.), *Cross-Cultural Approaches to Literacy*, Cambridge University Press, 1993

Street, J.C., and B.V., 'The Schooling of Literacy', in D. Barton and R. Ivanic (eds), *Writing in the Community*, Sage Publications, 1991

Sutherland, Gillian, *Elementary Education in the Nineteenth Century*, The Historical Association, 1971

The Teaching of English in England. Being the Report of the Departmental Committee Appointed by the President of the Board of Education to Inquire into the Position of English in the Educational System of England, HMSO, 1921. Known as 'The Newbolt Report'.

Thompson, Ann, and Helen Wilcox (eds), *Teaching Women: Feminism and English Studies*, Manchester University Press, 1989

Thompson, Dorothy, *Queen Victoria: Gender and Power*, Virago, 1990

Thompson, Flora, *Lark Rise to Candleford* (1945), Penguin, 1973

Thompson, Flora, *Still Glides the Stream* (1948), Oxford University Press, 1979

Turvey, Anne, 'Interrupting the Lecture: "Cox" seen from a Classroom', in Ken Jones (ed.), *English and the National Curriculum: Cox's Revolution?*, Kogan Page, 1992

Turvey, Anne, 'On Becoming an English Teacher', *Changing English*, 2, no. 1 (1994)

Urwin, Cathy, 'Constructing Motherhood: The Persuasion of Normal Development', in Carolyn Steedman, Cathy Urwin and Valerie Walkerdine (eds), *Language, Gender and Childhood*, Routledge & Kegan Paul, 1985

Viola, Wilhelm, *Child Art*, University of London Press, 1942

Vicinus, Martha, *Independent Women: Work and Community for Single Women 1850–1920*, Virago, 1985

Vicinus, Martha (ed.), *A Widening Sphere: Changing Roles of Victorian Women*, Methuen, 1980

Viswanathan, Gauri, *The Masks of Conquest*, Columbia University Press, 1989

Volosinov, V.N., *Marxism and the Philosophy of Language*, Harvard University Press, 1973

Walker, Alice, *The Color Purple*, Women's Press, 1983

Walker, Stephen, and Len Barton (eds), *Gender, Class and Education*, Falmer Press, 1983

Walkerdine, Valerie, 'From Context to Text: A Psychosemiotic Approach to Abstract Thought', in Michael Beveridge (ed.), *Children Thinking through Language*, Arnold, 1982

Walkerdine, Valerie, 'Dreams from an Ordinary Childhood', in Liz Heron (ed.), *Truth, Dare or Promise: Girls Growing up in the Fifties*, Virago, 1985

Walkerdine, Valerie, 'Sex, Power and Pedagogy' in *Schoolgirl Fictions*, Verso, 1990

Walkerdine, Valerie, and Helen Lucey, *Democracy in the Kitchen: Regulating Mothers and Socialising Daughters*, Virago, 1989

Weber, Sandra, and Claudia Mitchell, *'That's Funny, You Don't Look Like a Teacher'*, Falmer Press, 1995

Weiler, Kathleen, *Women Teaching for Change: Gender, Class and Power*, Bergin and Garvey, 1988

Weiner, Myron, *The Child and the State in India*, Princeton University Press, 1991

Weis, René, *Criminal Justice: The True Story of Edith Thompson*, Hamish Hamilton, 1988

Wellesley College Center for Research on Women, *The AAUW Report: How Schools Shortchange Girls*, AAUW Educational Foundation and National Education Association, 1992

White, Antonia, *Frost in May* (1933), Virago, 1978

Widdowson, Frances, *Going Up into the Next Class: Women and Elementary Teacher Training, 1840–1914*, Hutchinson, 1983

Wilder, Laura Ingalls, *These Happy Golden Years* (1943), Puffin Books, 1970

Wilder, Laura Ingalls, *On the Banks of Plum Creek* (1953), Puffin Books, 1973

Williams, Raymond, 'Cambridge English and Beyond', *The London Review of Books*, 5. no. 12, 7–20 July 1983

Williams, Raymond, *Politics and Letters: Interviews with New Left Review*, Verso, 1979

Williams, Raymond, *The English Novel from Dickens to Lawrence*, Chatto and Windus, 1974

Williams, Raymond, *The Long Revolution*, Penguin, 1965

Willis, Paul, *Learning to Labour: How Working-Class Kids get Working-Class Jobs*, Saxon House, 1977

Willmott, Peter, *Adolescent Boys of East London*, Penguin, 1966

Wollstonecraft, Mary, *Vindication of the Rights of Woman* (1792), Penguin, 1985

Wolpe, AnnMarie, and James Donald, *Is There Anyone Here from Education?*, Pluto, 1983

Wood, A.C., *A History of the University College Nottingham 1881–1948*, Blackwell, 1953

Worthen, John, *D.H. Lawrence: The Early Years 1885–1912*, Cambridge University Press, 1991

Wyndham, Violet, *Madame de Genlis*, André Deutsch, 1958

Index

Other Virago Books of Interest

CHILDHOOD, CULTURE AND CLASS IN BRITAIN: MARGARET McMILLAN, 1860–1931

Carolyn Steedman

Taking Margaret McMillan's life and work as a starting point, *Childhood, Culture and Class in Britain* illuminates a profound transformation in Western sensibility, and looks at the psychological and political fate of this woman who gave up her life 'for the children'. In this richly informative and widely researched book, Carolyn Steedman describes and explores the ways in which children – especially working-class children – became symbols of social hope for a better future at the end of the nineteenth century. More than just an account of one woman's life, this book considers major shifts in turn-of-the-century British social life, reflected in aspects of and attitudes towards politics and the new journalism; women's place within socialism; childhood and education; gardens and cities; bodies and minds; voices and legends.

BECOMING A WOMAN

And Other Essays in 19th and 20th Century Feminist History

Sally Alexander

Sally Alexander, one of Britain's most reputed feminist historians, has selected from her essays and papers of the past two decades. Writings on women and work in nineteenth-century London; feminism and social movements in Victorian England; subjectivity, memory and psychoanalysis; generation and history writing, all demonstrate the depth of her concern with the historical temporalities and imagery of feminism and sexual difference. Also charted and reflected here are the developments within feminism and feminist historiography. These exemplary papers offer us both a fascinating exploration of different historical moments and of the process of history writing itself.

HEARTS UNDEFEATED

Women's Writing of the Second World War

Jenny Hartley

'Jenny Hartley's brilliant anthology – moving, painful, funny by turns – is concerned with the range of ideas and emotions that were stimulated by the wartime trauma. It will be read by new generations of women, and men, who wish to discover the half of the tale that is usually forgotten . . . It will certainly become a classic' – *Ben Pimlott*

Featuring well over a hundred women, from well-known writers such as Rosamond Lehmann, Virginia Woolf and Beatrice Webb, to canteen workers and clippies, this fascinating collection unites their work for the first time. Ranging from lighter accounts of austerity to a chilling description of the 1938 Nuremberg Rally and Martha Gellhorn's devastating report of Dachau in 1945, *Hearts Undefeated* is an invaluable portrait of the war years, as seen through women's eyes.

☐	Childhood, Class and Culture	Carolyn Steedman	£16.99
☐	Becoming a Woman	Sally Alexander	£16.99
☐	Hearts Undefeated	Jenny Hartley	£9.99
☐	Talking From 9 to 5	Deborah Tannen	£7.99

Virago now offers an exciting range of quality titles by both established and new authors which can be ordered from the following address:

Little, Brown and Company (UK),
P.O. Box 11,
Falmouth,
Cornwall TR10 9EN.

Alternatively you may fax your order to the above address.
Fax No. 01326 317444.

Payments can be made as follows: cheque, postal order (payable to Little, Brown and Company) or by credit cards, Visa/Access. Do not send cash or currency. UK customers and B.F.P.O. please allow £1.00 for postage and packing for the first book, plus 50p for the second book, plus 30p for each additional book up to a maximum charge of £3.00 (7 books plus).

Overseas customers including Ireland, please allow £2.00 for the first book plus £1.00 for the second book, plus 50p for each additional book.

NAME (Block Letters) ....

....

ADDRESS ....

....

....

☐ I enclose my remittance for ....

☐ I wish to pay by Access/Visa Card

Number ☐☐☐☐☐☐☐☐☐☐☐☐☐☐☐☐☐☐

Card Expiry Date ☐☐☐☐